D307·76CHA

MEMORIES OF CITIES

Ashgate Studies in Architecture Series

SERIES EDITOR: EAMONN CANNIFFE, MANCHESTER SCHOOL OF ARCHITECTURE, MANCHESTER METROPOLITAN UNIVERSITY, UK

The discipline of Architecture is undergoing subtle transformation as design awareness permeates our visually dominated culture. Technological change, the search for sustainability and debates around the value of place and meaning of the architectural gesture are aspects which will affect the cities we inhabit. This series seeks to address such topics, both theoretically and in practice, through the publication of high quality original research, written and visual.

Memories of Cities

Trips and Manifestoes

Jonathan Charley
University of Strathclyde, Glasgow, UK

ASHGATE

Published by
Ashgate Publishing Limited
Wey Court East
Union Road
Farnham
Surrey, GU9 7PT
England

Ashgate Publishing Company
110 Cherry Street
Suite 3-1
Burlington, VT 05401-3818
USA

www.ashgate.com

British Library Cataloguing in Publication Data
Memories of cities : trips and manifestoes. – (Ashgate studies in architecture)
    1. Architecture and literature. 2. Space (Architecture) in literature. 3. Architecture and philosophy.
    I. Series II. Charley, Jonathan, 1959–

The Library of Congress has cataloged the printed edition as follows:
Charley, Jonathan.
    Memories of cities : trips and manifestoes / by Jonathan Charley.
        pages cm. – (Ashgate studies in architecture)
    Includes bibliographical references and index.
    ISBN 978-1-4094-3137-4 (hardback : alk. paper) – ISBN 978-1-4094-3138-1 (ebook) – ISBN 978-1-4094-7297-1 (epub)
    1. Cities and towns. 2. Architecture and society. I. Title.

    HT151.C522 2013
    307.76–dc23
                                                                2012038424

ISBN 9781409431374 (hbk)
ISBN 9781409431381 (ebk – PDF)
ISBN 9781409472971 (ebk – ePUB)

MIX
Paper from
responsible sources
FSC
www.fsc.org   FSC® C018575

Printed and bound in Great Britain
by MPG PRINTGROUP.

Contents

List of Illustrations

4.3 'Women construction workers, raise your productivity in the interests of building socialism'

5.1 'Imperial picturesque' – African fountain head in Marseille / Hindu soldiers in Glasgow

5.2 'Exchanging commodities'. Bourse in Marseille / Royal Exchange Square, Glasgow

5.3 'Slogans for a new order'. Graffiti in Marseille and Glasgow

5.4 'Machinery of creative destruction'. Demolition sites in Marseille and Glasgow

5.5 'Bridging concrete uncertainties'. Flyovers in Marseille and Glasgow

5.6 'Navigating the future'. Container port in Marseille / Shipyard in Glasgow

6.1 One of the few remaining buildings of the avant-garde, the legendary Club Russakova by Konstantin Melnikov, built in 1928 from a brief that had been developed in conjunction with workers

6.2 The pioneering Dom Narkomfina, 1928. A commune of a 'transitional kind' designed by Ginzburg and Milnius, it sought to articulate the 'new way of life'. 'Molodoi Chelovek, why are you taking photos of this ruin?', asked a war veteran. 'Because it is one of the most important buildings of the twentieth century' I replied

6.3 Tragedy and farce come to mind. Demolished in 2004, the Hotel Moskva has made a surreal reappearance worthy of Bulgakov, only this time without hammers, sickles, revolutionary motifs or, indeed, the different wings. Top image taken in 2010, bottom image: the old hotel in 1984

6.4 Studying carefully and enthralled by what Haussmann had achieved in Paris, Stalin's planners deliver infinity in the shape of Gorky Street, now renamed Tverskaya.

The top image was taken in 1988 before the advertising detritus of investment banks, gambling emporia and fast food chains covered its facades. Bottom image taken in 2004

6.5 Another iconic workers' club, Zueva, with its famous glazed circulation tower designed by Ilya Golosov in 1927. Still in use today as a cinema and for community activities

6.6 By 1989 something approaching 90 per cent of all new housing construction in the Soviet Union was being prefabricated out of concrete panels. The goal was to organise building production as a fully integrated and automated system in which there was a continual feedback loop from inception to completion. At its height it employed 13,000,000 workers. Photos taken in 1988

6.7 For all the promise of the avant-garde and the monumentalism of the Stalinist city, the twentieth-century history of Russian architecture really belongs to the industrialisation of the building industry and the development of the *mikrorayon*. These two are both on the outskirts of Moscow, taken in 1989

6.8 Top image from 1984, the glass and steel dome of the Yuri Gagarin Space Pavilion in what was once the Park of Economic Achievements – a Soviet-era theme park of pavilions celebrating the technological and economic development of Soviet society. Bottom: the old state supermarket GUM, now rebranded as an elite shopping arcade

6.9 The architecture of an absolutist state. Hostile towards modernism, the Soviet bureaucracy of Stalin's era preferred something rather more solid: two of the seven Stalin towers. Top image: a housing complex on the Moscow River designed by Chechulin and Rostovsky, 1952. Bottom image: Moscow State University, MGU

Preface

Everything always begins with a long hot summer and a confession. It was July 1975 and it was my first job on a building site as a scaffolder's mate. It was the beginning of an accidental career in architecture and building that somehow has continued for nearly 40 years. My confession is that unlike some of my contemporaries, who swear they woke up one day at an impossibly early age with a driving ambition to redesign the world, I fell into architecture almost by default. Like the drunk labourer who, after tumbling three stories from the scaffold, landed at my feet and then got up virtually unscathed, it was a lucky fall, in that architecture rather suited my wayward and diverse engagement with the world. In true renaissance fashion, it has allowed me to play music, read, write, travel, make pictures, design, build and teach. In other words, it has been more of an immersive osmotic field rather than a professional vocation. *Memories of Cities* reflects that scattered life in architecture and collects together nine essays developed over the last eight years that explore different ways of writing about the history of the built environment.

Employing a variety of narrative techniques including memoirs, letters, and diary entries, each essay tells a story about the political and ideological character of buildings and cities. The reason for the diversity of outputs is straightforward enough and reflects the idea that the form in which a story is narrated depends on the subject matter. Each chapter sets out to illuminate key forces that underpin the development of the capitalist built environment and to highlight attempts to forge alternative visions of how buildings and cities might be produced and experienced.

There are four themes that recur throughout the book: capitalism, empire, revolution and utopia. These function like territorial markers; reminders of what drives me and where one day we might drive to. I do not offer any comprehensive theory of capitalist urban development and am not an historian so much as someone who writes about history. But suffice to say that Marxism and critical theory have heavily influenced my thinking and writing and have taken me into intellectual territories that I have found forbidding but exciting.

Thirty-five years ago, when I was first an architecture student, there was relatively little urban and architectural history and theory that challenged how we might understand the field. Since then, there has been an extraordinary profusion of books on things architectural and urban and especially books with the word 'space' in the title; that strange euphemism for all manner of things and properties. This reflected not only an increased general interest in buildings and cities, but also the increasingly fuzzy boundaries between different disciplines. Social scientists began writing about space at more or less the same time as people from architecture ventured into the world of sociology and the humanities. This was captured by what was called the 'spatial turn,' which set out to give history a more explicit geographical dimension and to remind us that the co-ordinates of human existence were both temporal and spatial.

The changing mood was exemplified by the way in which students of architecture, politics, literature and sociology were reading the same books like Foucault's *Madness and Civilisation*, Adorno and Horkheimer's *Dialectic of the Enlightenment*, Lefebvre's *Production of Space*, Jameson's *The Cultural Logic of Post-Modernity* and so on. The essays here are embedded in this interdisciplinary cultural shift and as such, draw on a broad range of fields, economic theory, social history, literary criticism, and cultural studies. Although some of this reading was a pleasure, an awful lot of it was tortuous. So much theory and history is dry, leaden, and for me, at any rate, impenetrable. Consequently, one of my biggest concerns in putting this book together has been to produce texts that are enjoyable and engaging to read. How successful I have been in this is for the reader to judge. If I have an aspiration as a 'voice', then it is to be a polemical essayist who plays with prose without ever losing sight of the truth imperative. On this point the work of writers like Walter Sebald and Norman Mailer have been particularly instructive because of the way they blend politics, history and storytelling, and point to the possibility inferred by the subtitle to Mailer's Armies of the Night of 'History as a novel, the novel as history'. Such a proposition intrigues me and I am hardly the first to point out that literature can be as powerful in its critique of social history as the work of the historian, and in this respect it is undoubtedly true that my world view has been formed as much by reading Steinbeck and Zola as Marx and Engels. To which I would always add travelling and looking, those experiential elements in the formation of knowledge that are often overlooked.

Memories of Cities gives glimpses, then, of the journey that I have been on in recent years – a voyage of discovery that was both intellectual and material. All of the buildings and cities that I write about are places that I have visited, lived or worked in, and each text is illustrated with images that provide a parallel narrative. With the exception of Brazil, it has been a predominantly European tour, one in which cities like Glasgow, Moscow, Paris and Marseille have loomed large.

The essays are very roughly laid out chronologically in terms of historical time, although some of them naturally enough bounce back and forth. Each of the chapters is preceded by a short abstract that explains their origins and objectives in more detail. The book begins with 'The Glimmer of Other Worlds' that takes the form of an interview about the character of the capitalist city and alternative forms of practice. In a way it functions as an introduction, in that it introduces many of the key themes developed in other chapters. 'Violent Stone' takes us into the heart of the nineteenth century and is put together as a trilogy of short essays about the dialectical character of one the most pre-eminent institutions of the early capitalist city, the law court. This is followed by 'Paris: Ghosts and Visions of a Revolutionary City', an obligatory and inevitable engagement with a well-worn subject that I try and give a new twist by presenting it as a succession of dramatic 'Acts' that explore the spatial dimensions of an urban revolution. This takes us to the turn of the twentieth century and 'Letters from the Front Line...' that is presented as the notes and letters of a journalist who is witnessing the changing nature of the Russian building industry as the revolutionary idealism of the 1920s gives way to dictatorship. Next comes 'Foreign Bodies', which is the oldest chapter in the book and imagines Marseille and Glasgow as two old men reminiscing and writing letters to each other about their rise and subsequent decline in the latter half of the twentieth century. 'The (Dis)Integrating City' returns to Russia and is one of two chapters in the collection that reflect a shift in my interests over the last five years towards the literary dimensions of the architectural and spatial imagination. It is composed as a series of notebooks and weaves a narrative between the Russian literary and architectural avant-garde in the context of the 1917 Revolution. 'Sketches of War II' is in some ways ahistorical, in that it deals with the antithetical history of architecture as a history of violence and destruction and takes us on a tour of places in which this relationship is acutely exposed. Chapter 8, 'The Shadow of Economic History II' brings us up to the present day, engages with economic theory and places the recent crisis in the building industry in an historical context. The final chapter, 'Scares and Squares II', plays with the boundaries between fiction and non-fiction and journeys through the architecture of utopian and dystopian literature from Thomas More to J.G. Ballard and Philip K. Dick, at which point the journey is interrupted.

As for acknowledgements, my particular thanks, of course, to my long-suffering family, but also to my teachers, friends, students, and unlucky casual acquaintances who have been forced to listen to me and who, in their different ways, have contributed to this endeavour. My thanks also to Valerie Rose and Emily Ruskell at Ashgate for supporting this project. All faults are, of course, my own.

Jonathan Charley

1

The Glimmer of Other Worlds: Questions on Alternative Architectural Practice

INTRODUCTION

'The Glimmer of Other Worlds' was prompted by my experiences as a teacher attempting to explain to students what the idea of an alternative to capitalist building production might mean. It struck me that one way to address this was to ask a series of questions that are typical of the kind I have received over the years. In effect, it is an architectural and political manifesto that addresses a specific politically engaged meaning of alternative practice understood as anti-capitalist resistance. More broadly, it summarises ideas that I have been preoccupied with ever since I first left architecture school in 1980 and was lucky enough to find work in the firm Collective Building and Design. A cooperative – or more precisely, a self-management collective – I worked there for seven years. It was very much a formative experience and an apprenticeship in how to produce architecture in a different way. I left in part because of a desire to study more seriously the political economy of the built environment, and it was after completing a Masters at University College London that I went to Moscow for a year to begin my research into the history of Soviet architecture and construction. These questions then have been fermenting for a long time. As for the answers, these are works in progress. 'The Glimmer of Other Worlds' was first presented at the Alternate Currents Conference at the University of Sheffield in 2007, and published in the *Architecture Research Quarterly (ARQ)* in 2008.

1.1 'Architects of
the world unite'.
Marx in front of the
Bolshoi Theatre

1

*Can there be a greater spectacle or drama than the seizure of a city during the midst
of a major protest or rebellion? St Petersburg, a metropolis framed by a skyline
composed of glistening cupolas and belching toxic chimneys, sways with intoxicated
expectation that a rent in time is about to appear. The cobbles crack with the sound
of falling statues. Horses dangle from lifting bridges. Barricades mesh across streets.
A panic-stricken government official searches for his nose and briefcase. Jealous civil
servants, Francophile aristocrats, and vengeful generals are feverishly engaged in
settling accounts, closing their shutters and securing safe passage out of the city.*[1]

Q1. What is meant by the phrase alternative or alternative practice?

Alternative or alternate are politically neutral words that suggest something to do
with notions of difference, opposites, or choice. Like any words, they acquire their
meaning through context and association, such as in the expressions 'the alternative
society', 'alternative medicine', or 'alternative technology'. Here I want to deal with a
very specific politically engaged meaning: alternative practice understood as anti-
capitalist practice. By this I mean a way of doing things, including making buildings,
which is not defined by capitalist imperatives and bourgeois morality. This has two
aspects: first, in the sense of resisting the environmentally damaging and socially
destructive aspects of capitalist urban development; second, in terms of engaging
with embryonic post-capitalist forms of architectural and building production.

2

*Murderous young men and women are hopping over the walls of back courts and
thousands of subterranean proletarians with molten metal teeth pour out of the
yards and factories, all of them searching for redemption. It is a perfect stage set*

1.2 'The trickle-down theory of capitalist urbanisation'. Squatter camp, 'Jardim de Paraguai', São Paulo

for the outbreak of a revolution, its illuminated enlightenment boulevards poised over rat-infested basements. Till the moment before the cannon roars it continues to parade its cathedrals, boulevards and illustrious terraces with a Potemkin-like contempt for the rest of the city. The flâneur, the prince, the banker, and the priest cannot believe that the history of their fundamentally implausible city has entered a new phase in which they will be relegated to bit parts.

Q2. But aren't you swimming against the tide, against received wisdom?

We should always be sceptical of received wisdom, or in its rather more dangerous guise, common sense, which is often little more than 'naturalised' ideology. One example of this is the 'common sense attitude' that socialism is finished and that human civilisation ends with the combination of free-market capitalism and liberal parliamentary democracy. It is a conclusion reinforced by the ideological consensus sweeping across the political parties that neo-liberal economic theory is the panacea for the world's ills.

Such 'ideological common sense' resembles a powerful virus that attacks the nervous system, destroying the powers of reason. Such is the germ's strength that it induces a dream-like state of narcosis in the corridors of power. The rallying cries of dissent become ever more ethereal and faint. The memories of ideological disputes about alternative worlds or concepts of society that had dominated political life in earlier generations become increasingly opaque until they take their place alongside the myths of ancient legend. Showmen and peddlers of bogus medicine sneak along the passageways and slide into the vacant seats of philosophers and orators. Investigative journalists and rebel spies cower in the shadows. They are visibly terrified, as if haunted by Walter Benjamin's comment that one of the defining features of fascism is 'the aestheticisation of politics'.[2] Surely this cannot be happening here? But it is, and in the Chamber of the House applause indicates that the garage mechanics are all agreed, there is no doubt that the engine works. The differences of opinion revolve around what colour to paint the bodywork and which type of lubricant should be used to ensure the engine ticks over with regularity and predictability. This is a profoundly depressing situation and we should neither believe nor accept it.

3

A detailed map of the city is laid out on the table. Hands sweep with a dramatic blur across the streets and squares. One of them picks up a fat pencil and begins to draw on the paper. The fingers compose two circles, one at a 500-metre radius from the Winter Palace the other at a 1,000 metres, and proceed to plot a series of smaller circles indicating the key places and intersections to be targeted in the coming insurrection. Strategic crossroads, the railway stations, the post and telegraph offices, bridges, key banking institutions and the Peter and Paul Fortress – the map of the city becomes a battle plan.[3]

Q3. But this is all politics, what about architecture?

There are exceptions, but historically architects have tended to work for those with power and wealth. It was in many ways the original bourgeois profession, so we should not be surprised that many a professional architect is happy to be employed as capitalism's decorator, applying the finishing touches to an edifice with which they have no real quarrel. As for the would-be rebel, even the architect's and builder's cooperative fully armed with a radical agenda to change the world for the better is required to make compromises in order to keep a business afloat. All alternative practices working within the context of a capitalist society still have to make some sort of surplus or profit if they are to survive in the market place. This said, there are ethical and moral choices to be made. It would be comforting to think that the majority of contemporary architects' firms would have refused to design autobahns, stadiums and banks with building materials mined by slave labourers in 1930s Germany. How is it, then, that seemingly intoxicated by the promise of largesse and oblivious to the human degradation and environmental catastrophe unravelling in the Gulf, architectural firms are clambering over bodies to collect their fees from reactionary authoritarian governments and corrupt dictators who deny civilian populations basic democratic rights?[4] Why is it that so many firms, in order to satisfy a 'werewolf hunger for profit', are happy to ignore the labour camps holding building workers in virtual prison conditions? There is no polite way of describing what amounts to amnesiac whoredom. But on this and other related matters the architectural and building professions remain largely silent, an unsettling quiet that is paralleled in Britain by the absence of any socially progressive movement within the architectural community that questions and confronts the ideological basis of the neo-liberal project.

1.3 'Architects, don't work for repressive regimes and dictators'. Third Reich Air Ministry, Berlin

4

Tearing up the theatrical rulebooks on the relationship between actors and audience, workers transform the steps of the Winter Palace into what looks like a set from an Expressionist film. A giant three-dimensional version of Lissitsky's print, 'Red wedge defeats the whites', a collision of cubes, pyramids and a distorted house are constructed to camouflage the pastel blue stucco facade. This is the stage on which the revolutionaries re-enact the occupation of the Royal Palace and the arrest of Kerensky's provisional government on a nightly basis with a cast of thousands. Something special had been unleashed. It makes perfect sense. 'We workers will no longer listen to our bosses in the factory, so why should we listen to them in the art salons and galleries? Away with the grand masters, away with the worship of experts, art into life, art into the street, the streets are our palettes, our bodies and tools our implements.

Q4. But isn't the Left dead and aren't you trying to raise ghosts and spectres?

There is perhaps an element of necromantic wishful thinking. It is probably true that the Left in Europe, despite the anti-capitalist movement, has scattered, punch-drunk and still reeling from the ideological battering ram unleashed against it. Like whipped autumnal leaves spread across the fields after high winds, it waits for a rake to pile it into a recognisable and coherent shape. But new alliances form at the very moment when all seems lost. The reclamation of the lost, buried and hidden is the subject matter of archaeology. But we also need to conduct a careful archaeological dig to reclaim the oft forgotten historical attempts to forge an alternative to capitalism. Central to this project of rebuilding opposition is to rescue the word socialism from its association with the violent state capitalist dictatorships of the former Soviet bloc. With careful scrapes and incisive cuts our archaeological dig reveals a library full of eminently modern and prescient ideas like equality of

1.4 'Architect, are you?' Graffiti, Glasgow

opportunity, social justice, the redistribution of wealth, the social ownership of resources – concepts that are easy to brush off and reinvigorate. The excavations continue and we discover that anarchism, far from its infantile representation as an ideology of chaos and disruption, offers other extraordinary ideas that can be added to the library index. Infused by a resolute defence of individual liberty, it speaks of self-management, of independent action, of autonomy, and of opposition to all forms of social power, especially that wielded by the State.

5

> *Comrades, take the time to read, digest and enjoy the declaration on land. Savour these words, 'the landowner's right to possession of the land is herewith abolished without compensation'.[5] Does that not sound magnificent? It is not poetry in the sense of Pushkin or Lermontov, but it possesses a timeless lyrical quality. We have achieved something that no other people in human history have managed. We have socialised the land on behalf of all of society's members at the same moment as occupying all the key buildings of the state and capitalist class. It is an act that, if it were to all end tomorrow, would nevertheless resound through the ages like the tales of Homer and Odysseus.*

Q5. But I've heard it all before, capitalism this, capitalism that, shouldn't we just accept that the best we can do is to ameliorate the worst aspects of capitalist building production? I can see why one might become anti-capitalist, but shouldn't we learn to accept that's just the way the world is?

That is indeed how the world is. The question is, do we think it should be? Is the capitalist system really the best way of handling human affairs and organising how we make and use our buildings and cities? It is true that capitalism has proved to be remarkably resilient and even in moments of profound economic crisis, has

1.5 'The miraculous appearance of no place like home.' Billboard, Glasgow

managed to restructure economic life so that capital accumulation can recommence. Yet it remains dominated by the contradictions that arise from a social and economic system based on the private accumulation of capital and the economic exploitation of workers. It is a 300-year old history disfigured by slavery, colonial domination, socio-spatial inequality, and fascism – scars that are viewed as aberrations arising from some other planet, rather than what they are, structural features of capitalist economic domination. Despite this history of social and psychological violence, we are told that the organisation of a mythical free market in land and building services and the relentless commodification of all aspects of the built environment are the best ways of building our villages, towns and cities. Simultaneously, attempts to provide a critique or offer alternative models for social and economic development are dismissed as the utopian dreams of the sleeping dead.

6

What we have achieved through our proclamation represents a continuation of the struggles of French revolutionaries to give the idea of a commune, and of communal property, a modern urban character. And they in turn were indebted to English revolutionaries a century before. It is comforting to think that a full 265 years before our declaration on land nationalisation, the Diggers, as the militants liked to call themselves, intended once and for all to 'level men's estates'. On a spring Sunday in 1649, a small band of revolutionary soldiers declared the abolition of the Sabbath, of tithes, magistrates, ministers and the Bible. Proceeding to dig local wasteland collectively, they loudly proclaimed that it was not a symbolic action but a real assumption of what they considered to be their rightful ownership of common lands. It was a radical vision of the future in which neither God nor powerful property owners had a place. Agricultural production outside London would have been collectivised in the common interest and a programme launched to build schools and hospitals for the poor throughout the country.[6]

1.6 'Exploding myths – don't believe the hype.' CCTV camera, Glasgow

Q6. So what are the main contradictions within the contemporary built environment that we should try and tackle?

A by no means exhaustive list might begin as follows: 1) The private ownership by capitalists of the means of building production; 2) The unstable character of urban development and the employment insecurity of workers that results from the endemic cycles of boom and slump within the building industry; 3) The history of 'geographical' uneven development and socio-spatial inequality; 4) The divisive patterns of social segregation that result from the privatisation and fortification of land and buildings; 5) The way in which the commodification of everyday life exacerbates our alienation from nature, each other and the products of our labour; 6) The subordination of social need and the environmental destruction caused by capitalists prioritising profits over all other requirements and desires; 7) The tendency towards the homogenisation of architecture as building producers economise so as to maintain the rate of profit; 8) Ever-increasing levels of spatial surveillance and control designed to create a 'purified city' and ensure that the process of capital accumulation remains uninterrupted. All of these characteristics and others that we could add to the list are accepted as a price worth paying and would have been more than recognisable concerns to social commentators 100 years ago. (It is worth remembering that in the nineteenth century, the construction industry was one of the test beds for laissez-faire economics.) The purpose of criticism then is quite simple – to challenge capitalist hegemony and to open up the imagination to the possibility of a liberated concept of labour and space.

7

Here in Russia, some workers and peasants have interpreted the new laws quite literally and have appropriated buildings, land and machinery in a quite

1.7 'Architects, say no to privatisation, defend public services'. Govanhill Pool occupation

spontaneous manner through direct action. Take for instance this proclamation nailed to posts and hoardings in the Ukraine: 'To all the workers of the city and its environs! Workers, your city is for the present occupied by the Revolutionary Insurrectionary (Makhnovist) Army. This army does not serve any political party, any power, and any dictatorship. On the contrary, it seeks to free the region of all political power, of all dictatorship. It strives to protect the freedom of action, the free life of the workers against all exploitation and domination. The Makhnovist Army does not therefore represent any authority. It will not subject anyone to any obligation whatsoever. Its role is confined to defending the freedom of the workers. The freedom of the peasants and the workers belongs to themselves, and should not suffer any restriction.'[7]

Q7. How do I begin to think about different forms of practice?

The first thing is to draw a map or a matrix of the things you think are important and locate yourself within it. Capitalism might appear relentless in the ingenious ways in which it carves up the world, but so are our abilities to resist it. If, generally speaking, the ruling ideas of any epoch tend to be those of the ruling class, there have always been other histories. These are the unsung stories of individuals and social classes engaged in the struggle to realise the hope that another world is possible. Where one looks for inspiration tends to be idiosyncratic, very much a journey that has to do with what you read, where you travel, who your teachers are and your identity in terms of race, class and gender. These are all lenses through which a view of the world is either clarified or obscured. One way of thinking about forms of resistance is to compose a simple map of a capitalist economy that describes the process of production and exchange through which the built environment is made and comes into use. This is helpful, because it allows us to locate and plan strategies for alternative practices in a coordinated and coherent fashion. So for instance, if we think of the 'sphere of production', we might discuss the struggles of architects, building workers, and planners to organise and envision a different way of making buildings and cities. If we think of the 'sphere of exchange and consumption', we might look to the struggles by tenants, users, and consumers to manage and use our built environment in a non-capitalist manner. Implicit in this model is that we place the activities of architects within a broader context and, indeed, it is fairly meaningless to talk of an 'alternative architectural practice' that is anti-capitalist unless it takes into account that what an architect does is only one small link in the chain of command by which buildings eventually emerge out of the ground. An example in Britain of how this might be realised can be found in the activities of Lubetkin, Tecton, and ATO. They endeavoured to produce an architecture of social commitment that was meticulously designed and engineered.[8] They worked closely with tenants and other organisations in the building industry and simultaneously engaged with the struggle against fascism.

8

> And so Comrades, we have a unique situation on our hands. We have the very real opportunity to fundamentally rethink what we understand by urban construction. The land has been nationalised, the operations of the real estate market and the phenomena of differential rents have been abolished, building workers have expelled the contractors and set up democratic workers' collectives on site and in factory, the bourgeois state has been smashed – and so we can now turn to the vexed question of what we should build on the ruins of the capitalist city. There are it seems two immediate ways of addressing the problem. The first is a directly political and economic issue that concerns questions about the ownership and control of how buildings will be produced and used. The second is a qualitative question that concerns what types of buildings and spatial organisation we should be thinking about and what form they might take.

Q8. So where do we look for alternative models to the capitalist production of the built environment?

I think that it is timely that we reflect critically on the legacy of social democracy and historical moments when the socialist movement has been strong enough to tip the balance of the 'use- exchange' value of the commodity in favour of social need. In twentieth-century Britain there were two periods worth recalling. The first was the epoch of municipal socialism 100 years ago, manifest in the architectural programmes of local authorities. In London, this gave birth to the first significant experiments in the production of rented social housing. In Glasgow, it brought about the construction of an extraordinary network of public and social facilities across the city that included bathhouses, schools, and libraries. Emboldened by the growing strength of the trade union movement, it was the first time that the state had directly intervened to regulate and sponsor the production of buildings with an explicit social mission. The second period coincided with the foundation of the welfare state and the post-Second World War national programme to build a new infrastructure of educational, social and cultural facilities. While we might question the quality of some of the architecture, the level of social commitment among the

1.8 'Rebuild an architecture of social commitment'. Early twentieth-century municipal library

architectural community contrasts sharply with the opportunism that dominates the profession today. Many a forgotten hero and heroine threw themselves into the task of building a New Britain and however misguided some of the results might seem, it is difficult not to be moved by their sense of idealism. However, as we know from the ideological assault on the legacy of the welfare state by both Tory and Labour administrations over the last 30 years, the gains that are fought for sometimes over decades can be quickly unravelled. All attempts to ameliorate or develop alternative practices within the context of a capitalist economy eventually come up against this contradiction. Despite this, voices can still be heard from the frontier making demands for the democratic social regulation of how we make and use our built environment so as to tip the balance of commodity production in the interests of disenfranchised users and social organisations. Listen closer, and you will hear distant echoes of other more radical voices, which, from the edge of the wilderness, still dream of the socialisation of land and the building industry.

9

In front of us we have a programme for a decentralised 'disurbanist' type of spatial development. What would happen if these plans were implemented? The idea of the monumental construction of a capital city would be consigned to books dealing with the urban history of class societies. Moscow would still remain the symbolic heart of the country, but the social and spatial contradictions that dominate the capitalist built environment would be eradicated. For the first time in human history, the connection between political power and urban construction would be smashed. It also suggests a quite different agenda for the design of individual buildings. It implies an architecture that emerges out of concerns for infrastructural networks, temporality, flexibility and mobility. It suggests ideas about architecture and urbanism that are open-ended rather than closed, changeable rather than static, and which celebrate chance, liberty and

1.9 'Architects, destroy the symbols of injustice and oppression'. Decapitated saints, France, 1789

fun, an architecture that is no longer obsessed with formal canons but thinks about strategic programmes, kinetic buildings, and about an urbanism born out of an understanding of social and technological change.

Q9. So where do we look next?

Everywhere and anywhere. I have focused on four of the more profound European attempts to challenge capitalist hegemony, so as to unravel the architectural or building programmes within them – the English Revolution of the seventeenth century, the French Revolutions of the eighteenth and nineteenth centuries, the Russian Revolution in the decade after 1917 and the Spanish Revolution in the mid 1930s. These are known primarily as political and social revolutions. However, all of them were implicitly spatial and opened up what Henri Lefebvre referred to as an oeuvre on a different world in which the tactics of 'spatial resistance' were transformed and developed.[9] Tactic one involves organisation – the exchange of ideas, the draughting of texts and manifestos, and the forging of bonds with fellow travellers. Next comes action – the organisation of strikes and the occupation of land and property as a prelude to the seizure of the city and its institutions. Third comes preparation – drawing up plans for new building programmes and forms of social and spatial organisation. Fourth comes construction, the development of post-capitalist labour processes and the practical task of converting the dream world of limitless possibilities into a something material, real and practical.

10

'Comrade Aleksei Gan, perhaps you would like to comment on these plans?' 'Most certainly, they are worthy but still a little timid. We should not be content with half measures, we should unequivocally demand the complete democratisation

1.10 'Keep the memory of other realities alive'. Commemorative plaque to the French anarchist, Montmartre, Paris

of planning and the development of new forms of artistic labour in which the revolutionary festival, would be re-conceptualised as a mass urban action. Imagine, my friends, an event in which the entire proletarian masses of Moscow would be able to enact their own vision of the Communist city of the future in real space-time, filling not only the entire city of Moscow but even its outskirts.'[10]

Q10. But hang on a minute, all the experiments you refer to failed! In fact, one might argue that the most lasting legacy in terms of socialised building construction did not come from Russia, it came from Sweden.

Yes and no. You are right that the achievements of the Scandinavian countries in prioritising social need, in building integrated transport systems, childcare facilities and good quality rented accommodation puts a lot of what we build to shame. However, it is a type of social democracy that many find rather uncomfortable and disturbing, even spooky – too sure, too right, too regulated, too ordered. In contrast, in the Barcelona of 1936 or in Paris in 1871, we find something very different, in which carnival, joy, freedom and self-determination are the goals of political struggle rather than sensible administration. As Henri Lefebvre reminds us, people fight revolutions to be happy not to produce tons of steel. The question of failure and failed experiments is an interesting one.

For instance, much has been written about the Paris Commune.[11] Manuel Castells called it the most repressed rent strike in history. In contrast Marx, Engels and Lenin heralded it as the first attempt by a proletarian revolution to smash the bourgeois state.[12] Whilst Guy Debord considered it revolutionary urbanism in action, arguing that although it ended in slaughter, for those who lived through the six weeks when the Communards controlled much of the city it was a 'triumph', in that they gained an unprecedented insight into how everyday life might be organised in a non-capitalist manner.[13] George Orwell was similarly effusive in his praise of the situation in Barcelona when anarchists took over the city, creating not another form of state power, but an opening on a quite new world of creative possibilities.[14] Like the Paris Commune, there was no reported crime in Barcelona and similar to the actions of French Communards, workers inspired by a libertarianism firmly rooted in the tradition of Bakunin and Kropotkin had actively begun to experiment with self-government and forms of self-management before the city fell to the Fascists. Although in recent times nothing quite as radical has happened in Britain, there have nevertheless been many experiments in independent self-government; from the setting up of workers' councils to organising daily life during the General Strike of 1926; to the communes and cooperatives of the late nineteenth century and the post-war counter-culture; to the peace camps of the nuclear protest campaign; and to the more recent sit-ins and occupations of the environmental movement. In their varied ways they all began to draw a different 'architecture' of Britain. That such movements fail to achieve their aims does not alter the fact that through such actions, the idea of a different political space is kept alive.

11

> Let me explain. The social condenser is conceived as being a part of, or all of, a building or complex, in which the development of a new way of life and of collective and cooperative organisation would be encouraged, an environment in which women in particular would be liberated from the burdens of domestic labour. As such, a collective laundry, a childcare establishment, as well as the more general categories of the housing commune or workers' club, can be considered as social condensers. Such a theory stresses the transformative and educational possibilities of architecture. As Lissitsky has commented, 'It is to the social revolution, rather than to the technological revolution that the basic elements of Russian architecture are tied.'[15]

Q11. But what has any of this really got to do with architecture?

Everything. Political movements that create an opportunity to experiment with new forms of social organisation are implicitly spatial. It is true that in both Barcelona and Paris more obviously spatial events took place – toppling monuments, changing the use of churches, occupying factories, taking over theatres, and organising rent strikes. But in the long term, if they had succeeded and lasted beyond their few months of existence, such forms of government would have opened up quite new possibilities for both imagining and making architecture. Successful social revolutions are automatically spatial revolutions that create new pre-conditions for the production of architecture. This is both organisational in meaning, in the sense of cooperatives of builders, architects and tenants (e.g. the idea of socialism as a network of collectives and cooperatives), and object-orientated in the imagination of new types of buildings and forms of spatial organisation. The most sustained attempt to do this was in the Soviet Union in the decade after the Bolshevik Revolution. Unlike in Spain and France, opportunities arose not just to 'negate'

1.11 'Change the politics of architecture'. Before and after Burger King was dismantled by urban guerrillas, Glasgow

capitalism but to spatialise a socialist democracy, to organise a socialist building industry, and to create and carry out socialist programmes for architecture. Building workers actively campaigned to abolish the wages system, to eradicate Taylorism, to dismantle 'one man' management and to develop a labour process based around production communes. Architects designed sophisticated housing communes that liberated women from domestic labour, workers' clubs for trade unions, and settlements that contradicted the idea of a city of concentrated political power. The fact that by the end of the 1920s the programme of the Soviet avant-garde had been largely destroyed does not diminish its significance. It is there to remind us that to engage politically with the idea of another world is possible, is a precondition of imagining 'another architecture' and a genuinely alternative practice. Architecture is already political; the point is to change its politics.

NOTES

1   The excerpts in italics that preface each question are taken from my *Fragments of a Moscow Diary*, a collection of notebooks, essays and anecdotes that I have been collecting and writing since I first went to Moscow in 1984 and published my first article on Soviet architecture way back in 1988. More details and references to this work are contained in Chapters 8 and 9 of this volume.

2   'The logical result of Fascism is the introduction of aesthetics into political life'. Walter Benjamin, 'The Work of Art in the Age of Mechanical Reproduction' in *Illuminations* (New York: Schocken, 1985), p. 241.

3   There are probably more essays and books published on the Russian Revolution than any other event in recent world history. There are a good number of volumes devoted to the experiments of the avant-garde, but for capturing the urban and spatial dimensions of the insurrectionary movement there is little that matches the

power and visual impact of the films of Sergei Eisenstein, such as *Strike* and *Battleship Potemkin*. The film *October*, released in 1927 on the tenth anniversary of the revolution, is unique in that it brings for the first time to a mass audience the full drama of an urban revolution in a spectacular display of the visual imagination that has remained a bench mark in the history of film.

4   See for instance Mike Davis, 'Fear and Money in Dubai', in *New Left Review*, 41, September–October 2006, pp. 47–68.

5   The decree on the nationalisation of land on 26 October 1917 was one of the first acts of the Soviet government. See Vladimir Ilyich Lenin, 'Economics and Politics in the Era of the Dictatorship of the Proletariat', in *Selected Works* (Moscow: Progress, 1977), p. 494.

6   For copies of original documents from the momentous years that surround the English Revolution, see Christopher Hill, *The World Turned Upside Down* (London: Penguin, 1991).

7   The full version is retold along with other proclamations in Voline, *The Unknown Revolution* (New York: Free Life Editions, 1974), p. 628. First published in France in 1947. Another version reads 'The freedom of the workers and the peasants is their own, and not subject to any restriction. It is up to the workers and peasants themselves to act, to organise themselves, to agree among themselves in all aspects of their lives, as they themselves see fit and desire...The Makhnovists can do no more than give aid and counsel...In no circumstances can they, nor do they wish to, govern.' Peter Marshall, *Demanding the Impossible: A History of Anarchism* (London: Fontana, 1993), p. 473. For an excellent introduction to revolutionary Barcelona see Chris Ealham, *Anarchism and the City: Revolution and Counter-Revolution in Barcelona, 1898–1937* (Edinburgh: AK Press, 2010).

8   See, for instance, Peter Coe and Malcolm Reading, *Lubetkin and Tecton: Architecture and Social Commitment*, (London:Arts Council of Briain, 1981). And for a comprehensive monograph on Lubetkin, see also the reprint of John Allan, *Berthold Lubetkin: Architecture and the Tradition of Progress* (London: Black Dog Publishing, 2011).

9   See, for instance, Henri Lefebvre, *Writings on Cities* (Oxford: Blackwell, 1996), *Critique of Everyday Life* (London: Verso, 1991) and *The Urban Revolution* (Minneapolis, MN: University of Minnesota Press, 2003).

10   See Catherine Cooke, 'Avant-Garde or Tradition? The Revolutionary Street Festivals,' in *Russian Avant-Garde, Theories of Art, Architecture and the City*, (London: Academy Editions, 1995), pp. 23–4. See also John Bowlt, *Russian Art of the Avant-Garde: Theory and Criticism, 1902–1934* (New York: Viking Press, 1976).

11   Along with the Russian Revolution, the Paris Commune in particular is one of those events that every political theorist and essayist has at some point passed comment on, myself included, and it is the focus of Chapter 6 in this volume.

12   Vladimir Ilyich Lenin, 'The State and Revolution. Experience of the Paris Commune, 1871' (1918), in 'Selected Works, pp. 286–301. Karl Marx, *The Civil War in France* (Peking: Foreign Languages Press, 1970), pp. 72–3.

13   Guy Debord, Attila Kotanyi and Raoul Vaneigem, 'Theses on the Paris Commune,' in K. Knabb (ed.), *The Situationist International, Anthology* (California: Bureau of Public Secrets, 1981), pp. 314–17.

14   Equally controversial is the legacy of the Barcelona commune of 1936. George Orwell visited the city during this period and published his thoughts in his *Homage to Catalonia* (Harmondsworth: Penguin, 2000, originally published in 1938). For a good introduction to the history of anarchist thought, see Peter Marshall, *Demanding the Impossible: The History of Anarchism*. For reprints of original anarchist manifestos

from the Spanish Civil War, see Daniel Guérin, *No Gods, No Masters: An Anthology of Anarchism*, Vol. II (Edinburgh: AK Press, 1998).

15   El Lissitsky, *Russia: An Architecture for World Revolution* (London: Lund Humphries, 1970).

2

Violent Stone: The City of Dialectical Justice –
Three Tales from Court

INTRODUCTION

In its geographical reach and typological inventiveness the spatial revolution of the nineteenth-century bourgeoisie was unprecedented in human history. It was all-embracing and affected every aspect of the architecture of daily life. As Marx famously commented: 'The bourgeoisie, during its rule of scarce 100 years, has created more massive and more colossal productive forces than have all preceding generations together.'[1] This spectacular story of progress and invention was from the outset scarred and deformed by its relationship with imperialism, slavery and colonial exploitation. In three interconnected stories about Glasgow, Liverpool and Brussels, 'Violent Stone' explores the pivotal role that their respective law courts played in providing a juridical and ideological foundation to this history. It is a tale in which reason was shadowed by ignorance, civilisation by barbarism and monumental institutions by diseased hovels. This is a version of a paper first given at the conference Architecture and Justice, held in Lincoln in 2010.

2.1   County
Court, Glasgow

GLASGOW – SUGAR, TOBACCO, AND THE OLD COURT

*Legally, government by bureaucracy is government by decree, and this means
that power, which in constitutional government only enforces the law, becomes
the direct source of all legislation. Decrees moreover remain anonymous (while
laws can always be traced to specific men or assemblies), and therefore seem to
flow from some over-all ruling power that needs no justification.[2]*

Like an unstoppable storm of creative destruction, the bourgeois revolution tore
through the familiar terrain of town and country, spitting out the space–time
certainties of old lives and reassembling them in unrecognisable forms. Vast new
landscapes of production emerged out of ancient commons and felled forests,
whilst terrifying institutions crept out of the smog to categorise and discipline the
unruly and unwilling. And at the epicentre of this urban revolution were buildings
devoted to the rule of law and the circulation of money and commodities. In an
unprecedented pageant of judicial and pecuniary imagination, all manner of banks,
trading houses, notary and lawyer's offices filled the streets of rapidly expanding
cities, and in the midst of all this sat the emblematic monarchs of modern political
economy, the stock exchange and law court.

Law and money became inseparable twins and with their institutional merging,
all the economic endeavours that financed the construction of the nineteenth-
century city, whether it was reaping tobacco, cutting sugar cane, manufacturing
cloth, building ships or smelting pig iron, in a flash of a quill pen and a wax seal were
objectified as legal documents and commodities. Contracts were signed, property
rights were assured, tobacco smoked, sugar eaten, a wage paid, and slowly but
surely the real social origins of commodities became clouded in the mysteries of
the fetish world.

The monumental architecture of the nineteenth century played a crucial role in this process of camouflage. Every city competing to become a fully-fledged capitalist metropolis was required to elevate the houses of legal contract and money to a status hitherto reserved for cardinals and royalty. 'City fathers' accomplished this task with varying degrees of success, measured by how well such institutions dominated the city. For money, they built temples to Mammon. And for the law, no expense was spared. The bigger the better, for it was the job of the new courts fashioned in glorious antiquity to confer the grandeur, authority, and legitimacy that the bourgeoisie so desperately craved. It was also the court's task to silence incendiary talk about self-regulating communes and workers' rights, and to approve the legislation necessary to ensure the smooth progress of capital accumulation.

One of the first examples in Glasgow of this new architecture of legal might was William Stark's sombre justiciary court and gaol built at the Saltmarket in 1809. Its foundation was opportune because it coincided with a marked increase in threats to civic order. Indeed, a year after its inauguration, the Glasgow Commission of Police issued an alarm about roaming gangs of 'Thieves, Rogues, and Vagabonds' who were posing a threat to both persons and property.[3] Exacerbated by repeated outbreaks of labour militancy, typhus and cholera, Stark's court and gaol soon proved inadequate to the task of meeting the disciplinary and punitive demands of a rapidly-expanding capitalist economy and metropolis. The solution was to commission the construction of the monumental County Buildings and Court Houses. Built nearby in the merchant city in the 1840s at the height of the Irish famine and the attack on Chartism, this old centre of government, itself superseded by the City Chambers 40 years later, bears few signs of its original function and now houses boutique flats, up-market shops, restaurants, and the Scottish youth theatre. It is still surrounded by old merchant warehouses, but these, too, have changed their use and are no longer scented with the odour of tobacco and boiling molasses, but by perfumed real estate. Like many of the city's nineteenth-century institutions, it is a neo-classical building dressed with giant Corinthian and Ionic columns. Such facsimiles of the architecture of the ancient world reflected the deeply held bourgeois conceit that they were somehow the legitimate heirs to a democratic tradition that could be traced back to classical antiquity.

Reaping the rewards of plantation and proletarian labour, the early nineteenth-century bourgeoisie liked nothing more than to imagine themselves dressed in togas, defending private property and upholding laws of contract that declared the capitalist and the labourer as 'free' and equal traders in commodities.[4] Accordingly, carved into the blond sandstone wall on its southern elevation that sits beneath a raised portico of fluted columns, is a mixed-up allegory of classical Greece and the death of Jesus that represents bourgeois law and government as high-minded, honourable and in tune with universal laws of nature and history.[5] To reinforce this vision of the timeless qualities of bourgeois justice, the sculpture features an impressive cast of characters judging and dispensing wisdom that includes disciples, sages, jailors, executioners, manacled prisoners, a prostrate man and a mourning woman.

There is, however, a far more insidious connection between Glasgow's merchant class and the ancient world to which they aspired. Much of the wealth of the Athenian Republic came from agricultural slavery. Plato even barred artisans from the polis, considering such labour to be the antithesis of what it meant to be human.[6] Similarly cognitively displaced in an unknown hinterland, the source of much of the finance needed to construct the grand streets and mansions of the merchant city came from the slave economy of the New World. In 1807, a group of prominent merchants gathered in a local meetinghouse to discuss the foundation of the West Indian Association to defend their commercial interests. Like their Liverpool counterparts, they were opposed to the abolition of slavery, expressing both concern over the 'comfort, health, and happiness of the negro population' if abolition was passed, and anxiety over 'the effects of emancipation on a race prone to indolence and idleness.'[7]

The pivotal roles slavery and the plantation economy played in the development of capitalism in Scotland have yet to be fully acknowledged. But the evidence of Glasgow's relationship is strewn across the city. One part of the city atlas is composed of prominent family names. There is Buchanan of Buchanan Street, owner of vast plantations in Virginia, who later became Lord Provost, along with Ingram, Glassford, Dennistoun, Oswald, Mitchell, Speirs and Wilson, all of them either tobacco, sugar or cotton merchants who saw no moral contradiction between their belief in Calvinism and laissez-faire economics and their activities in the plantation economies of the southern United States and Caribbean. Dissecting the urban grid are other names that without conscience commemorate the locations of their estates. It is a roll call of colonial interests – Jamaica, Kingston, Virginia, Plantation Quay, and the ghostly apparition of vanished Antigua. Together they scatter the pink coloured streets with soap, fine cigars, chocolate, sweetened tea and coffee; a culinary and confectionary mix of 'sugar and spice and all things nice.' That is what empire was made of.

LIVERPOOL – FEVER SHEDS, FAMINE AND ST GEORGE'S HALL

> By taking the form of law, right steps into a determinate mode of being. It is then something on its own account, and in contrast with particular willing and opining of the right, it is self-subsistent and has to vindicate itself as something universal. This is achieved by recognising it and making it actual in a particular case without the subjective feeling of private interest; and this is the business of a public authority-the court of justice.'[8]

It is 1838, a mere eight years after the abolition of slavery. It is a momentous period in British political history. Working-class militants, bitterly disappointed by the failure of the Reform Act of 1832 to introduce universal suffrage, had turned to revolutionary syndicalism. Owenite building workers in Birmingham had drafted a plan to reorganise society along cooperative communist lines, and the People's Charter was about to be launched.[9] And it is in the midst of this proto-revolutionary shift in English political sensibilities, in spitting distance of smokestack and dockyard chains, that the Liverpool bourgeoisie embark on their own quest to

2.2   St George's
Hall, Liverpool

build their belief in the eternal nature of capitalist morality and justice. Glaswegians claim their city as the second city of empire. Bengalis claim Kolkata. Scousers insist it is Liverpool. All of them have good reason. I stepped out of Lime Street Station in the low autumnal sun and was dazzled by what was once the biggest and strangest civic building in Britain, a combination of concert hall and court of law.[10]

It is true that when I visit medieval cathedrals, my mind jams with a cacophony of sheep, indentured serfs, fearful labourers, maniac priests and tyrannical landowners. But I also see extraordinary spatial engineering, delicate craftsmanship, and the building labour of love and devotion. Similarly here, in front of this homage to Athens the landscape glitters with the trowels of heroic stonemasons whilst nostrils contract with the odour of choleric fever sheds.[11] And as the city fathers sought immortality in the foundation of St Georges, they commissioned the construction of prison cell and workhouse dormitory that were planned with the same attention to detail as the hold of a slave ship. Here capitalist reason is stripped bare. Planning the distribution of bodies on bunks as preparation for labour in sweatshop or plantation becomes a question of maximising the number of human commodities that can be crammed into every cubic metre.

Simply obeying instructions in the same way that 200 years later, they would plan housing estates and office blocks, architects and engineers drew meticulous plans and sections in which individuals become abstract blobs between lines. Meanwhile in a subterranean world of gloomy and banal offices hidden up back streets and alleyways, armies of accountants, solicitors and bank clerks compile inventories of every conceivable kind. Bureaucratic administration is elevated in importance and becomes the essential modus operandi of the 'great game of expansion,' both domestically and abroad. In a blink of the eye, capital accumulation and conquest become logistical operations that can be precisely detailed in leather-bound ledgers and legal documents. Neutralised in words and numbers, the administrators' archives conceal a rule which, 'out of sight and out of mind' – and therefore unrestricted by social and ethical values – 'exploded with the suddenness of a short circuit in the phantom world of colonial adventure.'[12]

Confident that they were conducting God's work and reassured by the classical economist's vision of a bourgeois utopia founded on the notion of 'free' wage labour, the Liverpool merchant class and bourgeoisie embraced Hegel's idea that law should be made universal and inviolate in the foundation of a 'court of justice'. Their conceit was breathtakingly audacious. With the exception of Roscoe, all of Liverpool's MPs at the turn of the nineteenth century were either slave traders in their own right or defenders of the trade in Parliament.[13] Like Glasgow, Manchester and Bristol, Liverpool's street names and architecture heap praise upon the triangular trade and plantation system, inadvertently reinforcing the argument that such economic activities provided up to 50 per cent of the capital that propelled the industrial revolution and funded the construction of the nineteenth-century city.[14] Only eight years before the foundations for St George's Hall were laid, civic leaders, merchants and politicians drank a toast on the king's birthday. Attired in the finest Egyptian cotton and Syrian mohair, glasses brimming with Portuguese wine and Jamaican rum, they clouded the drawing room with flumes of Cuban tobacco. Staring through the window at the profiles of African children neatly embossed in the entrance to a bank, they announced: 'Prosperity to the African Trade, and may it always be conducted with humanity.'[15]

Forty years later, without malice or irony, they carved their governing ideals into the east elevation. In a burst of utopian delusion they declared the foundation of a new 'world supported by knowledge and right,' and of a society in which 'Justice is relieved of her sword by virtue and the scales of concord.' Their ideal of a natural and God-given justice knew of no limits, for it was born out of 'righteousness and the crown of immortality.' Drunk on ideology, they proselytised from pulpits a concept of justice that was to be pure and untainted by the trappings of 'wealth and fame.' But words of 'conscience and wisdom' were not enough. The Greek goddess of blind justice, Diké, and a supporting cast of angels, are summoned to command this cosmic ambition to plant the kingdom of divine law on earth. Swaying in the folds of Grecian gowns, they sport wreaths, wings, weapons, globes and scales. In a brilliant combination of sculpture and text, the city fathers feminised and eternalised their concept of law and justice as if such demonstrations of state power were in time with history and at one with the universe.

Whilst the friezes of St George's were unveiled to the public, Marx was dying in London. His first writings on alienation and estrangement marked the inception of St Georges, and the development of his critique of political economy coincided with its opening. As discipline and punishment were meted out to the sound of choirs and violins, Marx unleashed his concept of the 'fetishism of commodities,' in which he describes a spectacularly upside-down world where the social relations between human beings assume the 'fantastic form' of a relation between objects seemingly imbued with mystical powers.[16]

Fantastic indeed was the form of St Georges and its sister institutions, and between the law court where property was defended, and the stock exchange where it was traded, there emerged 'an enchanted, perverted topsy-turvy world, in which Monsieur Le Capital and Madame La Terre did their ghost walking as social characters and at the same time as mere things.'[17] As they performed their spectral dance, they whispered the words, 'capital, land and labour'– a semantic trilogy in which 'the secrets of the social production process', profit, rent and wages were hidden.[18] It was an ingenious act of camouflage reinforced by the sacred words that decorated St George's. The magician completes his trick, 'Legal fetishism complements commodity fetishism.'[19] The result was a new and mysterious vocabulary of economic and juridical categories constructed from 'distorted, mystified mental images', in which the reality of capitalist exploitation was obscured in fog.[20]

And it was the same fog that provided much of the cover for dubious acts of exchange in the seaports of Britain; nowhere more so than in the Albert Docks. During the 1890s, long after the 'formal' abolition of slavery, Liverpool had a monopoly on all shipping to the Congo, and it was a clerk for one of the shipping companies, despatched to Antwerp, that came across a horrible secret. The ships being filled with commodities were not listing in the water with the weight of textiles and copper pans, but with guns and armaments. I, too, was on my way from Liverpool to a Belgian city that reminds me of a 'whited sepulchre.'[21] Joseph Conrad's Marlowe in Heart of Darkness does not mention the city's name, but we know where it is, because he looks at a giant map on the wall in the company's offices and realises, 'I am going into the Yellow dead in the centre.' How the foreign secretaries must have argued over the colour to mark their possessions – a grotesque parlour game in which the scramble for Africa became a board game with dice and gun. Pink for the British, purple for the Germans, orange for the Portuguese, green for the Italians, blue for the French, and yellow for the Belgians.

BRUSSELS – RUBBER, OIL AND THE PALAIS DE JUSTICE

> The bourgeoisie has stripped of its halo every occupation hitherto honoured and looked up to with reverent awe. It has converted the physician, the lawyer, the priest, the poet, the man of science into its paid wage labourers. It has been the first to show what man's activity can bring about. It has accomplished wonders far surpassing Egyptian pyramids, Roman aqueducts, and Gothic cathedrals; it has conducted expeditions that put in the shade all former exoduses of nations and crusades.[22]

Still early on a damp morning the Grand Place was almost empty of the steady stream of tourists who arrive throughout the day to admire the gothic Hôtel de Ville and the opulent baroque homes of the merchants and guilds that laid the foundations for Belgium's claim to be the first industrialised economy in continental Europe.[23] Tucked away in a corner there is a bar where Marx, following his expulsion from Paris, met Engels. Peering at the framed views of the guild houses that flank the square, Marx puts pen to paper, and begins to draft one of history's most influential documents, the 'Communist Manifesto'. As his infectious and lyrically political narrative grows, the legacy of his youthful commitment to

legal struggle fades. By now he is convinced that the battle will not be won by the rhetoric of courtroom gowns, but by the class struggle. He flippantly depicts the law as an epiphenomenon of capitalist society's superstructure, and the lawyer, which was once his intended profession, as little more than a paid wage labourer.[24] One hundred and fifty years later and I am standing in front of a small plaque on the wall of the Maison de Cygne that commemorates his stay, pondering the irony of predicting world revolution whilst surrounded by the extravagant architectural display of capitalist economic and political invention.

A short walk from the Grand Place will take you past the Bourse and Opera House – a convenient arrangement so that having first secured the deal and traded on it, the bourgeoisie could relax to the sound of Wagner and Verdi. But my route proceeds down the hill to the old working-class district of Marolles, with its terraces of red-brick housing named after professions like cooper, carpenter and sweep. Once out of the narrow streets linked by arched tunnels, you have to creep furtively lest you are spotted. Even then, there is little chance of remaining concealed.

I stole a glance up an alley in the shadow of a modern council housing scheme with an advert for David Lynch's Eraserhead glued to the lamppost. But the Palais had seen me.[25] It glowers with the same sepulchral silence with which the Sacré Coeur in Paris sends shivers through the descendants of the Communards.[26] It is a grey and unforgiving monument to cruelty and murder. Inaugurated by Leopold the II in 1883 at the very moment when his expeditionary forces delivered gun and sword justice to the indigenous peoples of the Congo, it was the biggest building constructed in the nineteenth century. It was even larger than St Peter's Basilica in Rome. As an unambiguous ideological expression of state power, it is no surprise that Hitler admired the Palais and he instructed Albert Speer to draw it in detail as a candidate for the new Germania plan for Berlin.[27]

As he dreamt of Brussels acquiring an imperial crown, Leopold could rely on Belgian taxpayers to foot the bill for civic buildings like the Palais. But to furnish his private universe, the lavishness of which rivalled that of absolutist monarchs and embarrassed visiting dignitaries, he required a source of revenue that was unrestrained by the demands for political reform sweeping Europe.[28] The Belgian working class, that lived and laboured in some of the most miserable conditions on the continent, were becoming increasingly militant and organised a wave of strikes and riots in support of universal suffrage in 1886 and 1893. Both uprisings were met with military force, mass arrest, and mounted gendarmes wielding sabres. It was the same Belgian sabre that would glint and sparkle in the African sun as Leopold II's mercenaries dispensed punishment, severing the hands of recalcitrant Africans who ignored demands to increase the production of rubber and who refused to accept European authority over their lands. From the very beginning, extraordinary levels of violence marked the European invasion of the Congo delta led by Leopold's adventurer agent Morton Stanley, who boasted to having in no time at all 'attacked and destroyed 28 large towns and four score villages.'[29] In contrast to Stanley's moral ambivalence, other stories filtered back of unspeakable horror.[30] It was Casement, soon to be executed by the British, who met Joseph Conrad and warned him of things 'I have tried to forget, [of] things I never did know.' One of these was the story of Van Kerckhoven, the collector of African heads, the inspiration for Conrad's Kurtz and Coppola's Brando, who was said to have surrounded his compound with a palisade of human skulls, and whose expeditions were described by a contemporary as a hurricane that passed through the countryside leaving nothing but devastation behind it.[31] Meanwhile back in Belgium, unperturbed by any of these tales, Leopold prepared for the grand opening of the Palais de Justice. In the background his ministers and propaganda department hastily set about building his reputation as a philanthropist king, friend of the African and anti-slavery crusader.

During the construction of imperial Brussels, the population of the Congo delta declined by a half, with an estimated 10,000,000 people dying through the combined effects of murder, starvation, exhaustion and disease.[32] The violence, speed, and scale of the Congo conquest, along with all the other crimes that litter the history of the colonisation of Africa, India and the Americas, are almost impossible to grasp. But by inventing concepts of race and bureaucracy the European managed to create a 'refined atmosphere' through which the tragedy of this real history became geographically and historically displaced.[33] Whether it is possible through a plaque on a wall or a piece of public art to evoke the memory of imperial crimes and the suspension of the rule of law is an open question. But unlike the attempt to objectify the memory of the holocaust in camp museums and commemorative landscapes, there is no trace in Brussels of the African genocide, and very little – it should be added – in British cities that speak of the crimes of empire.

Whether Leopold had ever seen St George's Hall, I am not sure. But Lord Leverhulme, MP for the Wirral, philanthropist and founder of the model worker's village at Port Sunlight, certainly visited the Congo where he followed in the footsteps of the Belgian monarch and set up his own private kingdom based in

Leverville that was reliant on forced labour to provide palm oil for his soap business.[34] There was, however, to be no model philanthropic village for the Africans.

The public career of the soon-to-be Lord Lever of Hulme survived his Congo expedition, as did the Palais de Justice. Nowadays the Palais performs a number of civic duties. But there is no hiding its origins in the megalomaniac vanity of one man who was oblivious to the idea that justice might have anything to do with Wallonian miners, let alone native Africans.

The prosperous merchants and wealthy bankers of the Belgian bourgeoisie had urged Leopold to build the Palais's 1,000,000 cubic metres of corridors and staircases, and were delighted with the citadel of secrets in which to defend their property and provide their profits with a legal foundation. The Palais, like St George's, seemed to prove Evgeny Pashukanis' contention that bourgeois capitalist property need no longer be contested weapon in hand for it had been 'transformed into an absolute, fixed right…and which, ever since bourgeois civilisation extended its rule to encompass the whole globe, had been protected the world over by laws, police and law courts.'[35] But others were less than impressed with Leopold's gift to justice, particularly the local proletarians shuffling in the streets below and the former inhabitants of the area, who had been forcibly evicted to make way for the Palais. Incandescent with rage, they ran to the Swan Bar where, under the watchful eye of the ghost of Marx, they joined the recently formed Belgian Workers' Party.

By the general strike of 1902, Brussels was shaking with the tremors of insurrection. Socialists fought running battles with police as they paraded the streets, 'smashing the windows of churches and cafés, firing revolvers and singing revolutionary songs.'[36] They retreated to the Maison du Peuple, the art nouveau masterpiece designed by Victor Horta, where they tore up tramlines and constructed barricades. But other residents resorted to more macabre acts of revenge and if the legend is to be believed, there was a witch who could be seen at dusk wandering the back streets busily sticking needles into an effigy of the Palais's architect Poelart with a relentless ferocity that greatly hastened his descent into terminal insanity.

THE WITHERING OF THE COURT OF LAW

> The state is not 'abolished'. It dies out. This gives the measure of the value of the phrase 'a free state', both as to its justifiable use at times of agitators, and as to its ultimate scientific insufficiency; and also of the demands of so-called anarchists for the abolition of the state out of hand.[37]

Engels wrote that the: 'The central link in civilised society is the state', of which one of the central institutions is the law court. Indeed, Glasgow's Old Court, like St George's and the Palais, ostensibly captures the idea of a civilised society governed by law. But he added that the state, 'in all typical periods is without exception the state of the ruling class and in all cases continues to be essentially a machine for holding down the oppressed, exploited class.'[38] For those that dream of the parliamentary reform of capitalism, the idea of the state and the

2.4   Marx in
Brussels

legal system as little more than a weapon designed to maintain the hegemony of the ruling class is crude and unsophisticated. They will point to evidence that shows that although courts can be places where draconian judgements are delivered or, indeed, where the rule of law is abandoned altogether, they have also been the forum where progressive legislation has been passed. By necessity they cling to the belief that however terrifying a court may be when controlled by political criminals, however intimidating its scale and size, and however grim its origins as the legal face of a repressive and exploitative system, changing the regime that resides within can alter its metaphorical associations. However in the latter half of the nineteenth century, before universal suffrage, when the courtrooms of Glasgow, Liverpool and Brussels echoed with black skins, tubercular workers and wigged rhetoric, Engel's depiction of the state and its legal machinery as an adjunct of capital made absolute sense.

The meanings we attach to buildings are unstable and transitory. Transformations in use, ingenious forms of camouflage, and the distortion of memory have softened and fundamentally altered the significance of old buildings like the courts of the nineteenth-century city. Glasgow's County Court becomes a chic place to live. St George's doubles up as a dance hall and cultural centre, and the Palais de Justice becomes a picture postcard… Meanwhile, light years away from faith in courtly dialogue or civilian changes in use, the anarchists of the Spanish Civil War dreamt of a society in which all forms of authority, discrimination, and punishment would be abolished.[39] In this stateless world there would be no need for such things as a court of law, a prison or the headquarters of the secret police. Such institutions would simply be allowed to disintegrate until they were indistinguishable from a ruined garden.

NOTES

1   Karl Marx and Frederick Engels, *The Communist Manifesto* (London: Penguin Classics, 2002), p. 224–5.

2   Hannah Arendt, *The Origins of Totalitarianism, Ideology and Terror* (London: Harvest, 1976), p. 243.

3   See Tom Devine, *The Scottish Nation, 1700–2000* (London: Penguin, 2000), p. 224.

4   'The slave is exactly subservient to his master. This is why this exploitative relationship requires no specifically legal formulation. The wage worker, on the contrary, enters the market as a free vendor of his labour power, which is why the relation of capitalist exploitation is mediated through the form of contract.' Evgeny Pashukanis, *Law and Marxism: A General Theory* (London: Pluto,1989), pp. 110–13.

5   See Arendt, *The Origins of Totalitarianism*, pp. 461–5.

6   See P. Anderson, *Passages from Antiquity to Feudalism* (London: Verso, 1974), pp. 18–28.

7   For the statements of Glasgow merchants see, J. MacLehose, *Memoirs and Portraits of 100 Glasgow Men* (Glasgow, 1886), p. 130 and other entries. See Glasgow Digital Library, http://gdl.cdlr.strath.ac.uk/mlemen/mlemen101.html. For a brief snapshot of the West Indian Association and black history in Glasgow, see D. Dabydeen, J. Gilmore and C. Jones (eds), *The Oxford Companion to Black British History* (Oxford: Oxford University Press, 2008), pp. 189–91.

8   Georg W.F. Hegel, *Philosophy of Right* (Oxford: Oxford University Press, 1967), p. 140.

9   For a general commentary on the European and British dimensions of political militancy, see E. Hobsbawm, *Age of Revolution* (London: Abacus. 1997). For a history of labour in the nineteenth-century construction industry, see Raymond Postgate, *The Builders' History* (London: The National Federation of Building Trade Operatives, 1923).

10   Architectural historians like Niklaus Pevsner claim St George's as one of the finest and most important examples of neo-classicism in the world. See, for instance, Quentin Hughes, *Liverpool: City of Architecture* (Liverpool: Bluecoat Press, 1999), p. 59.

11   For first-hand details of living conditions in Liverpool in the mid nineteenth century, see the *Liverpool Journal*, 24 November 1849, htttp://www.old-merseytimes.co.uk.

12   Arendt, *The Origins of Totalitarianism*, p. 190.

13   See, for instance, G. Cameron and S. Cooke, *Liverpool: Capital of the Slave Trade* (Liverpool: Birkenhead Press, 1992), p. 44.

14   See Robin Blackburn, *The Making of New World Slavery: From the Baroque to the Modern, 1492–1800* (London: Verso, 1998), pp. 517–18.

15   See G. Cameron and S. Cooke, *Liverpool*, p. 72. See also M. and K. Sherwood, *Britain, The Slave Trade and Slavery from 1562 to the 1880s* (Liverpool:S avannah Press, 2007), pp. 73–7.

16   See Karl Marx, *Capital*, Vol. I (London: Penguin, 1990), pp. 163–7.

17   Karl Marx, *Capital*, Vol. III (London: Lawrence and Wishart, 1984), p. 830.

18   Ibid., p. 814.

19   Evgeny Pashukanis, *Law and Marxism: A General Theory* (London: Pluto, 1989) p. 117.

20   Ibid., p. 73.

21 'I was crossing the Channel to show myself to my employers, and sign the contract. In a very few hours I arrived in a city that always makes me think of a whited sepulchre. Prejudice no doubt. I had no difficulty in finding the company's offices. It was the biggest thing in town, and everybody I met was full of it. They were going to run an overseas empire, and make no end of coin by trade.' Joseph Conrad, *Heart of Darkness* (Oxford: Oxford University Press, 2002), p. 110.

22 Karl Marx and Friedrich Engels, *The Communist Manifesto* (London: Penguin Classics, 2002), p. 222.

23 Eric Hobsbawm, *Age of Empire* (London: Abacus, 1987), pp. 41–2.

24 Karl Marx and Friedrich Engels, *The Communist Manifesto*, p. 82. See also the infamous and often misunderstood passage that begins: 'The totality of these relations of production constitutes the economic structure of society, the real foundation, on which arises a legal and political superstructure…' Karl Marx, *A Contribution to the Critique of Political Economy* (London: Lawrence and Wishart, 1981), p. 20.

25 For a description of the Palais see Walter Sebald, *Austerlitz* (London: Penguin Books, 2001), pp. 38–9.

26 See David Harvey, *Paris, Capital of Modernity* (London: Routledge, 2006), p. 311.

27 See Albert Speer, *Inside the Third Reich* (London: Phoenix, 1997), pp. 78–9.

28 Adam Hochschild, *King Leopold's Ghost. A Story of Greed, Terror, and Heroism in Colonial Africa* (London: Macmillan, 1998), pp. 293–4.

29 Stanley added that: 'The blacks give an immense amount of trouble; they are too ungrateful to suit my fancy.' Hochschild (1998), p. 49.

30 Reports relayed by Roger Casement, Morel the Liverpool shipping clerk and Williams the African American journalist. 'This officer's…method…was to arrive in canoes at a village, the inhabitants of which invariably bolted on their arrival; the soldiers were then landed, and commenced looting…after this they attacked the natives until able to seize their women; these women were then kept as hostages until the Chief of the District brought in the required number of kilograms of rubber.' Hochschild, *King Leopold's Ghost*, p. 161.

31 Ibid., pp. 196–8.

32 That took place between 1880–1920. Ibid., pp. 225–34.

33 The ability to forget about Africa, to 'create a vicious, refined atmosphere' around such crimes was institutionalised within the European mind through what Arendt suggests were the concept of race, a mechanism to explain 'other' human beings 'who no civilised European could understand', and through the great game of bureaucratic administration, the essential modus operandi of the 'great game of expansion'. Arendt, *The Origins of Totalitarianism*, pp. 185–90.

34 See Jules Marchal, *Lord Leverhulme's Ghosts – Colonial Exploitation in the Congo* (London: Verso, 2008).

35 Pashukanis, *Law and Marxism*, p. 115.

36 *New York Times*, 11 April 1902.

37 Friedrich Engels, *Anti-Duhring* (Moscow: Progress Publishers, 1978), p. 341.

38 Friedrich Engels, *The Origin of the Family, Private Property, and the State* (London: Lawrence and Wishart, 1981), p. 235.

39   See for instance, Murray Bookchin, *The Spanish Anarchists. The Heroic Years 1868–1936* (Edinburgh: Cassell, 1998), pp. 269–70. In addition, for reprints of various libertarian manifestos from the Iberian anarchist tradition, see Daniel Guerin, *No Gods, No Masters*, Book 2 (Edinburgh: AK Press, 1998).

3

Paris: Ghosts and Visions of a Revolutionary City

INTRODUCTION

I had been following in the footsteps of Walter Benjamin, rambling through the arcades from the proletarian haberdashery of the rue St Denis to the consumption theme park of the Passage de Panorama. Exiting into the brittle February morning, I retreated across the road into a small bistro, the Café Le Croissant. It was here in 1914 that Jean Jaurès, philosopher, socialist and founder of *L'Humanité*, had stopped to gather his thoughts before heading for a meeting of the Worker's Internationale. He never made it, and a plaque outside commemorates his death at the hands of an appropriately-named assassin, Villain. As the sleet smeared the windows, it seemed the perfect place to sit for an afternoon and ponder the spatial tactics of urban revolution, in particular that of the Paris Commune, which like an otherworldly phenomena possessed of uncertain qualities and shifting form, has been pored over, researched, and theorised from every conceivable angle.[1] Arguments over its significance and political character were a keystone in debates on the left during the twentieth century; one of the litmus tests, with which you could tell by the shade of red, where an individual stood in the historic disputes between Communists, social democrats and anarchists.[2] As might be expected, there is no consensus. For Engels and Lenin it was nothing short of 'the dictatorship of the proletariat in action'.[3] But for others, this is romantic and wishful thinking. The Commune might have been many things – a demand for municipal liberties, a viciously repressed rent strike, an anarchist rejection of authority, an angry outburst at the capitulation of Versailles to the Prussians, but a revolution it was not.[4] To which the Situationists replied: 'How would you know? For those that really lived it, it was already there.'[5]

3.1   Boulevard des Italiens

480   PARIS — Boulevard des Italiens
E. L. D.

ACT 1

The attempt to banish the memory of 1848. Paris is transformed into an outdoor cemetery. Preparation for a coup d'état and the inauguration of the Second Empire.

Enjoyed by Parisians and tourists alike, who come to sit on the randomly distributed chairs, the Jardin du Luxembourg is a tranquil enough place, and there is nothing on the information plaque that tells of its grisly history. If after 1789, the full programme for the socialisation of land and property had been implemented, then like all other private gardens of the aristocracy, it would have been planted with wheat and sunflowers. But there was to be no such picturesque fate for the Jardin. In marked contrast, in 1848 it was temporarily closed to the public because the giant pools of blood that had accumulated with the mass slaughter of insurgents had become impossible to hide. The Jardin du Luxembourg – one of the green lungs of Paris – had been transformed into a butcher's yard.[6] It was just one episode in a macabre 'saturnalia of reaction' that was unleashed across the city. Rivers of blood coursed down street gutters, mountains of corpses stood in squares, and prisoners were shot on the spot. The idea of a social republic was defeated and within days all the progressive laws that had been fought for, such as the tax on capital, on the restriction of the working day, and on the illegality of debt imprisonment, were repealed.[7] The repression was ruthless and thorough. On the eve of the revolution of 1848 there had been 300 socialist associations in Paris. By 1851, there were none.[8]

3.2   The Rue de Rivoli

ACT 2

The Prelude to the Commune. The dialectic of urban development. Paris is rebuilt as the Capital of the Second Empire to tumultuous acclaim and equally passionate condemnation.

I am standing on a traffic island in the middle of the Boulevard von Haussmann. In all such places I tend to stop, transfixed, camera in hand, and peer through squinted eyes along avenues that like the bourgeois determination to conquer and colonise the world seem to have no limits. Contemplating infinity is disorientating and unsettling. Time begins to drift and the vista fills with picks, rams and a phantom army of unemployed labourers busily demolishing the city's prehistory. Marshalling their activities is Haussmann, the Ahab of modern urban reconstruction, a man whose name would become synonymous with the relentless search for the ideal city of god, empire and capital.

Tourists flocked to the city from as far away as New York and Moscow to marvel at the elegant embodiment of the modern urban imagination. On a daily basis they left the city spellbound by tales of how the magician Haussmann had rescued Paris from 'moral epilepsy',[9] of how he had stimulated economic revival, restored France's world reputation, and improved the city's sanitation, infrastructure and transport.[10] 'Look,' they said, 'at how the new streets are fast, clean, airy, brightly illuminated, and safe from pickpockets and pimps.'[11] Most important of all, they left happy, comforted by the expert manner in which Haussmann had absorbed the monumental propaganda and urban surveillance techniques of Ledoux and Boullée and made the city 'unfavourable to the habitual tactic of local insurrection'.[12] The pursuit of profit and autocratic government had created a city that encapsulated the bourgeois worldview, and if the forces of progress smashed antiquated patterns of life, this was simply the work of the immutable law of creative destruction in which the ends justified the occasional errors of means.[13] So admired was his blueprint for an imperial city of order and authority, that it was copied and speedily dispatched to the endangered ruling class across Europe. In Madrid, Budapest and Berlin, bankers, priests and the siblings of fallen absolutist monarchs knelt and gave thanks for the restoration of the holy cross and private property. In turn, they, too, set about building their own Parisian facsimile.

But there is another version of events in which the noble city of empire, smashed together in great haste, has begun to crack and fade like the paint on a hurriedly finished canvas. The fairy lights and flowers that once festooned the streets flicker and wilt. The furious clapping that celebrated the mythic restoration of order subsides. Majestically illuminated tenements and arcades are plunged into darkness as the whole panorama is enveloped in a mucky grey. Damned is the empire. The roars of conquering cannon struggle to compete with the groans of Africa and the curses of unemployed insurgents. Haussmann's name plaque, once securely fastened to the wall as a signal of his restoration as a hero of France, has slipped and is dangling precariously. Another history begins to emerge. This one has no happy ending. It speaks not of valour and pride but of financial corruption, unregulated speculation and politically motivated urban vandalism. It speaks of urban dictatorship.

Paris is now condemned as 'a plague of senseless constructions in which unknown thousands lost their lives'. Far from a demonstration of the mason's art or the tectonic wonder of modern construction, it has mutated into an ugly pile of stones shifted 'by the hand of despotism' that lacks 'all social spontaneity'.[14] No longer the capital of romance and poetry, it has become an 'eternal prison' of endlessly repeated details that 'represses all forms of organic self-development and individuality'.[15] In this version of events, Haussmann is the villainous urban dictator who, with the full backing of the emperor, bypasses the planning commission and co-opts the unelected municipal council to suit his will.[16]

He is no longer the enlightened urban planner, but a criminal manipulator who masterminds the operations of a secret cult of public officials, financiers, bankers, builders, developers and landowners.[17] Together they hatch a plot to rebuild the city but in a way that would personally assure them of vast fortunes. To fund their scheme, they build an elaborate and impenetrable financial system specialising in credit.[18] Fictitious capital and mythical bonds create money out of nothing. Architecture assumes full commodity form as a nameless money object.[19] Leases are fabricated out of thin air. Lawyers are happy to make it all legal.[20] Recently bought property is suddenly expropriated and the landowner, a member of the inner circle, laughs all the way to the bank as if he has won the lottery.[21] Haussmann's wife is heard joking; 'It is curious that every time we buy a house, a boulevard passes through it.'[22] And for 20 years the banquet of unrestrained speculation and pleasure seeking continued.[23] Then in 1870, it came to an abrupt end in a financial scandal that revealed that debt charges constituted over 44 per cent of the city's budget.[24] Haussmann and his friends had bankrupted the city and mortgaged the future.[25] The culprit ends up in the dock, accused along with the directors of financial companies and contracting firms of defrauding the city of Paris.[26]

5. Hôtel de Ville incendié – Grande Façade

3.3   The ruins of
the Hôtel de Ville

But the trial would have to wait. By July of the same year France was at war with Prussia – a conflict that would culminate in one of the most celebrated and controversial episodes in urban history.

ACT 3

> *26 March. The real action begins. The city votes and citizens pour into the streets. The city is seized. The town hall is occupied and the ruling class flee to Versailles.*

The temptation that lurks in romantic exaggeration is matched in equal measure by the desire to forget. Defeat should never be confused with failure. The Commune might never have seized the Bank of France – a single act that would have stopped the vengeful bourgeoisie in its tracks, but as Marx reflected, 'the great social measure of the Commune was its existence'.[27]

In 1848, captured revolutionaries were starved to death in the cellars of the Hôtel de Ville. Twenty-three years later, their former comrades returned to occupy its debating chambers and raise the red flag from its roof that they claimed was not only the emblem of the Commune, but the flag of the World Republic. It was from a platform in front of the main façade bedecked in red streamers and banners that on 28 March 1871 the Commune was proclaimed and the greatest festival of the nineteenth century began.[28] A massive crowd had assembled to celebrate the results of the election in which over a quarter of a million Parisians had participated. All manner of romantics, fantasists, liberals, radicals and revolutionaries thronged the square and surrounding streets, parading their beliefs in an ideological carnival, vying with each other in their claims to be speaking on behalf of the people. Many had voted simply for the right to a municipal democracy, and for the fair and just administration of the city. They had lost their patience with the emperor, were seething with resentment at the theft of public money, but had no interest in the overthrow of the capitalist state. A spokesman held forth: 'Friends, there is no need for arms. Capitalism can be reformed by peaceful means without us threatening private property or attacking the principles of the free market.'

But the mood of the crowd had decisively shifted away from such timorous talk towards the songs of ardent revolutionary socialists, 29 of whom had just been elected to the new municipal government and who promised a quite different political future. Re-emerging from the shadows and political catacombs of two decades of repression, they were determined to rekindle the memories and programmes of 1848 and 1789. Ridiculing the idea that the political and economic system, which they held to be morally corrupt, could be reformed, they dreamt instead of the 'levelling of wealth', and of a 'communism of land, industry and commerce', in which at long last an individual would have 'the right to the produce of his or her labour'.[29] Armed with glue and hastily printed posters, they covered the city with manifestos that demanded in a prefiguration of future plans for the socialisation of property, the establishment of a Republic that would 'guarantee political liberty through social equality – by handing over to the workers the tools of their production'.[30]

Kropotkin had argued that the soul of the 1789 Revolution was to be found in the Communes that abolished feudal dues and appropriated what had formerly been communal lands from the lords.[31] Now, after a century maturing in the political imagination, this spirit of collective self-organisation had been reborn in the occupation of the city and in a succession of famous decrees announced over the next four weeks that included: the formal separation of Church and State, the suspension of rent payments, the requisitioning of empty houses, the closure of pawnshops and the handover of abandoned factories to workers' cooperatives.[32]

ACT 4

> *11 April. An invading army surrounds Paris. The Commune tries to protect itself by building barricades. Its streets, parks and construction sites are pillaged for anything that can be used as building material. Women take to the streets in their thousands to defend their new found civil liberties. Patriarchs choke with fury and are met with abuse.*

The appearance of barricades announces that an urban revolution has begun (but is also under threat). Thousands were built in the revolutions of 1830 and 1848, in spectacular examples of collective urban construction that consumed millions of paving stones.[33] Some of them, inspired by medieval fortifications, 'towered like mountains' and stretched 'to the level of the rooftops'.[34] In the Rue St Jacques alone, a steeplechase of 38 barricades was built along its length to defend the area around the Panthéon where, in 1848, students and workers had sparked the revolution. It was an epic building enterprise, but despite their number and structural ingenuity, they were to prove no match for Cavaignac's troops, who took them one by one

1. Barricade des Fédérés
Place Vendôme et Rue Castiglionne

3.4   Barricade des Fédérés

as revolutionaries retreated to the balconies of the dome. From there, flitting amongst the columns, they fired their last bullets as a fatal fusillade of cannon fire ripped through the door of the former church and blew off the head of the statue of immortality. As Engels was to point out in the aftermath of 1848, barricades had been shown to be obsolete in the face of modern weaponry.[35]

However, completely undeterred by such history lessons, barricades sprang up again in 1871, first in Belleville, the Rue de Charonne and the Fauborg du Temple, and then all over the East and the Left Bank. Once more the city was transformed into a real time construction site, in which all manner of experimental structures appeared. Their proliferation was helped by the fact that construction workers were the biggest occupational group amongst the Communards, or at least, in the list of those arrested and deported.[36] Some were little more than hastily-built barriers piled up out of stolen building materials and whatever objets trouvés the city could offer: carts, carriages, fences and street furniture. But others, like the Barricade de Fédérés in the Rue de Castiglionne, were elegant engineering works, meticulously detailed and as picturesque as the Beaux Artes terraces that they bridged.

It was the twenty-first time since 1789 that the streets of the city had been barricaded. If inanimate objects could speak or a forensic archaeologist could diagnose chips and cracks, many of the cobblestones could tell of how they had been repeatedly used as missiles or construction materials. But why such madness if they were of little military use? Because the barricades were like magic charms, moral fortifications, a highly-charged and symbolic declaration that 'the city is ours'. They might not stop bullets and cannonballs but that mattered little to those that waited behind them, ready and intoxicated by a 'crazed ecstasy of senseless expectations'.[37]

And it wasn't just men that waited either. So often marginalised from the political history of such events, women were at the forefront of the Commune. They mobilised the people, organised neighbourhood meetings and demonstrations and were some of the most enthusiastic barricade builders.[38] In the midst of them was the spiritual godmother of Emma Goldman and Alexandra Kollontai, the anarchist poet Louise Michel, nicknamed the Red Virgin. Touring the barricades she read Baudelaire to students, who sat enthralled by the legends of her fearlessness and revolutionary ardour and by her reputation as an advocate of free love.[39] Like a phantom, she was seen everywhere from Montmartre to Belleville. One moment she was chairing a meeting, the next she was seen waving a red flag, standing fearlessly on top of a barricade with gun in hand, firing on the Versailles troops.

There was little that the conservatives, monarchists and right-wing republicans hated more than revolutionary women. Delacroix's romanticised painting of a noble bare-breasted Liberté was bad enough. But the reality was far worse. Nothing could be more offensive than mothers, sisters, and daughters demanding equality between the sexes, sexual freedom and the right to divorce. For a century, 'creatures from the underworld', 'nameless harpies', atheists, communists, and 'middle-aged women who should no better', had offended God and the sanctity of the family. Their ranks had spawned the hideous *petroleuses* who, dressed in black with red bandanas, would bare their genitalia at the bourgeoisie and for ten francs throw a milk-can full of kerosene into a house. Equally terrifying was the sight of women demonstrating at the Hôtel de Ville over rising bread prices and soaring rent levels – women who were ready and willing to tear the city apart if their demands went unmet.

ACT 5

> *The end of April and early May. Everyday life in the city is transformed. Buildings are squatted and turned over to new uses. The volume of programmes and manifestos turn the cogs of the printing presses white-hot. Cardinals flee as the revolution mounts the pulpit.*

For a while at least Paris was like a mythological city bursting with strange and unfamiliar phenomena, in which the profane had replaced the normal rules and conventions of civic order and behaviour.[40] Ordinary citizens forgot the causal promenade and immersed themselves in the tactics of urban rebellion. Shop-keepers, buildings workers and teachers became students in the art of barricading streets, and in occupying and changing the use of key buildings and government institutions. They altered place names, destroyed the symbols of repression and authority, and in place of the cherubs and chariots of imperial monuments, there emerged a 'terrifying' architecture of constructive negation. It was as if the city's inhabitants had willingly agreed to participate in an epic drama, a pageant of retributive justice that they somehow knew would be remembered for centuries. The optimism was contagious. After all, the city had been released from the suffocating stranglehold of imperial rhetoric. It had begun to breathe again. And yes, the people drank and sang, as is to be expected at the celebratory wake that follows the death of tyrants.

PARIS APRÈS LE SIÈGE ET LA COMMUNE

3.5   The destruction of the Vendôme Column

There was, then, far more at stake than simply the right to vote. A different sort of city fluttered in the imagination of urban revolutionaries, who could draw upon a tradition that included Fourier's Phalansterie, Godin's Palais Sociale and Tony Moilin's plan for a socialist Paris.[41] Artists such as Courbet joined in, and carried away with the emotion of the moment, painted a portrait of a Paris liberated from all exploitation where everyone would be 'engaged in unfettered genius', remaking the city into the international capital of Europe. No longer governed by the 'pretensions of monsters', Paris would become a creative idyll that offered 'arts, industry, trade, and transactions of all kinds' to refugees from repressive regimes.[42]

Political bleach and a broom had swept the city clean of the rich and powerful, leaving barely a trace of 'the meretricious Paris of the Second Empire'. It was no longer the rendezvous of British landlords, American ex-slaveholders and Russian boyars.[43] The ruling class had fled, along with the thieves and murderers. Paris had begun to police itself. Nocturnal burglaries and robbery had virtually ceased, and for the first time since February 1848, the streets were safe. Gendarmes were nowhere to be seen inside the barricades.

A pressure valve had blown; this much we know. Newspaper stands overflowed with new titles such as the *Vengeur* and *La Commune*. The *Cri de Peuple* alone had a circulation of 100,000. Pamphleteers, political artists and caricaturists were hard at work and the kiosks displayed cartoons ridiculing and satirising the opponents of the Commune. The Corps Legislatif was cleared of politicians and transformed into a sandbag factory. The red flag flew from the glass dome of the Bourse.[44] Theatres staged benefit concerts for the wounded. The Opera performed revolutionary hymns. Where once Bonaparte had been entertained in the Salle de Marechaux, now Mademoiselle Agar recited Victor Hugo's poetic condemnations of imperial grandeur. Great works of music drove away the 'musical obscenities of Empire'. The Museum de Louvre was opened to the public, and the Place de Bastille hosted a bizarre gingerbread fair.[45]

As in previous revolutions, clubs became the home of political life and were organised in halls, rooms and appropriated buildings across the city. Windows rattled as the streets and squares resounded with the noise of passionate debate on women's rights, the role of trade unions and the idea of producer and consumer cooperatives.[46] Dance halls, that only a few weeks earlier had heaved to the sound of bands and orchestras, were transformed into revolutionary debating chambers. It was reported that in the Montmatre Club, one could hardly see for the clouds of blue smoke or hear for the tumult of voices. An extraordinary cross-section of Parisian society, national guards, suburban philosophers, women of the people, prostitutes, girls in red hoods, 'all of them red from the insides of their hats to the uppers of their shoes',[47] had gathered underneath the chandeliers to argue and dance to a new way of life. For that is what the Commune promised – a quotidian revolution in which nothing was sacred and just as in 1789, when churches and chapels were turned into Temples of Reason, so once again they were secularised, as God was pronounced dead.

Like their revolutionary ancestors, many Communards saw little distinction between the crucifix and the time clock of the bourgeoisie and attacked both with equal force. The pulpits, draped in scarlet and bathed in blood-red candlelight, were transformed into revolutionary stage sets. In place of humble submission, quite different ideas of moral authority echoed down the aisles. Psalms and promises of salvation were replaced by demands for freedom from exploitation. The altars shook with threats to despotic employers, who considered workers as 'production machines' and who failed to pay them the full value of their labour.[48] The anti-clerical and revolutionary sentiment was contagious. In the St Severin Church, the club chairman announced his intention to once and for all 'crush the bourgeoisie' and 'take over the Bank of France'.[49] At a meeting in the Trinité, a speaker rose from the pews and promised the audience of women that the factories, all means of production and profits, would be fully socialised, but that to achieve such goals they must make 'an immediate and total break with the insane superstitions that are preached in this building'.[50] Meanwhile, from the St Ambroise Church of the XI arrondissement, the Club Prolétaire distributed its own revolutionary newspaper in which they demanded the abolition of all special privileges and religious instruction, and the introduction of workers' control and universal primary school education.[51]

ACT 6

16 May. The antithesis of architecture. In time-honoured fashion insurgents attack the symbols of oppression. With the applause of the Communards ringing in his stone ears, Napoleon Bonaparte is toppled from his perch. The city burns. Versailles blames vandals. Communards blame it on the cannon fire of Versailles as they flee in an effort to escape the execution squads.

Throughout the short-lived Commune, apoplexy, indignation and panic had filled the corridors of Versailles. Outraged clerics and factory owners fearing damnation declaimed the Communards with all their might: 'They planted crops in our

10. Palais des Tuileries incendié
Vue Générale

3.6   The burnt-out remains of the Tuileries

gardens, burnt the royal throne, and made a bridge out of the ruins of our prison. They decapitated the statues of apostles, and ridiculed us. Now they have shot our generals and plan to demolish not only the Nôtre Dame but also the Chapel of Atonement built to make amends for their execution of Louis XVI. Is there no end to their ungodliness?'

On 16 May, as the fate of the Commune hung in the balance, the Parisian workers, in one of their last acts of defiance, decided to carry out the decree of 12 April and demolish the Vendôme Column, an event that was to become as famous in urban history as the storming of the Bastille. Forged out of the cannons of defeated armies and etched with images of the debris of war, angels, eagles, and Roman standards, Napoleon's column was considered an affront to the civilised world and democracy.[52] An estimated 15,000 onlookers thronged the square, hung out of windows and sat on rooftops. The column was sawn above the pedestal, a pulley was attached and with a drawn-out moan, it was dragged to the ground. The bands played the *Marseillaise*, as the 'head of Bonaparte rolled on the ground, and his parricidal arm lay detached from the trunk.' Immediately after, a red flag was hoisted on the 'purified pedestal'.[53] If the council hadn't prevented the massive crowd from picking up pieces of the column as mementoes, the Versaillese would have been unable to put Napoleon back together again, and the pedestal would have remained empty as a permanent reminder of the folly of war and empire.[54]

Toppling the Vendôme was an outrage. But what happened next was worse. Had Versailles not attacked the Commune with such ferocity, then Paris might well have escaped unscathed. The Communards were in retreat. There would be no time to build a new city, but just enough to strike at the heart of the body politic and French history by torching the Town Hall and the Royal Palace. With 12 remaining Communards, Jean Louis Pindy, an anarchist carpenter who would later represent the Paris construction workers at the Second International, led the defence of the last barricade in front of the Tuileries. Facing certain defeat, he instructed the others to set fire to the palace. As the flames ripped through the salons and galleries, he proclaimed: 'Let the imperial palace, this shame of France, perish in flames, and never rise again from the ashes.'[55] He was successful. The Tuileries, ruined beyond repair, was never rebuilt and the Louvre courtyard lost its western façade.

Its charred husk was still there when Kropotkin visited the city in 1878. Overwhelmed by the sight, as if it presaged the dawn of a newly-liberated Europe, he talked of how its broken pediments, crumbling stone and empty windows, already overgrown with 'new vegetation, were the most beautiful monument in Paris'. 'How fine it was', he said, 'that in at least one city of Europe the dwelling place of emperors should be a scenic ruin.'[56] These were the last days of the Commune. Flames licked the Hôtel de Ville, and quickly consumed the Rue de Rivoli, the Palais Royale and the left bank all the way up to the Palais de Justice and Prefecture de Police. Before long, the whole of central Paris was burning in an unexpected son et lumière, in which 'the caprices of the fire displayed a blazing architecture of arches, cupolas, and spectral edifices'.[57]

Although much of the firestorm was the result of the cannon fire of Versailles, the Communards were inevitably blamed for the desecration of Paris – an act that confirmed that these godless rebels were no better than a horde of barbarians, who should be dealt with accordingly. Retribution was swift and violent, proving Marx's contention that the value placed on human death lies in inverse proportion to the value placed on the destruction of property. For that was certainly the case in the reaction to the burning of Paris that accompanied the fall of the Commune, when '(t)he bourgeoisie of the whole world, which looks complacently upon the wholesale massacre after the battle', was 'convulsed by horror at the desecration of brick and mortar'.[58]

ACT 7

The city of Hope gives way to the city of vengeance. Unspeakable savagery takes place. The rest of Europe looks on in shock at the unjustifiable blood lust of the bourgeoisie.

The meanings that we attach to buildings, built out of some warped notion of retributive justice or to satisfy the megalomaniac conceit of rulers, can soften and alter over time. Few of us worry that the mediaeval cathedrals and monuments of the ancient world required armies of conscripted labourers and the forcible taxation of civilians. There are, however, some buildings that retain all of their horror. Franco's tomb at El Valle de Los Caídos is one. And such is the case with the Sacré Coeur, whose only hope of redemption is when it is turned into a revolutionary theatre or a climbing centre. From the top of the Eiffel Tower it resembles the upturned teats and udder of an un-milked cow. It was famously located and built to be unavoidable. In the sun, its white stone shimmers like a daylight spectre. At night, floodlights illuminate its facades and transform it into a pale cadaver that casts a sickly glow across Montmartre. Commissioned in 1873,

3.7   Mur des
Fédérés, cimetière
Père Lachaise

for the faithful it signifies the victorious restoration of the Church after the defeat of the blasphemous Commune – architectural penitence for a century of defiant anti-clerical sentiment in which holy places had been defamed. This is also why it is despised. As construction workers wound their way up the hill to lay the foundation stones they ran a gauntlet of taunts from surviving insurgents, who sang 'Long live the devil' and the 'The good lord in the shit'.[59] Some say that the Sacré Coeur 'hides its secrets in sepulchral silence'.[60] But for those sympathetic to the aspirations of the Commune, it remains a loud and permanent reminder of the slaughter conducted by General MacMahon. The descendent of an Irish doctor from Limerick, the Duc de Magenta, a favourite of Napoleon III, orchestrated the murder of 30,000 Communards in response to the loss of 700 Versailles troops. The rapidity, brutality and bloodthirsty madness of Versailles's revenge traumatised a nation. However, not content with the reclamation of the living city, the bourgeoisie had one last act to perform – the occupation of the city of the dead. In tune with their imperial ambitions, figures like Thiers and Haussmann are interred in a hybrid architecture of classical antiquity and Egypt. Not surprisingly, they are located off the main avenue in the centre of the cemetery Père Lachaise. In marked contrast to the pompous memorial of the rich and powerful is the Mur des Fédérés in the far eastern corner. This was the last stand of the Commune and after a ferocious gun battle amongst the gravestones, 147 Communards were executed and buried in a communal pit at the foot of the wall.

EPILOGUE

…Three ghosts stand looking at the carved inscription, each proffering an answer to the question: so what was the Commune? The first speaks:

'It was the political form at last discovered under which to work out the economic emancipation of labour, and had it survived, it would have undoubtedly abolished the capital and the class which makes the labour of the many the wealth of the few.'[61]

The second demurs:

'But to the best of my knowledge my friend, it neither declared itself socialist, nor did it expropriate capital. It didn't even take stock of the general resources of the city, let alone break with the tradition of the state. It could be nothing but a first attempt.'[62]

The third tries to provide a conclusion:

'It was as far as I am concerned the only realisation of a revolutionary urbanism to date, that attacked on the spot the petrified signs of the dominant organisation of life, and understood social space in political terms, refusing to accept the innocence of any monument...'[63]

NOTES

1   Such as Marx, Lenin, Lefebvre, Debord, Castells, and Harvey, to name but a mere handful.

2   Along with the history of the Russian Revolution and Spanish Civil War.

3   Engels quips, 'Gentleman; do you want to know what the dictatorship looks like? Look at the Paris Commune. That was the dictatorship of the proletariat'. Frederick Engels, 'Introduction' in Karl Marx, *The Civil War in France* (Peking: Foreign Languages Press, 1970), pp. 17–18.

4   "To many then and now the Commune was not a revolution at all, but an anarchist parody of what had begun as an old-fashioned bourgeois rejection of ossified authority.' G. Marcus, *Lipstick Traces: A Secret History of the Twentieth Century* (Cambridge, MA: Harvard University Press, 1989), p. 125. It was a 'spontaneous, patriotic and democratic outburst' at the capitulation of Versailles to the Prussians. See Eugene E. Schulkind, *The Paris Commune of 1871* (London: Edward Arnold, 1971), No. 78, p. 7. It was Castells who described it as the most 'repressed rent strike in history'. M. Castells, *The City and the Grassroots: A Cross-Cultural Theory of Urban Social Movements* (London: Edward Arnold, 1983), p. 23.

5   Guy Debord, Attila Kotanyi and Raoul Vaneigem, 'Theses on the Paris Commune' in *The Situationist International Anthology*, ed. and trans. by K. Knabb (California: Bureau of Public Secrets, 1981), p. 316.

6   Eric Hazan, *The Invention of Paris* (London:Verso, 2011), p. 289.

7   Karl Marx, *The Class Struggles in France 1848 to 1850* (Moscow: Progress Publishers, 1972), p. 57.

8   David Harvey, *Paris, Capital of Modernity* (London: Routledge, 2006), pp. 76 ff.

9   Hazan, *The Invention of Paris*, p. 232.

10   The urban historian Peter Hall tries to give what he considers a balanced view of Haussmann's works, emphasising in particular the necessary infrastructural

improvements. P. Hall, *Cities in Civilizsation: Culture, Innovation and Urban Order* (London: Phoenix, 1999), pp. 708 ff.

11   Jules Simon comments in *Le Gaulois* in 1882: 'There were cries that he would bring on the plague; he tolerated such outcries and gave us instead – through his well considered architectural breakthroughs – air, health, and life.' In Walter Benjamin, *The Arcades Project* (Cambridge, MA: Harvard University Press, 2002), p. 127.

12   In the words of Marcel Poëte in 1925. Quoted in Walter Benjamin, *The Arcades Project*, p. 121. On this Hazan writes: 'By an amalgam that is characteristic of the spirit of our time, the (useful) re-appreciation of nineteenth-century architecture has led to a positive revaluation of Haussmann, to the point of a ridiculous minimisation of his anti-insurrectionary concerns, just as it is good form to present Napoleon III as a philanthropic Saint-Simonian.' Hazan, *Invention*, p. 106. It was Ledoux who designed the 'ideal' Panoptican salt works city of Chaux, whilst Boullée was the author of the monumental cenotaph for Isaac Newton and the Biblioteque Nationale.

13   Hall, *Cities*, p. 718.

14   Blanqui issued an extraordinary denunciation of Haussmann's plan, a lengthy extract of which is quoted in Benjamin, *Arcades*, p. 144 ff.

15   In Benjamin, ibid., p. 122.

16   Harvey, *Paris*, p. 132. Harvey has written extensively on the history of nineteenth-century Paris. In particular, *Paris: Capital of Modernity*, which offers an extensive political economy of the urban reconstruction of the city. See also Harvey, *Consciousness and the Urban Experience: Studies in the History and Theory of Capitalist Urbanisation*, (Baltimore, MD: Johns Hopkins University Press, 1985), pp. 70–90, for a shorter excellent overview.

17   As Harvey says, Haussmann put together, 'a well organised monopolistic form of competition with him at the top of the hierarchy. It was, he argued, "best to leave to speculation stimulated by competition the task of recognising the people's real needs and satisfying them." To this end he forged an alliance between the city and a coterie of financial and real-estate interests (builders, developers, architects, etc.) assembled under the umbrella power of "associated" or "finance" capital.' Harvey, *Paris*, p. 134.

18   The financiers and bankers were the bloodline ancestors of the financial moguls of the late twentieth century, who were similarly adept at setting up a baroque financial architecture heavily laden with bizarre acronyms and clandestine details.

19   Powerful commercial landlords who could buy and sell whole urban blocks and for whom property was no more than a financial asset quickly dominated the real-estate market. With regards to the general shift in the organisation of the construction industry and the commodity form, Harvey comments; 'a form of fictitious capital whose exchange value, integrated into the general circulation of capital, entirely dominated use-value.' Harvey, *Paris*, pp. 125–7.

20   If there were any impediments to planned demolitions, there were plenty of barristers who could provide the necessary documents for the expropriation of property and who could fabricate leases on antedated sheets of paper bearing official stamps. Benjamin, *Arcades*, p. 123.

21   Quoted in Hall, *Cities*, p. 738.

22   Benjamin, *Arcades*, p. 132.

23   Benjamin, ibid., p. 135.

24   Hall, *Cities*, p. 737.

25   The 'ideological' situation was not unlike the way in which neo-liberal ideology encouraged individuals to believe that boom time would last forever. But the mid 1860s, the warning signs were already there as Haussmann's efforts to camouflage the growing state debt began to fail. He had in effect mortgaged the future, in a manner similar to the way in which bankers and speculators bankrupted nations in the early twenty-first century.

26   For Marx there could be only one verdict on the rule of the Baron – it was a series of 'colossal robberies committed upon the city of Paris by the great financial companies and contractors.' Karl Marx, *The Civil War in France*, pp. 78–9.

27   Marx, *Civil War*, p. 78.

28   Which is how the Situationists described it.

29   Of all the burning questions of the revolution of 1789 was that of land, on which the radical Dolivier in his 'Essai sur la justice primitive' declared 'two immutable principles: the first, that the land belongs to all in general and to no one in particular; and the second, that each has the exclusive right to the produce of his labour.' Adding 'the land…taken as a whole, must be considered as the great common-land of nature'; the common property of all: 'each individual must have the right of sharing in the great common land (au grand communal). One generation has no right to make laws for the next, or to dispose of its sovereign rights.' Peter Kropotkin, *The Great French Revolution 1789–1793* (London: Heinemann, 1909), p. 494. Sections of the Communes preached like the Diggers in England for the 'levelling of wealth' and vociferously denounced property owners, merchants and monopolists in general.' In addition, they advocated fixed prices for grain and food – not just equality before the law but equality in fact (égalité de fait) and wage equalisation between labourers and deputies.' Kropotkin, ibid., *The Great French Revolution*, pp. 354–7, and p. 488.

30   Schulkind, *The Paris Commune of 1871*, p. 88. One of the proclamations fly-posted around the city was issued by the Democratic and Socialist Republican Club of the 13th arrondissement. Article 3: 'The purpose of the club…is to study all political and social problems which relate to the liberation of labour, the emancipation of workers; to pursue their solution by revolutionary means.' Schulkind, ibid., p. 77. It was a sentiment shared by the newspaper *La Lutte* that declared, 'We believe that workers have the right today to take possession of the tools of production just as in 1789, the peasant took possession of the land.' Schulkind, ibid., p. 39.

31   '…The soul of the revolution was therefore in the Communes, and without these centres scattered all over the land, the revolution would never have had the power to overthrow the old regime…' Kropotkin, *The Great French Revolution*, pp. 180–84.

32   In addition, it placed a moratorium on the payment of commercial bills, limited the salaries of civil servants, decreed that labour should be allowed to participate in the setting of working conditions, forbad employers from deducting penalties from wages, and decreed that bakery workers no longer had to work nights.

33   Benjamin, *Arcades*, p. 139.

34   Michael Bakunin, 'The Revolution of February 1848, as seen by Bakunin', in D. Guérin, *No Gods, No Masters: An Anthology of Anarchism*, Book 1 (Edinburgh: AK PRess, 1998), p. 108.

35   'Rebellion in the old style, street fighting with barricades, which decided the issue everywhere up to 1848, was to a considerable extent obsolete.' Frederick Engels, 'Introduction' in *Class Struggles in France*, p. 18.

36   Manuel Castells, *Grassroots*, p. 16.

37 Bakunin, *The Revolution*, p. 109. In 1991, just after the attempted coup, I was visiting Moscow and went down to see the barricades around the Beliye Dom. Heroic ensembles of urban debris, they could have been mistaken for works of street art. The students who maintained their camp and were holding a vigil in defence of democracy asked for them to be left as a memorial. Overnight they vanished, no match for a bulldozer, let alone a tank.

38 Castells, *Grassroots*, p. 19. Women were in the vanguard of the revolutions of 1789, 1848, 1917 and 1936 and it was women who led the rent strikes in Glasgow, 1914 and New York, 1931.

39 See for instance A. Hussey, *Paris: The Secret History* (London: Penguin, 2007), p. 289, Hazan, *The Invention of Paris*, p. 236, and Peter Marshall, *Demanding the Impossible* (London: Fontana Press, 1993), pp. 396–409.

40 For the Situationists, it 'was the biggest festival of the nineteenth century', Debord et al., *The Situationist International*, p. 314. Writing in 1947, Henri Lefebvre fell out with orthodox communists by emphasising this aspect of the goals of any revolution. 'It is ludicrous to define socialism solely by the development of the productive forces. Economic statistics cannot answer the question: what is socialism? Men do not fight and die for tons of steel, or for tanks or atomic bombs. They aspire to be happy, not to produce…To put it another way, socialism (the new society, the new life) can only be defined concretely on the level of everyday life, as a system of changes in what can be called lived experience.' H. Lefebvre, *Critique of Everyday Life* (London: Verso, 1991), pp. 48–9.

41 See for instance Charles Fourier, 'New Material Conditions: The Establishment of a Trial Phalanx', reprinted in J. Beecher, and R. Bienvenu (trans. and ed.), *The Utopian Vision of Charles Fourier: Selected Texts on Work, Love and Passionate Attraction* (London: Jonathan Cape, 1972), and T. Moilin, *Paris en l'An 2000* (Paris: Librairie de Renaissance, 1869). Ahead of his time, Moilin advocated the complete socialisation and state ownership of the housing stock.

42 Quoted in Louise Michel, *La Commune* (Paris: Editions Stock, 1978) (1898), p. 222.

43 His address to the General Council of the International Working Men's Association in London, K. Marx, *The Civil War in France*, p. 423.

44 It is suggested by Marx and others that this single act – the seizure of the state treasury and all of its bullion – would have prevented the slaughter.

45 Oliver Lissagaray, *History of the Paris Commune of 1871*, pp. 239–45.

46 Harvey, *Paris*, p. 214.

47 Taken from a journalist's observations of the activities of one of the clubs quoted in R. Baldrick, *The Siege of Paris*, (London: History Book Club, 1964), p. 61.

48 Schulkind, *The Paris Commune of 1871*, pp. 126–9. In the church of St Nicholas des Champs, the only illumination came from the reading desk that faced the pulpit and was hung with red, as the people chanted the *Marseillaise*, launched into 'fantastic declamations', discussed the events of the day, censured the members of the Council, and voted on resolutions to be presented at the Hôtel de Ville the next day. Lissagaray, *History of the Paris Commune of 1871*, p. 244.

49 Schulkind, *The Paris Commune of 1871*, p. 128.

50 'The factories in which you are crowded together will belong to you; the tools placed in your hand will belong to you; the profit that results from your labour, your care, and the loss of your health, will be shared by you.' Schulkind, ibid., p. 129. Another speaker

proposes to forcibly enter the homes of the rich to seize bed linen for the wounded workers and soldiers defending the Commune.

51   The aims of the Prolétaire were the '…Abolition of all privileges and special prerogatives and their replacement by the law of ability, in order that the worker may truly enjoy the fruits of his labour.' Not only that, but the club called for the 'complete abolition of all religious instruction', and the introduction of 'universal free primary school education'.

52   'The Paris Commune, considering that the imperial column in the Place Vendôme is a monument to barbarism, a symbol of brute force and false glory, an affirmation of militarism, a denial of international law, a permanent insult directed at the conquered by their conquerors, a perpetual attack upon one of the three great principles of the French Republic, decrees the column in the Place de Vendôme shall be demolished.' 'Decree of the Commune to Demolish the Column in the Place de Vendôme, April 12th 1871' in Schulkind, *The Paris Commune of 1871*, p. 159.

53   Lissagaray, *History of the Paris Commune of 1871*, p. 236.

54   See introduction by Engels, *Civil War in France*, p. 394. It was not the first time in history that the monuments of tyrants had been toppled and certainly not the last. Like the removal of the tsar from his pedestal in Sergei Eisenstein's film *October*, it has become an iconic moment in the history of urban revolution.

55   Kropotkin, 'Western Europe', in *Conquest of Bread and Other Writings*, (Cambridge: Cambridge University Press, 1995), p. 226.

56   'The window holes affording glimpses of the sky in a framework of greenery were highly artistic. As the young plant life increasingly took possession of the cracked walls, they would have become, more and more artistically resplendent.' Kropotkin, 'Western Europe', pp. 226–7.

57   Lissagaray, *History of the Paris Commune of 1871*, p. 281.

58   'The working men's Paris, in the act of its heroic self-holocaust, involved in its flames, buildings and monuments. While tearing to pieces the living body of the proletariat, its rulers must no longer expect to return triumphantly into the intact architecture of their abodes. The government of Versailles cries, "Incendiarism!" and whispers this cue to all its agents, down to the remotest hamlet, to hunt up its enemies everywhere as the suspect of professional incendiarism. The bourgeoisie of the whole world, which looks complacently upon the wholesale massacre after the battle, is convulsed by horror at the desecration of brick and mortar.' Marx, *Civil War in France*, p. 92.

59   Hussey, *Paris: The Secret History*, p. 292.

60   Harvey, *Consciousness*, p. 249.

61   Marx, ibid., pp. 72–3.

62   Notes from Kropotkin, 'The Commune of Paris', in Schulkind, *Paris Commune*, p. 225. See also M. Bookchin, *The Third Revolution – Popular Movements in the Revolutionary Era* (London: Cassell, 1998), pp. 225–35.

63   G. Debord, R. Kotanyi and R. Vangeim, 'Theses on the Paris Commune' in *Situationist International Anthology*, pp. 314–16.

4

Letters from the Front Line of the Building Industry: 1918–1938

INTRODUCTION

It should be self-evident that buildings and cities are not made by magic but are the result of the 'union of human labour with the objects and instruments of production.' However, it is rare in the conventional narratives of architectural and urban history that we ever hear much about building workers or, indeed, the *labour* of architects. Human labour might have a bit part, or be a passing reference, but it is seldom placed centre-stage. This antipathy towards 'history as labour' is all the more strange when we consider that what Marx called the *labour process* is the 'universal condition for the metabolic interaction between man and nature, the everlasting nature-imposed condition of human existence.'[1] 'Letters from the Frontline' makes a small contribution to this history of the human species as a history of the labour process. Written in 2011, it was assembled from notes collected in Moscow when the Soviet Union still existed. My research at that point was very much to do with the history of the labour process in the construction industry, and in particular, the Marxist critique of capitalist work practices. This naturally enough led me to look at how and in what ways the labour process had developed differently in the Soviet Union. The three 'letters' here, written as if I am a visiting journalist, chart a 20-year period from 1919 to 1938 – a tale of revolution and counter-revolution. To this day the question remains unresolved: what form will labour take in a post-capitalist society?

1. 1918

Spring comes to Samara on the mighty Volga – a fitting backdrop, for like its unstoppable currents, this history runs deep and strong – a report from the Conference of the All Russian Union of Construction Workers – Samara 12–15 May 1918 – excerpts from the historical annals of the building worker – close the churches – whitewash the icons – declare class war on priests, landowners and imperialists – peace, bread and electricity is the foundation of Soviet power – long live the Internationale – the painters are dismantling the world and putting it back together in colliding planes of colour – Malevic invites the workers of the world to unite with abstract typography laid over broken geometry – here we have it then, laid out bare on the slab, history is up for the making – what shall it be? – Lenin's 'network of producer and consumer communes'? – Bakunin's 'free federation of worker associations'?[2] – Kropotkin's Anarchist Communism, a carnival of independence, mutual agreement and cooperation? – Marx and Engels's futurist society in which class distinctions have disappeared and public power has shed its political character?[3] – the signpost on how to get there is revolving – the Communists say that to begin with workers must seize and occupy the institutions of the state and to use it to their advantage in completing their victory over the capitalist class – only when this has been accomplished does it make sense to speak of the state withering like a disease-ridden tree – the anarchists, on the other hand, would take an axe to the trunk tomorrow and abolish the state forthwith – time is pressing, and Alexander Bogdanov is wasting none of it – already he is thinking of an end to toil and of a new type of complex spiritual creative labour that unites mind and body[4] – perhaps this is what Marx meant by 'revolutionary practical critical activity.'[5]

Organise workers' councils at your place of employment

Every delegate is preoccupied with one question, the alarmingly simple and atrociously difficult, 'What form will labour take in a worker's state?' No longer fearful of arrest, building workers have moved beyond the pressing matters of wages and the working week, and are passionately debating as if the world might end tomorrow what Soviet power might mean for working life on a building site. They are poring over the decrees on workers' control that were announced in November last year. Extraordinary documents in the history of the labour movement, they guarantee the rights and authority of workers through the factory committees and trade unions to control the activities of enterprises.[6] Copies of Lenin's essays in which he lays out his plan for socialism are passing from hand to hand. His vision of the state losing its coercive nature and becoming an administrative department whose function is to coordinate a network of producers and consumers' communes, chimes with the aspirations of the ordinary carpenters, masons and bricklayers who have packed the hall.[7] It is both intoxicating and avant-garde. Boundaries are being transgressed. Convention dismissed. Neither are building workers restricting themselves to purely political questions. Utopia beckons. If work on a capitalist building site is back-breaking, repetitive, and ruled by the tyranny of piece rates, then surely they argue, work under socialism should be creative and based on co-operation and the sharing of wages?

2. БУДЕТ РОССИЯ ВСЕХ БОГАЧЕ
ЧЕРЕЗ НЕСКОЛЬКО ЛЕТ

4. НАМИ ДОЛЖЕН БЫТЬ
ПЛАНУ ХОД ДАН

4.1 'Comrades, we have a real opportunity to transcend the printed page and build a new world'

It would be a mistake to think that these themes have sprung up over night. It is certainly the case that the revolution has thrown them sharply into focus, but in truth they have been fomenting in the lap of labour for over 100 years. As quite literally the builders of capitalism's cities and infrastructure, building workers were in the front line of the development of the new ideology of laissez-faire. As ancient rules on craft and guild were torn to pieces, they were thrust into a system of vicious competition and contracting that was notorious for being unregulated and dominated by an authoritarian class of contractors.[8] They were also one of the largest sections of the industrial working class and one of the most militant. As long ago as the end of the eighteenth century, French building workers denounced their employers as 'ignorant, rapacious and insatiable oppressors.'[9] A few years later in 1833, the Operative Builders' Union in Britain fought for the creation of a builders' parliament and the introduction of a nationwide system of cooperative building production.[10] Inspired by the lessons of Robert Owen, they argued that the wages system should be abolished and that workers should control the building process, adding they were able to build better and more efficiently than any contractor. But that was not all. These were just steps towards their ultimate goal of creating a 'great association for the emancipation of the productive classes.'[11] This dream of a prototypical French Commune or Russian soviet was not the fantasy of a few individuals either. At the height of its brief existence, the OBU vanguard mobilized over 40,000 building workers who were possessed by a 'revolutionary temper',[12] and judging by the declarations and the debates at the conference here, their ghosts are mingling amongst the delegates.

The events in Russia, then, are neither an accident nor an aberration. They are the latest chapter in a wave of labour militancy that has swept across Europe over the last 30 years. Building sites in Siberia, Moscow and St Petersburg were convulsed by a succession of strikes in the 1870s and 1890s.[13] These were indicative of a growing sense of confidence in the organised workers' movement that famously culminated in the 1905 Revolution, when over 3,000,000 workers across the country laid down their tools. They included bricklayers, cement workers, carpenters, painters, and stonemasons.[14] Horrified by this turn of events, the tsarist authorities unleashed a violent storm of armed repression that forced workers' organisations underground. By 1910, police infiltration, mass arrests and imprisonment had succeeded in closing all of the fledgling trade union branches in the major cities and strike activity had dropped to a fraction of what it had been in 1905.[15] This trade union conference, then, is something of a phoenix, and a young one at that. For it was not until 1914 that a union representing the interests of construction workers and architects – 'The Society of Architectural and Construction Workers of the Moscow Industrial Region' – was able to operate in relative freedom from arrest and closure.

During the following two years, the union replaced the slogan 'Better wages' with '*Doloi gnet*': 'Down with oppression'.[16] Battle lines were drawn and workers knew instinctively that the situation had changed irrevocably.[17] Then on 2 March, paralleling the demonstrations in St Peterburg, Moscow exploded. Reports filtered through the city that workers from the Dinamo Plant had marched across the Yauza Bridge and swept aside the police cordons. By the end of the day, workers were in control of the post and telegraph offices, the telephone exchange, the Kremlin, the railways and the security police headquarters.

It was a turning point and during the next three months there was a dramatic rise in workers' unrest. Between May and October, on the building sites of St Petersburg alone 50 strikes took place.[18] Meanwhile in Moscow, new wage demands were sent out to all contractors.[19] They refused them and following a series of increasingly bitter confrontations, the Moscow Union called a city-wide strike that continued throughout September and involved over 12,000 building workers. In all, from April to November in the Moscow region, 21,000 building workers took part in strike action, with over a third of them raising directly political demands.[20]

As I write, Russia is in the midst of a civil war and of what senior Party officials have labelled 'war communism'. Many building workers have joined the Red Army. Some, such as the old Union of Plumbers, have entered the ranks of Mensheviks. However, despite the uncertainty and upheaval, it was felt that the union should continue to meet. So here I am in Samara, as an observer at the first-ever conference of the All Russian Union of Construction Workers. I have been a witness at a number of trade union gatherings, but none of them has ever come close to this, and its proceedings are there for all to read in a new journal *Stroitel* (Builder).[21] Relatively modest motions for the introduction of an eight-hour day, time-based wages, and educational programmes were passed in an instance, as was the decision to unite the disparate smaller unions of building workers into one organisation. But this was just the prelude to two momentous resolutions. The first called for the liquidation of private contractors and the second for the introduction of workers' control of production in all construction organisations employing more than 30 workers. There was still yet more to come. As if conscious that building workers across the world were listening, the conference closed with thunderous applause for the passing of a motion to fully socialise the building industry so that all of its branches would be brought under the organs of 'socialist state power'.[22]

2. 1927

> Tons of concrete – the proletarianisation of otkhodniki (seasonal workers)
> is accomplished – concrete and steel architecture springs from the earth – a
> planetarium is planned to conquer the cosmos – goodbye to the private
> contractor, your likes will not be seen again – agit prop street art and agit prop
> trains – spellbound and mesmerised, audiences watch Battleship Potemkin and
> Strike – propaganda and art unite to stunning effect, and not just in film – factory
> conductors stand on roofs and conducts symphonies of factory sirens – the
> People's Commissar of the Enlightenment, Lunacharsky, calls for the Institutions
> of Art education to be proleratarianised – a boy is born and is given the name
> Zavod, (Factory) – a girl is born next-door and is given the name Dotnara,
> (Daughter of the toiling people) – the iron sword of the working class will make
> sure that all remains peaceful – a confusing tension stalks – blind faith, for I have
> to believe, is battling with disillusionment – which way now? – the Soviet state
> has survived – but the state is getting bigger and bigger, it does not look likely
> to wither – who remembers Rosa Luxemburg's warning that if the expression
> 'the dictatorship of the proletariat' must be used, then it must be on the basis of

the 'most active, unlimited participation of the mass of the people, of unlimited democracy'[23] – it makes no difference, say anarchists – a dictatorship is a dictatorship is a dictatorship, regardless on whose behalf it is wielded – Comrade, don't read that book, it is ant-soviet and degenerate – Gorky is acceptable, but not that madman Bulgakov – still, the plans for workers' clubs look exciting – build social condensers for our time say the Constructivists – architects ask the users of the transitional commune how they imagine a new way of life – the ingenious metal rings of the Shabolovka Radio Tower broadcast its messages to the world, but what kind of messages are they? – Trotsky said he preferred monumental constructions to Tatlin's tower and that the modernist writer Bely is a corpse – he should be wary that a cadaverous fate doesn't await him as well – the anarchist artist Aleksei Gan has no time for pleasantries and accuses everyone except proletarians of being stricken by artistic podagrism.

'We didn't fight a revolution for piece rates and Taylorism', say building workers

The statistics department is working overtime. Its typewriters and reprographic machines spew smoke like a turbine hall. Numbers are everything and in purely quantitative terms, the New Economic Policy has been a success. Two thousand new factories have been built. Brick and cement production has recovered its pre-war levels. The number of workers in the building industry has increased four-fold. Gross production nearly ten-fold. The productivity of labour has increased 100 per cent.[24] Membership of the Moscow branch of the Construction Union has risen to 150,000.[25] Applause rings across the rooftops. The factory hooters sing their praises.

There is much else that the building industry has to be proud of. The first signs of what a socialist architecture might look like are emerging out of the ground. For most of the past decade, architects and urban designers have been restricted to working out on paper the theoretical shape of the urban revolution and the non-capitalist city. All manner of communes, workers' clubs, linear and flying cities jumped from the drawing board to stretch the public imagination and the boundaries of structural engineering. Now the task is to translate these ideas into reality and building workers are rising to the challenge. The foundations for the epic Dnieper hydroelectric dam have been laid. Glazed steel cylinders and flying cantilevered concrete workers' clubs raise a glass to the sky. Mossoviet has built its first project that integrates housing, a crèche, bath house, shops and school, and even the revolutionary newspaper *Izvestia* has a new headquarters: a fragment of modern poetry whose round steel windows look down over the statue of Pushkin. All of this is cause for celebration and from what I understand there are more plans for housing communes and workers' clubs in the coming year.[26]

But amidst the excitement at Moscow's new architecture and the impressive indices of economic growth, all is not well. Censors are banning books and a culture of authoritarianism is leaking like a toxin through government organisations and Party committees. It is a process of corrosion that has accelerated since Stalin consolidated his grip on the leadership of the Party. Six years, ago in the interests of revolutionary discipline the Party banned factions and launched a scathing attack on the millenarian demands of the Workers' Opposition and anarchists. Now it is convulsed again and eating itself from the inside. There is, of course, nothing about this that Voline, Arshinov and Shliapnikov hadn't already warned.

4.2　'In no time at all we shall surpass the West. All hands to the
pump in the industrialisation of the economy'

Power is seductive and is never voluntarily relinquished. For the anarchists, 'all political power inevitably creates a privileged situation for the men who exercise it.' And once the throne has been seized, then like an unfailing mechanical clock, the new incumbents will be '…compelled to create a bureaucratic and coercive apparatus.'[27]

On the labour front there has been an equally regrettable turn of events. Despite the efforts of Tomsky to maintain independence for trade unions, it looks increasingly likely that as of next year, they will become subordinate organs of the Soviet state. A mixed economy in which state ownership and a capitalist market co-exist is bound to produce mixed results and reactions. Even so, building sites are far from happy places. The reintroduction of capitalist contractors during the New Economic Policy, even if a temporary measure to kick-start the economy, has not gone down well with rank and file building workers, who can not hide their disappointment. As early as 1919, they criticised the way in which private contractors who, only two years before, they had thrown off sites in the 'carting off' ceremonies, were being given rights that ran counter to the workers' movement.[28] State building organisations are having to compete on tenders with the private sector and there is evidence of swindlers posing as contractors actually receiving cash advances. And if rumours are to be believed, some of the old contractors are even working in the State Offices for construction![29]

The contradictions mount. As NEP has unfolded over the last six years, many workers have looked on in confusion over the concessions being given to foreign building firms and the Party's reinforcement of the system of *edinochaliye* – one-man management. How, they legitimately ask, do we reconcile this policy with the principle that democratically elected workers' collectives should be running building enterprises? Equally contentious has been the introduction of the scientific organisation of labour – *nauchnaya organizatsia truda* (NOT). An adaptation of American Taylorism, it is being championed by Gastev, who is obsessed with discipline and is instructing workers to avoid fraternisation and sharp movements![30] Determined to raise productivity, his office has produced diagrams that purport to show the optimum way of moving hand and foot when laying a course of bricks. But bricklayers are not performing seals. Neither are they robots.

And it gets worse. Over a third of the construction workforce is unemployed, and for those that do have a job, how are they being paid? By piece rates and bonus schemes; the very wage form in which Karl Marx argued capitalist hunger is laid bare. Needless to say, the Party leadership rhetorically defends the system of one-man management, piece rates and Taylorism, arguing that under the conditions of a workers' state, they assume another character. Besides which, they insist, the construction industry is simply not in a strong enough position to dispense with the experience, achievements and techniques of capitalist society.[31] This is also the reason why they deride as utopian the anarchist demand for the immediate 'expropriation of private industry by the organisations of collective production.'[32] For support, they point to no greater authority than Lenin himself, who argued that in order to rebuild the economy, it was necessary to adapt elements of capitalist work practices, reminding workers that they always had recourse to political bodies if new labour laws were contravened.[33] So be it, but it doesn't make the situation any more palatable for building workers. Many still dream of a qualitatively different way of working and remember fondly the arguments of the Workers' Opposition and industrial unions on how they should be given complete freedom to develop their creative abilities whilst discovering and experimenting with new forms of production.[34]

Perhaps the strangest aspect of the first ten years of Soviet power has been labour unrest and the last few years have seen a marked increase in what are euphemistically being described as 'general conflicts.' As one might expect, many of these have occurred in the old artels and firms run by unscrupulous speculators who have been allowed back into the labour market. But a good number have been taking place in the state sector. Tales abound of 12- and 18-hour days, the usurpation of labour laws, and of wages not being paid.[35] In 1923, 75,000 building workers were embroiled in major disputes over contract arrangements.[36] The following year, an astonishing 22 strikes broke out in the building industry, with over 3,000 reported disagreements over wages. It was a pattern that was replicated in the first six months of 1925, when over 25,000 workers were again in disputes over wages and contracts.[37]

The high rate of incidents in state-run building organisations are particularly contradictory, since workers rightly expect that here at least new working conditions should be upheld. One can only hope that as the building industry becomes fully nationalised next year with the launch of the first five-year plan, such problems will be ironed out. Already in Moscow, virtually all new house building is being carried out by the 'socialised sector', the majority under the direction of the Moscow Soviet and its organisation Mosstroi.[38] The role of the private sector has been drastically reduced and in the building materials sector, 90 per cent of it is now state owned.[39] Progressive measures though these appear to be, Russian workers should be on their guard, for the state ownership of the means of production is no guarantee of democracy. This is why Shliapnikov asked with regards to the transition from the New Economic Policy to Socialism, the title of a series of lectures by Party economist Preobrashensky: 'By what means during this period of transformation can our Communist Party carry out its economic policy; shall it be by means of the workers organised into their class union, or – over their heads – by bureaucratic means, through canonised functionaries of the state?'[40]

3. 1936

> Nine years have passed since I was here last – Kagonovich opens the metro – Plastov paints life on a collective farm – it bears the crimson slogan, 'Life is happier under Stalin' – the knock – all artistic organisations brought under state control – marble is declared socialist – ideanost, partinost *and* narodnost – ideological content, party spirit and national character – these are the new slogans for the future – Novelist, are you celebrating the class struggle of the proletariat? If not, why not? – Painter, are your images of workers and peasants, figurative and noble? If not, why not? – farewell to the avant garde, gone are

*its sharp edges – welcome to proletarian classicism – Golosov, architect of the
constructivist worker's' club Zuev has become antiquarian – his new apartment
block has been praised as a fine example of revolutionary romanticism – delusion
charges across the city – exiled in Paris, Voline has christened the USSR the
USCR: the Union of State Capitalist Republics – the Party bureaucracy, he says,
is a ruling class that has 'totalitarianised, easily and quickly, the whole Russian
administration, and the organisations of industrial workers and peasants'[41] –
Arshinov condemns the Soviet state for transforming trade unions into organs
of police surveillance – their job, to discipline a working class labouring under a
regime of obligatory and militarised labour[42] – ironically, Trostky agrees and calls
the bureaucracy a 'privileged upper strata – a ruling Soviet caste'[43] – atomisation –
fragmentation – jackhammers are pounding away as new boulevards split
the city – strange facsimiles of renaissance Italy and ancient Greece adorn the
triumphal new streets – Doric, iconic, but never ironic – fluting columns and
Corinthian curls – the Palace of Versailles has been built underground – it is, it
has to be said, magnificent – a true dialectic, a cruel mix of exalted craftsmanship
and forced labour – the proletariat shall go to work through the palaces of
former kings – ideology is sealed in the stone tombs of the triumphal Lenin
library and five-point star plan of the Red Army theatre – Shliapnikov and the
economist Isaac Rubin have disappeared – 'Trotskyist theoreticians' are being
ritually unmasked with alarming regularity – on the architectural front line, two
recent victims of what is perversely being described as 'revolutionary zeal' have
vanished – Lisagor, who worked with Ginzburg and the Vesnins, and the radical
disurbanist Okhitovich.[44]*

**Exceed the plan targets and beware of saboteurs: Egalitarianism has been
banned by the Communist Party as a bourgeois idea!**

Two years ago, a new plan was launched for Moscow. The winning scheme
selected by the Central Committee after an international competition is intended
to amplify the neo-classical radial plan of the nineteenth century. Blessed by Stalin
and steeped in classical antiquity, academic masters from before the revolution
like Zholtoskvsy have re-emerged from the shadows of the avant-garde to claim
their place at the forefront of Soviet architecture. Bulldozers carve colossal new
boulevards that hurtle from the birch forests to the heart of the city. Eventually they
will be flanked by cliffs of uninterrupted parade-like housing of the kind that can
already be seen on Gorky and Chkalova Street. Existing avenues will be widened so
that they are broad enough to land aircraft and move army divisions. Standing at
the centre of the ensemble, in place of the recently demolished Cathedral of Christ
the Saviour, will tower the Palace of the Soviets that metaphorically, if not literally,
will be visible from the corners of every republic. The intention is unambiguous. It
is to create an aura of immutability, of theatrical grandeur. Moscow is to become
a monumental and triumphant city that broadcasts to the world the might of
the Soviet Union. The ideologues of socialist realism claim that it is only right
that the proletariat should enjoy architectural splendours that previously were
reserved for the aristocracy. Accordingly, there is barely a trace of the aesthetic
sensibilities or egalitarianism that informed the work of architects and urbanists in
the 1920s. I confess to finding the whole scheme profoundly depressing. For what

4.3 'Women construction workers, raise your productivity in the interests of building socialism'

kind of progressive socialist democracy is it that requires the plan of an imperial city and the pomp and bombastic scale of the Palace of the Soviets? It is as if the Central Committee are announcing in architectural form the concentration and centralisation of all power in the hands of the Party in Moscow. It's as if the stacked tiers of the palace are screaming in deafening stone that the State is no longer constructed by the people, it is built over and above them.[45] Given this, it is small wonder that the Communist Party under Stalin has declared wage levelling in the building industry as reactionary.

Many who remain committed to the long-term goals of the revolution think that the recent arrests and repressive measures taken by the bureaucracy against all internal opposition are merely passing irregularities. There is no blue print for socialism, they say. Unfortunate measures were taken for expediency's sake. Mistakes will inevitably occur, but lessons will be learnt. After all, revolutions have to be made, remade and then remade again. In time, all will be resolved. But there is little sign of this in action. The Communist Party has occupied all government departments and has assumed absolute control of the country's resources and decision-making bodies.[46]

Under the new system of economic management, directors of enterprises, not workers' collectives, are responsible for the carrying out of plan targets. In addition, directors have been granted complete authority in the appointment of staff, in the general running of the enterprise and in maintaining labour discipline.[47] In an even stranger twist, trade unions have been informed that 'they must not hinder directly in the running of the enterprise' and that their role is 'to assist actively in the carrying out and strengthening of one-man management.'[48]

Odd announcements indeed for a workers' state. The revolutionary declarations of 1917 might only be two decades old but they seem light years away, and it is difficult to reconcile the transitional idea of 'workers' control of production', let alone Lenin's vision of the next stage, of 'full workers regulation of production', with these new laws and policy statements.[49] But it gets even stranger. There are only two things that seem to matter. Discipline and productivity. Strange new tools have been introduced like plastering machines, double-handed two-metre long trowels and bizarre straight-edged buckets for pouring mortar along a brick course. But in the absence of significant advances in labour-saving technology, the Party has decided that there is only one way to extract more labour out of workers and that is through a combination of 'scientific' management, wage differentials, and competitive targets.

Accordingly, workers on building sites are increasingly being organised in hierarchical military-style brigades. They are led by a 'brigadier' foreman who is accountable to the 'enterprise director', who operates in much the same way as a divisional army captain. Gathering data from his field of operations, he passes statistics on plan targets and cadre training to regional offices, who then report to the high command in the Construction Ministry in Moscow. This militarisation of the labour collective is designed to ensure both political and economic discipline, and its ideological character is accurately captured by its name, *Khozraschotnie Brigadi*: cost-accounting brigades.[50] The intention is quite straightforward. It is to link wages directly to output, a system of performance-related pay that is being reinforced by the increased use of bonus schemes and piece rates.[51] The second weapon in the Ministry's armoury is *sotzialisticheskoe sorevnovania*, 'Socialist competition'. Cleaning their tools and preparing materials, one brigade issues a productivity challenge to another. The two then embark on a furious mission to exceed plan targets by as much as is humanly possible or, indeed, imaginable.[52]

High bonuses and medals await the record breakers, who are ceremonially paraded in front of ordinary mortals in full glare of spotlights and camera. The plasterer Golov is supposed to have raised his productivity by a factor of 25. By what means, no one is entirely sure. Comrade Orlov organised his own bricklaying school and showed young shock workers how to lay a scarcely believable 5,000 bricks a day.[53] Individual brigades are reported as having raised productivity by a miraculous 300 per cent. Some are so determined to exceed norms that they have worked flat-out in Stakhanovite fortnights.[54] Wonders never cease. The electrician Maria Maslova has improved her productivity by over 800 per cent,[55] and a steel worker by the name of Romanov is reputed to have processed 40 tons of reinforcing steel in a single day, exceeding norms by a staggering 1,250 percent. Not content with such earth shattering statistics, officials have discovered one individual who, in a Herculean feat of mythological proportions, is reported to have laid bricks at the staggering rate of 1,500 per hour.[56] Despite the claims of the Party, there are doubts about whether the combination of shock work, 'socialist competition', and Stakhanovism, has in actual fact raised productivity that significantly.

This has all been accompanied by a sustained attack by the Party bureaucracy against what are being described as 'left opportunists" who, as late as 1932, still supported the use of *produktoobmen* (product exchange) as a replacement for the use of money.[57] Also singled out as an 'ideological error' has been the continued popularity amongst young building workers of *Proizvodstvennie Beatovye Kommuni*, (Production Way of Life Communes), which are reported as still operating 'false principles', like wage sharing.[58] There is no irony to be found here, only tragedy. In what can only be described as a grotesque ideological inversion, Communist Party officials are out in force on building sites to ensure the liquidation of *uranilovka*, egalitarianism. For they claim that it is egalitarianism and 'the equalising policies of the old directors of the trade union',[59] that is the principle cause of all of the building industry's problems; its low productivity, poor record in improving workers qualifications, and in the lack of commitment to the fulfillment of plan targets.[60] At the moment the campaign against wage equalisation and egalitarianism is relentless. However, rhetorical attacks are not enough and new legislation has been passed that further increases wage differentials.[61] And so it has come to pass that 20 years after the revolution, the battle cry of *Uranilovka* is now deemed a weapon used by the enemies of the Stakhanovite movement, a 'distortion of the socialist principle of wages according to the quantity and quality of work', and, most extraordinary of all, of being 'petty bourgeois'.[62] Such is the insatiable appetite of the Soviet state for surplus labour.[63]

The Party would have everyone believe that Stakhanovism, NOT and 'Emulation' are the movements of the moment, a shining example of socialist labour. But for others it is a draconian regime that utilises many of the worst aspects of capitalist work practices and is undermining collective solidarity.[64] A deeply insidious system, it pits worker against worker in a competitive relationship, where mind and body are pushed to the limits of exhaustion. It has created a grotesque culture of the hero worker as part of a full-blown cultural counter-revolution designed to incarcerate hearts and minds through the hagiographic idealisation of everyday life. Like an ideological poison, this has bled into the rhetorical gestures of painting, sculpture, literature, and the ritualised displays of state power. It may not be a workers' state but at least it can be made to look like one. It is all very fantastic and it feels as if I have been on a bizarre journey that started in a city governed by the fetishism of the commodity and took me across the universe to a planet ruled by the fetishism of the plan where Superman is alive and well.

Myth as ever competes with reality in volatile and sharpened circumstances. But memory runs deep and even amidst the culture of fear, tales are leaking of opposition to the Stakhanovite movement.[65] Long gone are the critical letters in the construction industry journals. These are now devoted to technological questions and upholding the official Party line. But we can draw conclusions by what is not written and what is implied. The journal *Trud* (*Labour*) has been forced to admit that the Stakhanovite movement has remained weak in the construction industry, which has been hit by numerous incidents of what is being called 'sabotage'.[66] Meanwhile, *Stroitelnaya Promishlenost* is reporting that conflict is widespread on building sites. It includes a disturbing warning issued to building workers to be vigilant of the Trotsky-Zinoviev bloc who are described as fascist agents, of having organised the murder of Kirov and of perpetrating terrorist acts against the leadership of the Party. Furthermore, it warns that such saboteurs are actively 'spinning yarns' and 'spreading their bloody web on building sites', and that building workers should 'not forget Krivom Ross, Magnitogorsk and Zaporashtal', where the very same bandits 'have been carrying out their mean and base work.'[67]

We should have known when Lenin's body was embalmed, and his brain removed for study that things were taking a turn for the worse. Now his passionate plea for an 'immense expansion of democracy' is barely audible above the megaphones announcing Stalin's declaration that class antagonisms have miraculously been overcome. As for Voline's argument that the real substance of the revolution lay in an immense process of construction based on emancipated labour and fundamental equality, it is no more than the faintest of whispers.[68]

NOTES

1   Marx, 1976, *Capital*, Volume I (London: Penguin, 1976), p. 290.

2   Daniel Guérin, 'Bakunin on Worker Self-Management' in *No Gods, No Masters: An Anthology of Anarchism*, Book 1 (Edinburgh: AK Press, 1998), p. 182.

3   Karl Marx and Frederick Engels, *The Communist Manifesto* (London: Penguin Classics, 2002), p. 244, and Peter Kropotkin, 'Anarchist Communism' in Peter, Kropotkin, *The Conquest of Bread and Other Writings* (Cambridge: Cambridge University Press, 1995), pp. 31–40.

4   See Aleksandr Bogdanov, 'The Paths of Proletarian Creation', *Proletarskaya Kultura*, Moscow, No. 15/16, 1920, and 'The Proletarian and Art', *Proletarskaya kultura*, No. 5,

1918; both reproduced in John Bowlt, *Russian Art of the Avant-Garde, Theory and Criticism*, 1902–1934, (New York: Viking Press, 1976), pp. 176–82.

5   Karl Marx and Frederick Engels, 'Theses on Feuerbach' in *The German Ideology* (London: Lawrence and Wishart, 1985), p. 121.

6   'In order to provide planned regulation of the national economy, workers' control over the manufacture, purchase, sale and storage of produce and raw materials and over the financial activity of enterprises is introduced in all industrial, commercial, banking, agricultural, and other enterprises which employ hired labour or give work to be done at home. Workers' control is exercised by all the workers of the given enterprise through their elected bodies, such as factory committees, shop stewards' councils...Decisions of workers' control bodies are binding upon the owners of enterprises and may be revoked only by higher workers' control bodies.' Quoted in Tony Cliff, *Lenin – Volume Three. The Revolution Besieged* (London: Pluto Press, 1978), p. 10. See also Vladimir Ilyich Lenin, 'Can the Bolsheviks Retain State Power?' in Lenin, *Selected Works* (Moscow: Progress, 1977), pp. 371–4 . First published in 1918.

7   Vladimir Ilyich Lenin, 'The Immediate Tasks of the Soviet Government' in Lenin, *Selected Works*, p. 410.

8   Richard Price, *Masters, Unions and Men* (Cambridge: Cambridge University Press, 1980), pp. 25–31.

9   George Rudé, *The Crowd in History* (London: Serif, 1995), p. 127.

10   'The trade unions will not strike for less work and more wages, but they will ultimately abolish wages, become their own masters, and work for each other: labour and capital will no longer be separate but they will be indissolubly joined together in the hands of the workmen and work-women.' See the fantastic book by Raymond W. Postgate, *The Builders' History* (London: The National Federation of Building Trade Operatives, 1923), pp. 77–114. Also see Eric P. Thompson, *The Making of the English Working Class* (London, 1980), pp. 909–12 and Eric Hobsbawm, *Age of Revolution*, (London, 1997), p. 256.

11   '…to erect all manner of dwellings and other architectural designs for the public more expeditiously, substantially and economically than any masters can build them under the individual system of competition.'…to decide upon the amount of work or service to be performed, each day…in order that none may be oppressed by labour beyond their labour and powers.' Postgate, *The Builders' History,* pp. 463–6. Not only this, but the OBU looked far beyond their own interests and imagined the urban reconstruction of the whole nation in a manner that recalled the proto communist programmes of the Diggers, who in 1649 advocated the construction of hospitals and schools for the whole population.

12   Postgate, *The Builders' History*, p. 58.

13   For details of the early strike movement with numerous entries on building workers, see the Soviet era reference works, *Robochie Dvisheniye v Rosiiya v 19 veka*, (Workers' Movements in Nineteenth-century Russia), Volume II, Part II, 1875–1884 and Volume III, Part II, 1890–1894, (Moscow: Politicheskaya Literatura, 1950). For numerous entries on building workers strikes in the Petersburg area and northern Russia see various works by E.A. Korolchuk, *Rabochiye Dvisheniye v 1870–90-x Godov* (Workers' Movements between 1870–1890), (Moscow, 1939), and *Kronika Revolutzionovo Rabochevo Dvisheniya v Petersburg, 1870–1904*, (Chronicle of Revolutionary Workers Movements in Petersburg), (Leningrad: Lenizdat, 1940). Nikolai Bogdanov, et al., *Kratkaya Istoria Soyuz Stroiteli*, (A Short History of the Construction Worker's Union) (Moscow: TKVSSR, 1927) (Central Committee of the All-Russian Union of Construction Workers), p. 4. See also N. Bogdanov, *Organisatsia Strotlenik Rabochik Rossii I Drugik Stran*, (The Organisation of

Building Workers in Russia and Other Countries), (Moscow, TK VSSR) and A. Tararukin, *Rabota credi Stroiteli*, (Work Amongst Building Workers), (Moscow: Moskovski Rabochi, 1927).

14   Several building workers were elected to the Moscow Soviet and in Novorossiski, cement workers linked with railway and other workers to organise a Soviet of Workers and Peasants Deputies that was to stay in power for over two months. For a detailed analysis of the organised workers' movement in English see Victoria Bonnell, *Roots of Rebellion: Workers Politics and Organizations in St Petersburg and Moscow, 1900–1914* (Berkeley, CA: University of California Press, 1983), and S.A. Smith, *Red Petrograd. Revolution In the Factories. 1917–1918* (Cambridge: Cambridge University Press, 1986). In 1914, at a clandestine conference in Moscow, building workers called for the legal creation of a single united union, a library and lecture programme, an eight-hour day, and wages to be determined locally by trade unions on a time basis. The delegates voted to continue the struggle against the exploitation of seasonal workers, and against the undercutting practices of those artels willing to work on piece rates. In addition, they advocated the replacement of food by money wages, the introduction of a state insurance scheme, training schools, and argued that overtime should only be allowed where there was no unemployment. Bogdanov, *Kratkaya Istoria*, pp. 9–16.

15   See for the development of the construction workers union and its role in 1917, S. Sindeyev, *Professionalnie Dvishenie Rabochik stroiteli v 1917*, (Building Worker's Movements in 1917), (Moscow: Trud i Kniga, 1927)

16   Sindeyev, *Professionalniye Dvisheniye*, ibid., p. 39, B. Boev, *Stroiteli v Revolutzia* in *'50 let'- Slavnie iubeli Sovietskik profsoyuz* (Moscow: Profsoyuzdat, 1958), p. 183.

17   Matters in the construction industry were further complicated by the rise of unemployment and by soldiers returning from the war front willing to work for lower wages. This prompted the creation of a labour bureau and law office to deal with the unemployed, as well as the creation of a private contractors' organisation to fight the workers' union, not unlike the Association of Master Builders in London. Sindeyev, *Professionalnie Dvishenie*, p. 13.

18   Boev, *Stroiteli v Revolutzia*, p. 184.

19   Sindeyev, *Professionalnie Dvishenie*, pp. 15–21.

20   With a strike fund of 5,000 rubles, the Moscow workers appealed to peasants and out of town workers not to enter the city, as contractors had begun to organise strike breakers. Despite the attempt by employers to bypass the courts and approach the administrators of factories and sites demanding lists of activists and issuing threats to have workers sent to the war front, the then Moscow Commissar for Labour proposed a court of arbitration which eventually adjudicated in favour of the workers. Sindeyev, *Professionalniye Dvisheniye*, p. 30. See also Diane Koenker, *Moscow Workers and the 1917 Revolution* (Princeton, NJ: Princeton University Press, 1981), pp. 311–22.

21   *Stroitel*, No. 2, May 1918, pp. 1–15. For the OBU declaration published in full see Postgate, *Builders' History*, p. 463.

22   *Stroitel*, No. 2, May 1918, pp. 1–15.

23   Rosa Luxemburg, *The Russian Revolution* (Ann Arbor, MI: University of Michigan Press, 1961), pp. 76–7.

24   *Ten Years of Soviet Power in Figures. 1917–1927* (Central Statistical Board of the USSR: Moscow, 1927), pp. 236–7. This needs to be tempered by reports of the industry still being in a state of crisis, due to serious deficits in good quality materials and qualified workers, and due to the persistence of 'individualism' in design and the *kustarnie*

(handicraft) character of the building labour that had entered the industry. *Stroitelstvo Moskvi*, No. 8 (Moscow, 1928), p. 15.

25   S. Sindeyev, *Professionalnie Dvishenie*, p. 39.

26   During the 1920s and 1930s the majority of the projects of the avant-garde were published in two seminal journals: *Sovremennaya Arkhitektura* (Modern Architecture) that ran from 1926–30, and *Stroitletsvo Moskvi*, (Moscow Construction) that started in 1923 and continued being published throughout the Soviet period.

27   Voline, *Unknown Revolution*, p. 249.

28   *Stroitel*, No. 10/11 (Moscow, 1919), p. 7.

29   Generally speaking during the period of the New Economic Policy, the experiment in a mixed economy designed to kick start Russian industry, the structure of the building industry was a volatile and confused mix of old private Contractors, traditional artisan based *Artels*, new state contracting organisations, and co-operatives. For an overview of construction contracting organisations in the pre and post revolutionary periods, see D.N. Zvorikin, *Razvitia stroitelnovo proizvodtsvo* (Moscow: Stroizdat, 1987).

30   Obsessed with mechanisation and standardisation, one of his most famous essays was *Kak Nado Rabotat*, that was first published in the 1920s and reprinted in the 1960s. See Alexei Gastev, *Kak Nado Rabotat, Praktichecki Vvdenie N.O.T,* (How it is Necessary to Work: The Practical Introduction of the Scientific Organisation of Labour) (Moscow: Ekonomika, 1972). He openly advocated the adoption of Taylorism arguing that under Socialism it lost its class character, and also penned 'mechanistic' poems. For a summary of his influence on early Soviet life see, Stites, Richard, *Revolutionary Dreams: Utopian Vision and Experimental Life in the Russian Revolution* (Oxford: Oxford University Press, 1989), pp. 149–59.

31   *Stroitelnaya Promishlennost*, No. 9, 1924, pp. 233–4.

32   Voline, *Unknown Revolution*, p. 221.

33   Lenin, 'The Immediate Tasks of the Soviet Government' in *Selected Works* (Moscow, 1977), pp. 412–13. See also 'Left-wing Childishness and the Petty Bourgeois Mentality', ibid., p. 440.

34   Alexandra Kollontai, 'The Workers' Opposition' in *Selected Writings* (Connecticut: Lawrence Hill, 1977), p. 176.

35   *Postroika*, 21 July 1926, p. 12.

36   Rashina (ed.), *Trud v SSSR, Statistiko, Economicheski obzop, 1922–1924* (Moscow, 1924), pp. 214–40, on labour in the USSR.

37   *Rabota Soyuz Stroiteli*, p. 112.

38   However, for Moscow, whilst at its high point in 1923–1924 the private sector accounted for around a fifth of all capital investment in the housing stock, by 1925/26 this had shrunk to less than one per cent, and by 1927/28 it was insignificant, virtually all house building being conducted by the 'socialised sector', the majority under the direction of the Moscow Soviet but a good proportion by cooperatives. *Stroitelstvo Moskvi*, No. 10, 1927, pp. 6–7, and No. 10, 1928, p. 2.

39   *Ten Years of Soviet Power in Figures, 1917–1927* (Moscow: Central Statistical Board of the USSR, 1927), pp. 248–9. It has been pointed out that the most significant area of private industry was to be found in small-scale concerns, handicraft and workshop production.

This is particularly important for the house-building sector, where it is clear that many small builders reappeared in the construction of individual housing in the private sector. In the same years in the whole Moscow area only 27 per cent of the total number of new houses were built by the state and cooperative sectors, although they accounted for 61 per cent of the total quantity in square metres. Another source suggests that in the 1925 building season in 167 Russian towns, 87.5 per cent of all new housing was being built by *chastnie zastroishiki*, that is, private individuals either building homes for themselves or having them built. *Stroitelnaya Promishlennost*, No. 9, 1926, p. 619.

40   Alexander Shliapnikov, 'The Workers' Opposition' in *Selected Writings of Alexandra Kollontai* (Westport, CT: Lawrence Hill, 1977), p. 174.

41   Voline, *Unknown Revolution*, pp. 358 and 380. Voline argues that it is a process in which all semblance of independence for working class and peasant institutions has been abolished in a new class structure that has three estates. At the top, party functionaries, in the middle, privileged workers – that is, Stakhanovite pace-setters – and at the bottom, the broad mass of workers and peasants.

42   Peter Arshinov, *History of the Makhnovist Movement* (London: Freedom Press, 1987), p. 71.

43   His reluctance to label the bureaucracy as a ruling class was based on his estimation that they were not the *legal* owners of the means of production. He did, however, acknowledge that the bureaucracy through the state machinery has 'appropriated the proletariat politically'. Trotsky argued that state property was not the solution to a deficit of democracy; in fact, state property becomes socialist property in proportion to the extent it ceases to be state property. Adding that state ownership is not in itself sufficient to change the character and form of labour, new forms of fetishised social relations are quite possible, the transfer of property to the state changed the situation of the workers only juridically. Leon Trotsky, *The Revolution Betrayed* (New York: Pathfinder, 1989), p. 24 and pp. 237–49. See also Charles Bettelheim, *Class Struggles in the USSR, First Period, 1917–1923* and *Second Period 1923–1930*, (Brighton: Harvester Press, 1978).

44   *Arkhitektura CCCP*, No. 9, 1936, p. 2.

45   For the construction industry, like other economic sectors, the mid 1930s were a turning point. The comprehensive 1935 plan for the reconstruction of Moscow was the signal for the reordering of space (see below). The catalyst in the restructuring of time and labour arrived in the 1936 decree concerning the 'Improvement of construction matters and reduction in price of construction'. These documents are important. First, because they institutionalised within law Party control over the production of the built environment. Second, the plans for construction were actually carried out in practice, and third, the all-embracing and comprehensive character of the declarations set the framework for the development of the labour process and for the physical character of the city of Moscow for the next 30 years. *Reshenie Partii i pravitelstvo no xozaistvennom voprocam*, Vol. 2, 1929–1940 (Moscow, 1967). Postanovleniye Sovnarkoma CCCP i TsK BKP, *Ob uluchsheniye stroitelstvo i ob udeshevlenie stroitelstvo* (On improving and cheapening construction), 11 February 1936. See also, *O generalnom plane rekonstruktsia goroda Moskvi* (On the general plan for the reconstruction of Moscow), 10 July 1935, pp. 534–46.

46   *Reshenie Partii (Party decisions) i pravitelstvo no xozaistvennom voprocam*, Vol. 2, 1929–1940, 'O merax po uporiadoenniu upravlenia proizvodstvom i ustanovlenie edinonachalie' (Moscow, 1967), pp. 125–31. An investigation of the language of law is particularly revealing of the double act that the Party was required to perform. The decree of 5 September 1929 on 'The measures for the regulation of the management of production and the installation of one-man management' was perhaps the pivotal piece of legislation legitimising in law the development of the bureaucracy.

47   Whilst the regulations clearly stipulated that directors were required to seek the opinions of trade union and party organisations and to delegate smaller day-to-day running problems, the extent to which rank and file workers could intervene in the actual management of the enterprise was strictly limited.

48   *Reshenii Parti*, ibid., p. 128.

49   Lenin, 'The Immediate Tasks of the Soviet Government' in *Collected Works*, p. 410.

50   This is where groups of workers were organised into teams and received production tasks as part of the overall planned output for a construction trust. It is worth remembering here that an adapted form of this labour organisation was at the centre of economic policy in the perestroika period.

51   The piece wage, *sdelnaya zarplata*, is the most effective way of linking money to output and therefore one of the most effective way of accumulating surplus. The operation of such a system was followed later by the introduction of *progressivno-sdelnaya* (progressive piece wages), part of a general policy for widening wage differentials, which, with the addition of bonus schemes, was felt to be the most appropriate method of stimulating labour and raising productivity.

52   In 1930 it is reported that in the construction industry, 51 out of every 100 workers were operating on the basis of *sotz sorevnovania*, and 27 out of every 100 were involved in shock brigades. See *Soyuz stroiteli v zifrak i diagrammak* (Moscow, 1930) on the union of builders in diagrams and indices; V.D. Fedorov, *Formirovanie rabochik kadrov na novostroikax pervoi piatiletki* (PhD dissertation, Gorkovsky University, 1966), Avotreferat p. 15.

53   *Trud*, 9 February 1936, p. 2.

54   *Stroitelnaya Promishlennost*, No. 7, 1936, p. 9.

55   Ibid., p. 6.

56   *Stroitelnaya Promishlennost*, No. 6, 1936, pp. 5–6.

57   A. Barsukov and A. Kristalnie, *Khozraschot na stroike* (Moscow: Gosfinizdat SSSP, 1932), p. 4.

58   V.D. Fedorov, p. 13.

59   Y. Pak, *Organizatia truda i zarabotnaya plati v stroitelstve* (Moscow: Stroizdat, 1974), p. 171, on the organisation of labour and wages in the construction industry.

60   *Stroitelstvo Moskva*, No. 10, 1931, pp. 2–4

61   A brief history of wage forms in the construction industry from the October Revolution onwards is to be found in Y. Pak, *Organizatia truda*, pp. 166, and by the same author, *Ekonomika truda v stroitelstve* (Moscow: Stroizdat, 1978), pp. 192 ff on the economics of labour in construction.

62   *Trud*, 8 May 1936, p. 1.

63   Some have argued that since the employer (in this case there is only one – the state) 'does not confront the worker in the same way as the capitalist confronts the wage labourer, labour power in the Soviet Union is not a commodity.' Subjectively, if a worker is at the mercy of productivity targets in which the driver is the wage and is forced to endure, what is the meaning of labour under socialism? See Donald Filtzer, *Soviet Workers and Stalinist Industrialization* (London: Pluto, 1986), p. 259.

64   Filtzer, *Soviet Workers*, p. 118.

65   Ibid., pp. 200–207.

66   *Trud*, 9 February 1936, p. 2. An indication of how widespread the opposition was in other sectors can be gleaned by the reported incidence of 'sabotage' in the journal throughout April in places like the Cheliabinsk Tractor and Motor Factory, the Invanovna cotton factories and in the mining regions of the Donbass. *Trud*, 15 April 1936, p. 3, *Trud*, 18 April 1936, p. 1. *Trud*, 31 April 1936, p. 4.

67   *Stroitelnaya Promishlennost*, 15 October 1936.

68   Voline, *Unknown Revolution*, p. 247.

5

Foreign Bodies: Corps Etranger

You be careful in that city son. They'll slit your pocket open when you're sleeping on the bus. The place is awash with knife yielding godless vagabonds. Its streets pounded by angry proletarians with a thirst. Your uncle has the 'kiss' and the liver to prove it.

INTRODUCTION

'Foreign Bodies' was originally published in 2004 as an exhibition and limited edition colour picture book. Published in both languages, the French text was illustrated with photographs of Glasgow and the English text with images of Marseille. Here it is reproduced in edited form with only a small selection of the photographs used in the original. The narrative takes the form of an exchange of letters between two cities – Marseille and Glasgow. Like two old men reminiscing about the course their life has taken, they reflect on their mutual rise to a position of great wealth and splendour and their subsequent decline in old age. At first glance they would appear to have little in common. One is a Mediterranean city that is bathed in warm sun for most of the year and the other shivers in the far northwest. On closer inspection, however, there is much that they share. They both have a reputation for being political rebels, and are passionate about football and alcohol – one the home of pastis, the other of whisky. They are also obsessed by the weather. Marseille can be chilled by the mistral blowing in from the Massif Central and burnt by the North African sirocco. Meanwhile, Glasgow seems to alternate between dreek Atlantic squalls and blanket grey cloud. Both cities are also famous for verbal trickery, and enjoy trading on their stereotypes of notoriety, with Glasgow feared by London, and Marseille by Paris. Perhaps more importantly, they are connected historically by their roles as imperial and industrial cities that were pivotal in the development of capitalism in Britain and France; a history that has left an indelible stamp on the fabric and structure of both cities.

14 MARCH 2004 – MARSEILLE

Tattered Epaulettes / Epaulettes en Lambeaux

They say that for a 2,500 year-old city I wear my age well. In truth, I feel like an old aristocrat, one who has fallen on hard times and dreams of former greatness, slightly confused and embarrassed at having turned the family home into a tourist trap to pay the taxman's bills. However, I remain optimistic that I can cash in on the taxpayer's unquenchable thirst for heritage and nostalgia. Manufacturing history into easily digestible chunks is a profitable business and 'Theme park bouillabaisse in ancient Massalia' is not such a bad sales pitch. But my recent history is more problematic. For I know that most of what is 'mine' belonged at some point to someone else. It has always been like that, and I have learnt to cope with this divided self. Part of me gazes down from the Nôtre-Dame de la Garde and marvels at the city unfolding into a speckled panorama of luminous stone. But I am reminded that this spectacle only exists because of the super profits generated by commodities like sugar. By 1789, Marseille already boasted 12 sugar refineries, built to process the sweet trade arriving from Saint Domingue (now Haiti). This connection with cash crops is a common enough experience for nineteenth-century boom cities, one that I believe matches your own. It is difficult knowing that your prosperity was achieved on the back of other people's misery. But how do you address such histories? Would you return all profits and property to their rightful owners? Put up a statue? Screw a plaque on the wall? I have toyed with the idea. But addressing historical guilt is a messy process if you possess a past that has been scarred by the violent excesses of colonisation, revolutionary justice, and Nazi occupation.

21 MARCH 2004 – GLASGOW

Fêtes and Festivals on the Clyde / Fêtes et Festivals sur La Clyde

At least you have the warm sun to cushion you against the memories of war, thievery and violence. I am younger by 1,000 years but it is familiar territory. Like you, I don't believe in burying the awkward truths of my origins and accumulated wealth. It is just that it seems so long ago now. The passing of historical time compresses memory and alters the symbolic value that we attach to objects, events and buildings. Just look at how the sumptuous institutions of state and capital like banks, warehouses and mills have been transformed into bars, galleries and flats. Once a proletarian can freely enter the Empire Bank and drink a beer, the building no longer exists simply as an icon of nineteenth-century imperial prowess. It has become something else. Similarly, it is bizarre to think that only 250 years ago, it was considered entirely reasonable to exploit the labour of landless highlanders and unpaid slaves to build a city. This has been the case for most of human history and it is difficult to imagine the construction of cities like Marseille or Glasgow without the concentration and centralisation of political and economic power. The nineteenth-century bourgeoisie were drunk on self-belief and determined to celebrate it in spectacular fashion, not just through the construction of stone

5.1 'Imperial picturesque' – African fountain head in Marseille / Hindu soldiers in Glasgow

monuments but in the staging of industry and empire exhibitions held in Glasgow in 1888, 1901 and 1936. I think Marseille hosted similar events. They said it all really. In the spirit of imperial triumphalism they combined a fun day out with a lecture on the economic and political priorities of the British Empire. What appeared as a casual stroll in Kelvingrove Park was transformed into a lesson about European ideas of science, culture and racial superiority, a guided tour through a choreographed landscape in which the earth and all of its diversity had been captured into stalls and catalogues of artefacts. 'Damn it by God,' you could hear them exclaim 'the world must be rationalised. It can be understood. Nature will be martialled and natives tamed.' And all of this had to be shown. So as to convince wage labour at home, to intimidate rival metropolitan centres and to announce to all of the empire's subjects who was king. In this way the exhibitions were like ideological cement, reinforcing the sense of confidence with which the bourgeoisie went about accumulating the capital to finance an industrial revolution.

28 MARCH 2004 – MARSEILLE

Stealing History in the Sunshine / Spolier l'histoire en Plein Soleil

I remember the exhibitions well, helped by the fact that the original posters have been reprinted as post cards and are for sale on every street corner. Our first carnival of industry and empire took place in 1899 to celebrate the city's 2,500-year history. A veritable jamboree of real and imagined histories, it was a rehearsal for l'Exposition Coloniale in 1906, and l'Exposition Internationale des Applications de l'Electricité in 1908. This was a process of ritualised display crowned by the empire exhibition of 1922 held in the park that is now home to the Velodrome. As you point out, they were designed to overwhelm the visitor, who wasn't there just to be entertained. No sir, you were there to be instructed. And in all of this there was one incontrovertible point being made. This inventiveness, this mastery of maths and matter on display in the Hall of Industry and the Palais des Machines was European in origin. You and I know that to be false. It was the Arabs, along with the Chinese, who developed modern mathematics and algebra. But in such themed spectacles they were little more than curios, fetishised craftsmen making gifts for visitors. A local Communist visiting the empire exhibition's model African villages, Arab souks, and pagodas, commented that it 'symbolised all the thievery, all the murders, all the plundering that took place in the name of civilisation.'

1 APRIL 2004 – GLASGOW

Cultural Kidnapping / Rapt Culturel

Plunder indeed. Not everyone sees it quite like that, of course. There are a growing number of people who are trying to revise our imperial history, pointing out the benefits to other countries of constructing railways stations and town halls. When really pushed, they also like to take credit for instilling democratic values amongst native peoples. It is, as you might imagine, a contested terrain that provokes strong emotions at home and abroad. The Glasgow authorities recently returned stolen religious artefacts and clothing to Native Americans. And one wonders what else lies in the vaults of the Kelvingrove Museum. One group of urban militants, keen to confront historical injustices, have taken to defacing monuments and buildings. Of course, the angry and discontented have been spraying the walls of cities with the profane and insurrectionary since ancient Rome. It was perhaps not surprising, then, that they should attack the statues of the great and good burghers of Bristol. Statues that had been erected for services to…Well, that was the point, services rendered to whom? The graffiti artist was in no doubt – slave traders, all of them. But here in Glasgow? 'Surely not. It was the English who instigated all the ruthless acts of appropriation and land acquisition.' If this were true it would mean that the Scottish landed class and bourgeoisie were uninterested in the spoils of the factory system or the cultivation of tobacco and cotton. The reality is that Scots were enthusiastic participants in the imperial services. They worked obediently and in fear of God as the empire's policemen, overseers and managers, and as soldiers fought across the globe, following in the footsteps of Field Marshall Roberts, whose monument towers over Park Circus and details how he traversed the planet, 'maintaining the gleam of weapon…and the greatness of empire' in Kandahar, Afghanistan, Burma, Waterford, India, South Africa and Abyssinia.

8 APRIL 2004 – MARSEILLE

The Glory / La Gloire

It is no more or less shameful than any of history's imperial projects. But it's right that we revisit historical taboos. Not least because each new generation and ruling class tries to fashion history in their own image. Writing new books and making emblematic buildings are two of the ways of doing this, and for us in Marseille, the legacy of the French Empire screams from every rooftop. Despite this, I like to think that my transformation into a bourgeois metropolis did some good. History is not a simple tale of domination and resistance. It is messier than that, and not all of the capitalist entrepreneurs who bankrolled my urban construction and that of the colonial city were bloodthirsty vampires with a 'werewolves' hunger for surplus value'. Like it or not, the architectural monuments of my imperial past are some of the favourite stopping-off points for tourists. Do you think that the Americans disembarking at the quays along the way to l'Estaque are arriving for a taste of French Arabia or Vietnam? I doubt it. No, they are here to witness the pomp and imperial triumphalism of industrial capitalism. In the same way that tourists arrive in Glasgow to wander around the historic core rather than visit working-class life on your periphery, they come here to admire my collection of neo-classical buildings and boulevards. You can see them shuffling along a prescribed route that takes in la Canabière, Préfecture, Opera House, Bourse and Cathedral, stopping to buy mementoes in the pink limestone courtyard of the Vieille Charité, a seventeenth-century workhouse and religious centre, now transformed into a culture boutique.

5.2   'Exchanging commodities'. Bourse in Marseille / Royal Exchange Square, Glasgow

You see, I might be crumbling at the edges, but I was once magnificent. By the end of the nineteenth century, after 30 years of unprecedented economic and population growth, Marseille possessed all of the institutions necessary for a capitalist city with visions of imperial grandeur, a definitive statement of the bourgeois world view that was reproduced in London, Madrid, Moscow, Budapest and Berlin. They might have been corrupt and morally bankrupt, but at least the nineteenth-century empire builders were adventurous and audacious enough to engrave their vision on the ceiling of the Bourse with the immortal words 'Commerce, industry, navigation, and agriculture'. To which they should really have added the word 'God'.

15 APRIL 2004 – GLASGOW

Civilising the World with Scottish Iron / Civiliser le Monde avec le Fer Ecossais

It won't surprise you that the same words and sentiments can be found printed on the surfaces of Glasgow. As you rightly point out, the real crowning achievement of urban development was not to be found in exhibitions but in the theatrical urbanism of the Victorian and Napoleonic city. We too took commerce and navigation seriously and with the historical union of industrial production and imperial rule, Glasgow's engineering skills became famous all over the globe. It is said that MacFarlane's decorative ironwork, produced in the Saracen works in Glasgow, can be found 'in every city in the civilised world'. And I think you will find that I can match your archipelago of institutional buildings, from the most basic of mills to the most sophisticated of carpet factories. But these days any pretensions I might once have had to greatness have been reduced to heritage trails. The Royal Exchange is now an art gallery. The former stock exchange is up for rent. But at my height, at my height, well. 'Why shouldn't Glasgow become the second Paris?' dreamt Provost John Blackie, and in 1866 he duly dispatched a delegation to see what could be learnt from Baron von Haussmann. He might have been fanciful but I was a contender. How many other cities can boast a town hall like the City Chambers that rivals the Vatican in its excess of marble and alabaster? And it is not just in the construction of our respective imperial cities that we share a common history, but in the building of the colonial city. The Scots helped build versions of the British State in Australia and India. The French went building in North Africa, and together we built Belem in Brazil. We supplied the cast-iron structures for market halls and libraries, whilst you tried to create a semblance of civic order by planning streets, fountains, and squares. Most famous of all was our joint venture to build the Manaus Opera House, a tiny fragment of bourgeois culture in the Amazonian forest, complete with an early example of air-conditioning, timber from France, iron columns from Glasgow and rubberised paving stones. But that, as they say, is another story.

28 APRIL 2004 – MARSEILLE

Camouflaging the French Empire / Camoufler l'Empire Francais

I knew of the French connection with Brazil. Its name is included in the roll call of economic partners carved onto the walls of the Bourse. Like the Scots, the French saw it as their duty to export the virtues of God, capital and industrious activity to all four corners of the world. And the logbooks indicate that Marseille had trading links with other Brazilian cites like Salvador – an Afro baroque port situated further down the coast with a legendary reputation for carnival. (Incidentally, it was also from Marseille that Joseph Conrad, that chronicler of imperial nightmares, made his maiden voyage to South America as an apprentice aboard the Mont Blanc.) But I suspect that the ships that took the architects, engineers and planed timber to Belem departed from Nantes or La Rochelle, as did most of the slave and merchant ships bound for the Caribbean and the Americas. Of course, the true character of Marseille's relationships with these places remains largely camouflaged by exotic stereotypes, not least in the city's monuments and sculptures. Take, for instance, the seemingly innocuous water sculpture in front of la Banque de France. Passers-by often rest in its shade, seldom realising the significance of the idealised representation of the four continents and their inhabitants. Carved out of blonde stone, it depicts Africa, Asia and the Americas as if they were equal partners in the process of colonisation, rather than carefully mapped landscapes for capital accumulation in which native peoples, their culture and resources became commodities for European consumption and decoration. This is one of the ways ideology worked by representing the exploitative character of the political and economic relationships between Europe and the rest of the world as benign and picturesque.

5 MAY 2004 – GLASGOW

Sweet Traditions and Slavery / Douces Traditions et Esclavage

I can think of no better example of a picturesque mask than the sweetness of sugar and the smoky satisfaction of tobacco, two commodities that both cities produced in abundance. Can you imagine France without a slice of cake and a cigarette? Can you imagine Glasgow without 'tea, two sugars and ten fags'? This little trinity was one of the foundations of British life. Little matter that it was also a permanent reminder of the coordinates of the transatlantic triangle and colonial expansion, faithfully reproduced on every kitchen table. It is strange to think of life's pleasures in such a way. I'm not saying that anyone today should feel individually responsible for Mr Macpherson's 'profitable spell in St Kitts'. And it would be ridiculous to feel guilty every time you ate chocolate. But we have a blind spot when it comes to slavery, India and what is in many ways our very own 'Algeria' – the history of colonial rule in Ireland. Maybe we should name cities according to the labourers who built them and provided the booty for their construction. In this case you could call me an Afro-Irish-Highland city. I think of myself as a part African city, not because of the small black population that has lived here for over two centuries, but because my street names crack to the whip of a plantation overseer. It is a twisted story that is continued in the city's statuary that romanticises imperial violence and celebrates the leaders of church, capital and crown. In marked contrast, there is no monument to the shortened lives of the Scots and Irish that laboured in the yards, docks and factories producing coal, ships, and sewing machines, although their labour time can be found immortalised in the rolling stock that connects Santos to India. And I dare say that there is little that commemorates the lives of the ordinary workers that fabricated the oil products, chemicals, bricks and alcohol for which you were famous.

12 MAY 2004 – MARSEILLE

Multiple Identities / Identités Multiples

Historical amnesia means that eventually it will all be forgotten. In a way, we have to edit our nightmares and memories or at least understand them as complex and multi-layered. Colonisation is a reflexive process and not a simple tale of domination. The empire strikes back in many ways, not least in terms of food and music. It infiltrates the lifeblood of the host city and challenges concepts of historical and social exclusivity. Multiple personalities have never been a problem for me. I am comfortable with the fact that the meeting of Africa, the Orient and the wandering tribes of the Mediterranean coast have forged my hybrid identity. As an independent city-state I established a trading port at Acre as early as the twelfth century and became the 'de facto headquarters of trade with the Levant'. Of course, it hasn't always been a history of peaceful cooperation. The remains of bourgeois opulence testify to the 'other' nature of my relations with Africa and the Orient. But I have remained for all that a socially vibrant and ethnically diverse city, a melting pot that the SS found deeply offensive. Le Panier on the hills above the dock has always been home to refugees and successive waves of immigrants. It was where outsiders could hide and the Nazis knew exactly where they were heading when they landed in Marseille. They rounded up nearly the entire population from the crooked streets and transferred it to a concentration camp, returning to detonate everything but those buildings that reminded them of ancient Rome. Such an act of barbarism would be shocking in any time and space, but particularly here. It is a Marseillain cliché, but you should feast your eyes on the throng of nationalities that head down la Canebière to le Vieux-Port. Re-enact the Potemkin step scene by stumbling down the staircase from la Gare Saint Charles. Turn right down into the aromas of mint tea and roasting lamb in Belsunce or straight down le boulevard d'Athènes Dugommier. Not for me the likes of Le Pen. How dare he rally his troops in this city? Fascists need history to legitimise their ideological ambition, but their real desire is to destroy history altogether. It is difficult to envisage what their France would look like. They don't like anyone who is black, Semitic, Arab, gay or left-wing. What would I be without my richly layered tapestry of Armenians, Jews, Algerians, Vietnamese and Senegalese? I hope they remember this as they try and turn me into a Euromed pleasure port for the affluent global tourist.

5.3 'Slogans for a new order', Graffiti in Marseille and Glasgow

26 MAY 2004 – GLASGOW

'Stand Firm Against the Employing Class' / «Tenir Bon Contre la Classe des Patrons»

There is a little of everyone and everything in Glasgow too, and its distinctiveness is the product of successive waves of Irish, Italian, Jewish, Pakistani, and recently, African and East European immigration. Racists periodically try to stir up animosities between communities. But for the most part, they have always got on pretty well and I like to think that my reputation as a tolerant and left-wing city is not fictitious but has a real foundation in truth. I know what you are thinking, and it is true perhaps that we've never embraced radical left politics in the same way as the French but believe me, we have had our moments. It could all have been very different. Maybe it should have been. Motivated by a commitment to reform and a determination to quell discontent, Glasgow Council built bathhouses, libraries, primary schools and parks in almost all of the city's residential neighbourhoods between 1890 and 1914. The basic right to an education and to being clean was a concession the authorities were willing to make, but workers' rights in the factories and shipyards were another matter. In response, workers became organised, joined trade unions and the newly-formed Independent Labour Party and set up educational classes, where they read not only Robert Burns but Marx. And then in 1914, my streets and squares resounded with the noise of massive rallies organised by women, at which a city wide rent strike was announced. Against all the odds it culminated in victory and the drafting of new legislation to regulate the activities of private landlords. It helped trigger a wave of political and industrial unrest that quickly enveloped the local economy. In the space of four years, the industrial sector was hit by a massive 261 strikes in a movement that had begun to acquire a genuinely insurgent character. By 1919, Churchill, the government and many of the ruling class were in no doubt. Unless a contingency plan was formed, Glasgow would go Red and as 60,000 workers assembled in George Square at a rally to support a 40-hour week, troops and tanks rolled into the city. Workers were under no illusions as to the historical significance of the moment. Leaflets circulated by motorbike called on workers to 'stand firm in their disputes and to continue fighting against the employing class'. It was an undoubtedly dramatic chain of events and prompted the *Glasgow Herald* to publish a front page that described 'wild Bolshevik scenes' in George Square. The red flag was hoisted and two of the leaders, MacLean and Gallagher, travelled to Moscow to discuss the possibility of a full-scale workers' uprising with Lenin. Famously, he advised them to wait for the English – and the rest, they say, is history.

4 JUNE – MARSEILLE

Utopian Socialists in Marseille / Socialistes Utopistes à Marseille

I might have temporarily assumed the trappings of nobility, but I, too, come from humble origins and have been home to anarchists, trade unions and all manner of workers' organisations. You have to remember that even though Marseille prevaricated in 1789, revolutionary ideas about how we might live and organise ourselves differently have moulded my history, from St Simon's plan to replace the European aristocracy with a new industrial and scientific order to the schemes for ideal cities imagined by Fourier, Considerant, and Godin. Not forgetting my neighbour Lyon, who boasts of being the home of the first industrial workers' revolt in 1831, when under the cover of an anarchist black flag, weavers declared the independent Commune of the Croix Rousse. So this city has always been surrounded by and naturally receptive to radical ideas. In fact, it turns out that your Robert Owen had strong connections with Marseille. Inspired by his ideas on social reform and economic justice, Marseille workers put together a plan in the 1830s to organise direct labour exchanges. Led by the bakers, it was visionary scheme in which 'labour-time' credits would be swapped between producers without the circulation and use of money. It was championed by a Monsieur André, who, swept away by revolutionary idealism, called on workers to 'assume their natural birth right and unite to overthrow the menace that caused them such suffering and poverty.' And then came 1848, when Marseillan workers sided decisively with la République Sociale. And for a moment I gazed into the distant unknown along what Blanqui had said were 'the multiple paths that lead to a new social order'. But no sooner had I glimpsed this new city than the curtains were drawn in a fusillade of muskets.

9 JUNE 2004 – GLASGOW

Hope and Farce / Espoir et Farce

We never had such bloodshed, at least not on home soil. Instead, we had the utter fiasco of the 1926 General Strike, fiasco that is in terms of its defeat and betrayal. However, for those involved in organising the Councils of Action that were set up throughout Scotland and that in some areas had begun to function like prototypical Soviets, it was a resounding success. Red flags were unfurled as the workshops and engine houses of empire ground to a halt. In 'Red Motherwell' an atmosphere of 'peace and quiet' descended over a region in which all rail and road transport ceased and over which the Councils of Action, together with the Workers Defence Corp, established what was almost complete control. This was repeated in Methil, when the rallying cry of 'All Power to the Councils of Action' echoed between the pitheads. For a brief moment the region of Fife resembled a people's republic. Can you imagine it, the 'Worker's Republic of Fife'? I have often wondered what sort of city the workers would have built had they succeeded. Would they have been like the Russian Constructivists and planned communes and networks of linear cities? It is not as far-fetched as one might think. After all it was only 20 years later that the modernist architect Berthold Lubetkin went to work with the miners of Peterlee. Tragically, we were never to find out. The ruling class was organised. First they stationed battleships off all the main ports and industrial areas on the coast. Then something much simpler. They struck a deal with the leader of the trade union movement. To the utter astonishment of workers still on strike (and French journalists, who found the whole thing incomprehensible), the dispute was called off.

5.4 'Machinery of creative destruction'. Demolition sites in Marseille and Glasgow

15 JUNE 2004 – MARSEILLE

Close to a Revolutionary Commune / Proche de la Commune Révolutionnaire

It was strange indeed, and in a way tragic. But so was the fate of the last real attempt to transform me into a city of freedom and liberty during the short-lived Marseille Commune of 1871. It was the son of a bourgeois family, a monsieur Gaston Crémieux, and his anarchist comrade Bastelica, who inspired the workers to seize the Préfecture and proclaim a commune, as had happened in Paris. Flirting with the other class is a forgivable youthful folly. However, there are certain lines you do not cross; receiving advice from Mikhail Bakunin was one. And there was no way back after left-wing radicals mounted the steps to announce that 'we will make a revolution, an implacable and inexorable revolution, a revolution with all of its anger, its colours and patriotic fury, we will leave Marseille in arms…long live the revolutionary commune.' They were confident. After all, only 70 years before, two thirds of the Marseillain Jacobin Club had been workers. It should have been enough, drawing on a tradition of political opposition and the spirit of independence for which the city was renowned. But the forces of reaction were gathering. 'Communards, damn them, they are men escaped from hell', muttered the Pope. And as the insurgents seized la Préfecture, as they did momentarily in Lyon, the generals responded with cannon fire. Yes, the government loyalists were even willing to destroy their own house in their pursuit of vengeance. The ferocity of the retaliation against the communards was matched only by the events in Paris. Many militants were executed or exiled, and Crémieux himself was shot on the orders of Thiers at the foot of the Pharo fort. Even by the standards of the Catholic clergy and supporters of l'Ancien Régime it was an overreaction. At the turn of the twentieth century, Marseille rose again. The syndicalist movement that had swept Europe from Glasgow to Moscow caught the political imagination of French workers, including those in the Marseille area, and for a while they exerted considerable influence on local affairs. By 1914 200 French municipalities were being run by the SFIO, the French Section of the Second Internationale, and Marseille was one of them. I, too, began to wonder what a workers' city might look like. Although I hoped it wasn't going to be anything like Ledoux's Panoptican salt-works or the enforced austerity of Fourier's Phalansterie. The Russian Revolution had ignited the dreams of French workers, hopes that survived the struggle against fascism, and in the aftermath of the Second World War, there was a genuine belief that maybe its time had come again in the plans for urban reconstruction and in the renewed commitment to social justice. There was the big dockers' strike in the late forties, when what had started out as a series of minor grievances escalated and ended up with an employers' lock-out and a General Strike. And I suppose we shouldn't forget 1968. It was nerve-racking and exciting to hear new slogans bounce off the parapets. But la Préfecture and l'Hôtel de Ville were never going to fall once the workers had been separated from the students.

12 JULY 2004 – GLASGOW

New Town Dreams / Rêves de Villes Nouvelles

There was to be no great 1968 moment for me. As bankers and cement producers ripped through my historic core in the 1950s and 1960s, the Paris of love and revolution seemed an awfully long way off. With the 1952 Festival of Britain in their hearts and minds, the city architects and planners duly completed what the German bombing raids had started. I can still hear them. 'You would have done the same. There was no choice, and besides, we genuinely thought we were doing the right thing. The housing was beyond repair. You can romanticise the empire city as much as you like, but in 1945 it stank. It was rotten and the threat of cholera and typhoid still occupied living memories.' All of which is true, and it was difficult not to be swept along by the optimistic plans for urban renewal that reminded me of the improvement acts of the late nineteenth century, when the city was illuminated by streetlights, cast-iron market halls and glass arcades. Similarly, the 1945 Bruce Plan spoke of modernity like a flashing beacon of a new world to come. The architectural and social programme of the welfare state was certainly ambitious. New housing, schools and hospitals would be built as part of a new social contract with the British people. There was to be no return to the Depression years of the 1930s. The future beckoned. Modern houses didn't have sash windows. They had aluminium ones. They didn't have antique plaster, they had concrete or block work walls. Hollow plywood doors replaced solid timber. The fireplace gave way to the radiator. And most importantly, the new homes were to be prefabricated under factory conditions and laid out on the gridiron traces of the demolished Victorian city. What we got, of course, was something rather different from that created in the utopian imagination. I am sure that Bruce never imagined that the rational organisation of land as a 'grid' and building as 'concrete prefabrication' would become a crude device for obliterating difference and maximising the profits of building contractors. Unfortunately it is a logic that I experienced first-hand. I had more tower blocks than anywhere else in Britain. I had the tallest in Europe at 32 stories. And I had the largest urban population anywhere in Britain living in state housing. Not just in tall storeys, but in four-storey barracks linked by solitary access roads.

20 JULY 2004 – MARSEILLE

The Flip Side of Reason / Le Revers de la Raison

I, too, nearly became a *tabula rasa* concrete city of planned efficiency, a fate that I only escaped because of the outbreak of the Second World War. In 1936, Monsieur Greber unveiled his version of la cité industrielle for Marseille that was similar to Garnier's plans for Lyon. The new Marseille was destined to become a radiant orthogonal city of replicated blocks and streets. It is an urban vision that I confess I never found entirely convincing; too much like a mechanical device for selling real estate and organising police patrols; far too reminiscent of Haussmann's reign in Paris when, under the cover of cleanliness, his boulevards tore through independent working-class communities. On the other hand, there is no reason to presume that Cartesian grid plan towns need become 'surveillance' cities, although there remains something peculiar about laying peoples lives out in identically patterned streets and houses. I have always wondered whether the word 'rational' is a fitting term to describe this type of urban reconstruction. It doesn't seem like the modern city of reason to me, but more its deformed sibling. They say historical hindsight is easy. It isn't. It is not an easy thing to deal with. The knowledge that is, that the reason cities like yours and mine were torn apart in the 1950s and 1960s was the result of an appalling historical collision between five forces: the imperatives of post-war reconstruction; the profits which had become available with the technological shift towards concrete prefabrication; developer greed; corruption in local politics; and the romanticism of architects in thrall to the machine. It was a recipe for disaster.

27 JULY 2004 – GLASGOW

Bare Bones and Dynamite / L'Essentiel et la Dynamite

Disaster is a polite term, I think, for such historical myopia. It really shouldn't have ended as it did. A 'home as a machine for living in' always struck me as an enticingly modern idea. There was no intrinsic reason why such a concept should become reduced to the vulgar idea of a machine for printing money. Similarly, my peripheral schemes bear little relationship to the early ideas of avant-garde architects in Russia and Germany. They imagined housing communes that were integrated with high-quality social and cultural facilities. But capitalism tends to strip things of qualities that are too expensive or difficult to commodify. The contemporary architect who aspires to be a social reformer is confronted at every stage in the construction process by a ruthless techno-economic logic that has one priority: to maximise the return on capital, whether invested in the mass production of brick and timber-framed suburban housing or the prefabrication of concrete frames and panels. This fragile relationship between social engineering and social catastrophe was underlined a decade ago when 30 years after they were built, the Area C flats in Hutchensontown were demolished. Designed by Basil Spence, they were the incarnation of sixties optimism and a symbol of modern housing and social regeneration. Streets in the sky, deck access, pilotis. The people had running water at last. However, it wasn't only out of the taps but down the walls. It was the end of Le Corbusier in Glasgow. Now they're trying to reinvent the tenement and 'to make new communities'. But when will they learn that architects and politicians cannot 'make' communities?

3 AUGUST 2004 – MARSEILLE

Concrete Memories / Mémoires de Béton

Architects can't create communities. But they are certainly adept at helping destroy them. In many ways, I think it is a good thing that the old industrialised building systems and land use zoning systems from the 1960s have been discredited.

5.5   'Bridging concrete uncertainties'. Flyovers in Marseille and Glasgow

But equally problematic has been what replaced this perceived failure of central planning. As far as I can make out, the current generation of cost accountants and bureaucrats has no more commitment to reason than before. The politics are essentially the same and the urban consequences, if anything, have turned out to be even more disastrous. It gave me poorly-built schemes on the periphery like la Bricarde and shocking intrusions, like the shopping mall Le Centre Bourse that has defaced my historic core. In their desperation to apportion blame for the mess they have made of me, they have even accused concrete. It is, of course, absurd. Concrete can be monstrous or magnificent. It depends on who's using it and why. I can boast le Cercle des Nageurs, a monument to the civic use of concrete from the sixties, and the glorious silo in the dock – a triumphant essay on the relationship between form and function. I also think that some of the spaces under the flyover have a great sculptural quality. And we shouldn't forget that I have one of the best examples of the use of concrete in the world, l'Unité d'Habitation. It's the building that inspired Basil Spence and his contemporaries in Glasgow, and its sculpted surfaces and duplex flats, lit from both sides by the Mediterranean sun, put to shame the woeful new brutalism and post-modernism that scar the new Marseille.

10 AUGUST 2004 – GLASGOW

Luxury is a Tin Shed by a Motorway / Le Luxe Est une Baraque en Tôle Près de l'Autoroute

Le Centre Bourse could easily trade places with St Enochs, and our silos (now demolished) on the north bank of the Clyde would have slipped into your port area without a second thought. I have a similar collection of poorly-built new offices, retail parks, leisure centres and speculative suburban housing schemes. These unimaginative, soulless landscapes were supposed to be a critique of modernism, but I would like to ask the developers who are tearing me apart again exactly what it is they think they will be remembered for? It might be the case that the mansion houses of the city's south side and west end were impossible to construct without bale loads of tobacco from the Caribbean. But at least the builders understood what luxury might mean in terms of architectural space. They featured cathedral-like floor to ceiling heights. Houses with bedrooms so grand that lovers could lose each other. In contrast, in the 'ideal homes for ideal families' sprouting all over the city, you hit your head on the ceiling of the 'luxury bedroom' that has no space for a cupboard. No cast-iron, just badly galvanised weeping steel. No treated timber seasoned to last 100 years, just factory-farmed pine that is rotten before the glass is sealed into the frame. But what does anyone expect from a largely deregulated building industry that is beyond any real democratic control and that has left a legacy of rusting sheds, atrociously designed schools, sad hospital extensions, and 'public' buildings that appear to have been built by a petrol station subcontractor?

17 AUGUST 2004 – MARSEILLE

Cheap Hotels for Cheap Visions / Des Hôtels Bon Marché pour des Visions Bon Marché

Responsibility for my fate has long since been transferred to a meritocracy of management consultants and land developers. Their attitude to urbanism is to maximise the number of IBIS hotels in prime locations. They are for the most part vulgar individuals with a penchant for instant thrills. Are they serious that their sad little office blocks at la Joliette and along du Boulevard du Prado will still be there 150 years later to tell a story like the Bourse or the Palais de Justice? They seem quite unconcerned and are forging ahead with ambitious plans for the docks, for new plazas around the Cathedral and for the reconstruction and development of the beaches at Prado. The city marketing department is working overtime in its attempt to rebrand the city. Tourist footfall, big name architect, grand projet, trickle-down effect, knock on economic benefits – even the poor will prosper. The delusions pile up as high as the metal boxes in the container port that we are told will be the city's salvation. But depending on who you believe, unemployment in Marseille is anywhere between 25 and 40 per cent of the population. And a disproportionate number of them are black or Muslim. But such statistics don't seem to bother the modern urban aesthete feasting on the whole mythology of neo-liberalism, light salads and skinny lattes.

24 AUGUST 2004 – GLASGOW

Sad Imitations of the Bourgeois Utopia / Tristes Imitations des Utopies Bourgeoises

There is a logic to all of this. For if you really buy into the utopian concept of free markets then you should accept that the capitalisation of public assets should have no moral restrictions. Hospitals, housing, schools, railways, looking after the elderly – leave it all to the private sector. Unfortunately, this ideological putsch seems to have been particularly popular in Glasgow. It has been pretty merciless, and despite sit-ins and demonstrations, they have succeeded in closing many of the city's important social institutions. It was particularly ironic, given the city's high level of poverty and reputation as the sick man of Europe. And as they padlocked the doors to the swimming pool I looked back in time and wondered what happened to the idea of public space? At least the nineteenth- and early twentieth-century planners valued a public realm, even if it was designed to keep the body docile and under observation. In contrast, the current political class seems to believe that the right to public space and free access to a city's squares and buildings is both archaic and anachronistic as an idea. They say that people don't want public space any more. Or they insist that it never existed anyway. In which case, privatise everything. And God only knows where it will stop. Public toilets, street cleaning, why not charge entrance fees to use the parks and breathe clean air? If you want public space, then 'go to a retail park'. And if you are down on your luck, 'seek philanthropic charity. Maybe this is what they meant by a 'return to traditional values'.

28 AUGUST 2004 – MARSEILLE

On the Attack / A l'Attac

Privatisation is a ubiquitous phenomenon but not exactly new. The annexing of common land has been going on for centuries. Much of what people think of as the 'public' city is, in fact, private – especially the city of tourism. The Marina in Le Vieux-Port, the hotels on the coastal road, the luxury housing and expensive restaurants already represent a 'privatised' city that we are only allowed to enter on license. In terms of the broader political context of privatisation, it was as unpopular in France as Scotland. In fact, a similar plan for the privatisation of public services launched by Juppé in the mid nineties provoked a nationwide rebellion of proportions that brought back memories of 1968. What Juppé succeeded in doing was mobilising the left. In late 1997, unemployed workers occupied the benefit offices in Marseille, and in the following year, the organisation ATTAC (l'Association pour la Taxe Tobin pour l'Aide aux Citoyens) was founded to orchestrate resistance to neo-liberal reform. It grew quickly and branches were set up all over France, including ATTAC-Marseille. It looked like the multi-nationals were at last going to be called to account. And we shouldn't forget José Bové and his ritual dismantling of a MacDonald's up the road. It was an act of protest against rubbish food and rotten buildings of which I am proud. After all, you don't have to be a Communist to champion the French peasant farmer. You just have to like food. Closure, redundancy and unemployment are other words that we have come to know all too well in Marseille. But although I like the Art Deco curves and lines scattered around the waterfront, I'm not nostalgic for the reality of working life in the old docks. Despite the legendary tales of solidarity and political militancy, it was back-breaking, filthy and poorly paid work. Eventually all of Europe's dockyards, at least those like Marseille that had grown with ancient trade routes, have been forced to rethink and rebrand themselves. And with the decline of Marseille's industrial base, largely the result of collapsing markets and the relocation of capital to areas of cheaper labour, it looked for a while like it was really over for me. Not even the romantics in la Chambre de Commerce could prevent the closure of the last oil and soap factories in the 1970s. Marseille had lubricated the engines and bodies of capitalism and the French Empire. Only fragments survive. You can still buy soap and bricks, of course. But tourist gifts are not sufficient to keep an industrial enterprise in full production. It underlines the inability of national states to control the movement of capital. It was always a frosty relationship anyway. But international finance capital has no more loyalty to Marseille, soap and pastis than it has to anything else. Phase four they are calling it in the history of my relationship with the docks and ports. I don't mind tourists. But the mass production of bouillabaisse is a rather sad parody of a city once famous for industrial production and trade.

5.6 'Navigating the future'. Container port in Marseille / Shipyard in Glasgow

3 SEPTEMBER 2004 – GLASGOW

Bankrupt Boosterism / La Faillite d'une Promotion

It is bizarre to think that an economic strategy for the twenty-first century might be based on aniseed and fish stew. But you must have realised by now that it is not enough for me to be Glasgow, or for you to be just Marseille. No, in the race to attract the petty cash box of global capital I am required to be a 'City of Something'. It doesn't really matter what exactly, providing it attracts tourists and increases revenue. I have been city of gardens, sport, architecture, and shopping. And whereas once I was a world-famous city of industry and manufacturing, I am now a city of financial services. All a little dull and desperate, I have to say. They could at least have had some fun and made me the city of sex. It is a sad imitation of bread and circuses. And do the authorities really think that the people are duped by hanging banners everywhere proclaiming that Glasgow is now 'the style capital of Scotland'? The current city fathers are trying to emulate their nineteenth-century predecessors by matching their enthusiasm for the state orchestrated fête. But they have neither the same quantities of surplus capital to spend nor the political imagination. Do they really imagine that feeling stylish is going to make up for three decades of economic restructuring in which families and whole towns have been left out to dry? Do they really think that wearing smart clothes is going to alleviate the consequences of closing mines, steelyards and docks? One thing they have succeeded in doing, however, is to reproduce the same job insecurity in call centres and the service industry that could be found in the mills and factories of an earlier period of capitalist expansion. What was the word they used? Ah yes, flexibility. Flexible labour markets, flexible workers and flexible capital accumulation. Even I could understand the semantic camouflage. Flexibility doesn't mean very much when you can't pay your electricity bill.

8 SEPTEMBER 2004 – MARSEILLE

Luxury Prisons along the Coast / Prisons Luxueuses sur la Côte

It comes as no surprise. The point of new neo-liberal social and economic restructuring wasn't to bail out the poor. It was to rescue government finances and sure up the rate of profit. The rich and powerful have always looked after themselves, and are adept at representing their self-interest as being synonymous with public interest. Just as they have always tried to detach themselves from the real lifeblood of the city. Here in Marseille, as elsewhere, they are busily engaged in constructing twenty first-century facsimiles of the walled garden and country estate complete with pool and helipad. And if you take a bus around la Corniche du Président John Kennedy you can glimpse the fortified condominia that command views of sea and city. But they are happy in their middle-class prisons. They will even tolerate ethnicity, providing it is kicking a ball on-screen for Olympique Marseille or doing the garden. Not surprisingly, the lairy street culture of cinematic and literary fame that gives Marseille its kudos exists in other parts of the city. And much of it's still in the centre. The process of gentrification and real estate speculation on land values eventually means that the poor working-class populations that build and service the city get shunted outwards. Not necessarily in the famed polo mint formation of core and periphery; it sometimes happens in a more haphazard manner. But one thing is certain: the movement is always away from the frame of the post card maker. I am sure that the city authorities are making new signs. Cast in metal, painted in enamel, and very historic looking, banning certain types of activity and by implication people. 'No xxxx here'. Fill in the blank as you see fit. The tourist board can't afford to have hard-faced men harassinq rich American tourists spilling from cruise ships to buy African trinkets. Neither can they allow wisecracking football fans to upset Europeans down for the weekend to see if the city is as tough and wild as legend says.

18 SEPTEMBER 2004 – GLASGOW

Tickets Only / Entrées sur Invitation Seulement

I have heard that after a closed meeting of the Council Executive Committee, a new initiative is to be launched to allay fears that the city might be on the verge of disintegration. It is to be called CESPOP, shorthand for control, efficiency, security, predictability, order and profit – words that rather neatly capture the ideological priorities of neo-liberals. It is most likely just a rumour. But then nothing would surprise me. We already have 'No cameras. No bawdy behaviour. No loitering. No repetitive beats. No public drinking and No ball games'. Before long they will hang 'No proletarian' signposts from city gates, reinstalled after 600 years. It's show time on the Clyde, and show flats for everyone. They say that 20 per cent of the new housing being erected in the city will be 'affordable'. For whom I wonder? I am tired now. Exhausted by the urban vandalism called progress. Tired of the track marks of abuse. Fed up with the false promises of so-called development opportunities. I have still to fully recover from the devastating social and economic consequences of de-industrialisation. I am not sure that I ever will. Parts of the population have remained traumatised. I try to stay optimistic. We have Globalise Resistance, we had the poll tax rebellion, and in Glasgow the anti-road protestors even managed to set up a free state in Pollok Park. The older generation still look back fondly at the Upper Clyde Shipbuilders work-in in the 1970s. You see, when all's said and done, they can tart me up as much as they like, but I am happy to be a Red, and sometimes redneck, city of delight, danger and drunkenness. Anything is better than what is on offer now: the city projected as a media-friendly investment opportunity for paying customers only. Let's face it, 'Ne travaillez jamais', 'Dieu est mort', and 'Demandez l'impossible', are far more intriguing propositions than, how would it go? 'Workers of the world throw down your chains and let's go shopping.' No, it doesn't quite have the same ring to it.

6

The (Dis)Integrating City: The Russian Architectural and Literary Avant-Garde

INTRODUCTION

This chapter is an extended version of a paper first given in Moscow at a conference in the Academy of Architecture held to commemorate the ninetieth anniversary of Vkhutemas, the State Higher Art and Technical Studios. Set up in the aftermath of the Bolshevik Revolution in 1920, Vkhutemas was at the epicentre of an extraordinary ten-year cultural revolution in the arts and architecture. Many of the luminaries of the avant-garde, both Rationalists and Constructivists, passed through its doors, where they both practised and taught. Together with students, they helped build a creative revolution propelled by new social conditions that precipitated an unprecedented outpouring of innovative ideas in all areas of architecture and urbanism. It was closed like the Bauhaus at the start of the 1930s, but unlike its German cousin, has never enjoyed the same historical status. The conference in Moscow was part of an on-going quest to remedy that situation and to reinforce Vkhutemas' position as one of the most important chapters in the history of modern architecture. 'The (Dis)Integrating City' takes a particular route through this history and investigates the relationship between the architectural avant-garde and the architectural dimensions of Russian literary modernism, in particular the work of Andrei Bely, Yevgeny Zamyatin and Andrei Platonov.

A MEMORY OF THE FUTURE

The Endurance of the Soviet Avant-Garde

I can think of no better way of capturing the continued importance of the Soviet avant-garde as a memory that resolutely stamps its claim on the future, than to borrow this title from Krzhizhanovsky's collection of short stories.[1]

It is more than 30 years since I first became acquainted with the avant-garde as an architecture student in 1970s Britain. It was the era of punk rock and deepening economic recession. The country was gloomy and grey and neo-liberal ideology was gathering strength. The sirens warned of impending social disintegration and a general mood of political uncertainty and distrust of grand historical narratives had spawned the vocabulary of post-modernism.

It was in the midst of all this that I stumbled across the spectacular world of the Russian avant-garde.[2] Four years later in 1984, intoxicated by hope and idealism and armed with a few grainy images and an architectural map, I made my inaugural trip to Moscow. For the first time I stood in front of the crumbling ruins of the Dom Narkomfina and gazed in astonishment at the Club Russakova that I imagined landing like a spaceship as if it had stepped out of the pages of Bogdanov's utopian novel *Red Star*.[3] Like visiting a terminally ill relative, regularly checking up on the state of health of these two 'memories of the future' has long since become an obligatory ritual.

Back then there was little available in English that revealed the full depth and breadth of the early Soviet experience. Three decades later, what was once forbidden or obscure has now become mainstream and most courses on the history of art and architecture will feature a lecture or two on the avant-garde. Many of its most iconic images like Rodchenko's book poster, Lissitsky's graphics, or Malevics's formal compositions have now entered mainstream European culture, although more often than not as decontextualised commodities stripped of historical meaning and used to sell anything from vodka to music.

When I first visited the Soviet Union I was aware of the slogan 'Neither Washington nor Moscow', but I desperately wanted to believe that something of the revolution had survived. In a more general sense it seemed to me then, as it does now, that all of the crucial questions about the relationship between architecture, social freedom and individual liberty, civilisation and barbarism, politics and culture were played out with an intensity that was unique. My fascination with the avant-garde, a term that I have always reserved for ideas and projects that synthesise revolutionary social and formal programmes, has never faded.[4] It is not just architecture, art and other forms of cultural production however that can be considered avant-garde, but any theoretical and historical work that breaks the mould and challenges orthodoxies in whatever field they might reside, be it philosophy, political economy or literary theory. This is how I arrived belatedly at Mikhail Bakhtin and his collection of essays known as *The Dialogic Imagination*, in which he celebrates the godfather of avant-garde 'shock art', Rabelais, whose novel Gargantua and Pantagruel broke all previous conventions and shook the moral foundations of sixteenth-century France.

6.1   One of the few remaining buildings of the avant-garde, the legendary Club Russakova by
Konstantin Melnikov, built in 1928 from a brief that had been developed in conjunction with workers

CHRONOTOPIC SHIFTS

Ways of Thinking and Doing

Bakhtin introduces a theory of literary culture in which he suggests that one of the ways we can differentiate between genres is by the manner in which they organise and privilege conceptions of time and space. He argued that any literary work can be said to be characterised by a particular 'chronotope' – literally time-space – and that it is through the intrinsic connectedness of temporal and spatial relationships, that its narrative is revealed. 'Time, as it were, thickens, takes on flesh, becomes artistically visible; likewise, space becomes charged and responsive to the movements of time, plot and history.'[5] Far from being of marginal concern, for Bakhtin, 'a definite and absolutely concrete locality serves as the starting point for the creative imagination'. It follows that the geography and locus of a literary narrative, whether it is a city, village or a single room, is no mere abstract landscape or theatrical backdrop, but a 'real piece of human history, of historical time condensed in space', within which the plot and the characters are unfolded 'as if they were present from the beginning'.[6]

For the discussion of the relationship between architecture and literature these are tantalising propositions. They open up a new dialogue between the two disciplines and suggest the possibility of a different type of both literary and architectural history based on the space-time revolutions that define paradigmatic shifts in literary and architectural production. This is not so far fetched as it might seem, for one way of thinking about architects and novelists is to see them both as jugglers of space, time and narrative, and it is undoubtedly true that just as there is no work of literature that does not have some spatio-temporal dimension, there is no building that doesn't possess some kind of plot or narrative. The parallel histories of the architectural and literary avant-garde exemplify this common ground in that they are both defined by a chronotopic revolution that interrogated the varied narratives of the enlightenment and nineteenth-century city and projected them into the future.

Both architecture and literature in this sense are perpetually locked in a dialogue with history, a dialogue that is born out of conflict.[7] It could not be otherwise. Bakhtin tells us that the novel, in a manner similar to an architectural project, seeks to 'orchestrate all its themes, the totality of the world of objects and ideas depicted and expressed in it, by means of the social diversity of speech types and by the differing individual voices.'[8] As such, and as if beset by an unwanted virus, both literature and architecture are inevitably and inescapably 'ideologically saturated'. Like it or not, the writer and the architect are locked into the reproduction of a particular 'world view or concrete opinion',[9] that leaves them both stumbling across the dangerous terrain of ideology in which truth and objectivity is constantly under attack from myth and deception.

It is the critic's and historian's task to disentangle these ideological tensions and to comprehend the dynamic social forces that propelled the development of the modern city and which would naturally enough come to be reflected in both modern architecture and literature – spatio-temporal reconstruction, scientific and

6.2   The pioneering Dom Narkomfina, 1928. A commune of a 'transitional kind'
designed by Ginzburg and Milnius, it sought to articulate the 'new way of life'. 'Molodoi
Chelovek, why are you taking photos of this ruin?', asked a war veteran. 'Because it
is one of the most important buildings of the twentieth century' I replied

technological transformation, political revolution and hovering like a spectre over everything, the limits of reason.

The Russian literary and architectural avant-garde is embedded in this fundamental chronotopic shift in both ways of thinking and doing. What connects Dostoevsky to Bely, Bulgakov, Zamyatin and Platonov is that they can all be thought of as literary experiments, in which the conventionally understood social and space-time relations that govern everyday life are turned upside-down in terms of both narrative structure and form. They are driven by a markedly new chronotopic impulse that is resolutely urban in all of its aspects. City streets, alleys, squares, bourgeois mansions, workers basements and factories now occupy the centre of the novelist's stage. In a similar manner, the architects, urban designers and artists of the avant-garde, steeped in the wonders of new technology and materialist philosophy, set out to discover an 'architectural chronotope' that was appropriate to a rapidly-changing society. And it is precisely the manipulation of time and space that sweeps like a hurricane through the avant-garde, from the abstract paintings of Malevic to the drawings of Chernikov, the manifestos of Aleksei Gan and the built work of Melnikov and Ginzburg.[10]

HALLUCINATION

Andrei Bely, Vkhutemas and Space-Time Disjuncture

Irrevocable and seismic historical change provoked an outpouring of hallucinatory and surreal portraits of the city. It starts in many ways with Peter Petrovich in Dostoevsky's philosophical urban thriller, *Crime and Punishment*, who declares that 'we have irrevocably severed ourselves from the past.'[11] A few decades later, in *Novel with Cocaine*, Ageyev depicts the modern city as a descent into alienated addiction. In the *Quadraturin*, the surrealist Krzhizhanovsky tells us of the lonely Sutulin, who applies a mysterious oil to the walls and ceiling of his tiny room that slowly expands into infinity and renders him hopelessly lost. At the same time, Bulgakov creates an unforgettable portrait of modern Moscow as a theatre of the absurd resplendent with talking animals. It is also here, in this phantasmal space, that we encounter Bely's *Petersburg*, where 'everything, the sunlit glitter, the walls, the body, the soul, is collapsing into ruins, leaving in its wake delirium, an abyss, and bombs.'[12]

Bely's city is a city of shadows, 'of phosphorescent bolts, glimmering surfaces', and 'unembraceable infinities'. It is a 'bubbling vortex of corridors stretching off into an immeasurable expanse.'[13] He exaggerates this feeling of accelerating history and splintered space-time by abruptly cutting from one location and narrative scenario to another in a manner that predicts the structure of modernist classics like Dos Passos' *U.S.A* and James Joyce's *Ulysses*.[14] It is a narrative form and structure that is similar to the 'split screen' and 'cut and paste' techniques of Sergey Eisenstein, and Dziga Vertov, and is analogous to the early Dadaist experiments in montage art that depicted the city as a kaleidoscopic assemblage of colliding images and objects. If we were to try and picture Bely's Petersburg, it would resemble the distorted perspectives and warped dimensions of Umberto Boccioni's *The City Rising*, (1912),

6.3   Tragedy and farce come to mind. Demolished in 2004, the Hotel Moskva has made a surreal reappearance worthy of Bulgakov, only this time without hammers, sickles, revolutionary motifs or, indeed, the different wings. Top image taken in 2010; bottom image: the old hotel in 1984

George Grosz's *Metropolis*, (1917), Ludwig Meidner's *Apocalyptic City* (1914), or in Russia the asymmetries and dislocated geometries of Exter's *Dynamic City* (1921) and Lyubov Popova's *Space-Force* and *Architektonika* series, (1919–21).

THE LIMITS TO URBAN REASON

Bely Announces the Death of Geometry

Petersburg is teetering on the brink of revolution. The geometric ideal of the city is under threat, as are the dreams of social and spatial order that had been promised by the scientists and philosophers of the Enlightenment. Bely needs a champion to celebrate and mourn the vision of limitless ordered space, of a city of Nevsky boulevards, 'an infinity of the prospect raised to the nth degree.'[15] He finds it in Apollon Apollonovich, who is possessed by a hopeless nostalgia for the mythic geometric rationality of what is a terminally ill aristocratic world and who, in order to calm himself, contemplates a cube. As he hurtles across Petersburg, he dreams of proportion, symmetry and squares, as if the city really had been built according to Le Blond's rationalised fortress plan of 1707, a 'delirium of geometry, a delirium which nothing can measure.'[16]

For Apollon, ordered reason is everything. He would have admired Baron Von Haussmann's plan for Paris, just as he would have found a home in Hilbersheimer's Berlin and felt reassured by the 1935 plan for Moscow. These urban visions are his ideal – fusions of urban design and centralised state power. His own home consists of little more than a mechanical assemblage 'of walls forming squares and cubes into which windows were cut.'[17] All Apollon wants so as to forget his disintegrating life and adulterous wife is for his 'carriage to fly forward, the prospects to fly to meet him – prospect after prospect, so that the entire spherical surface of the planet should be embraced, as in serpent coils, by blackish gray cubes of houses.'[18] All that he desires is for the earth to be crushed by parallel prospects that intersect and eventually expand into the abysses of the cosmos in planes of squares and cubes: one square per 'solid citizen'. He is desperate for the certainty of a neat grid, but instead he looks out across the city and to his horror, spots Malevic, who is taking the ordered universe of platonic forms and twisting them into something unspeakable.

PARADOX

Disurbanism and Ordered Asymmetry

The extraordinary paradox of this is clear. History has been broken. The city is breaking. Chimneys had stopped spewing smoke and darkness had appeared on the Nevsky Prospect 'in the form of a Manchurian hat.'[19] A 'red domino' stalked the city streets and a 'crimson sun' arced in the sky. The neatly ordered hierarchy of ranks and privilege was under threat, and the idea of a rationalised urban plan parachuted in from the cosmos has been found wanting. A similar kind of

6.4   Studying carefully and enthralled by what Haussmann had achieved in Paris, Stalin's planners deliver infinity in the shape of Gorky Street, now renamed Tverskaya. The top image was taken in 1988, before the advertising detritus of investment banks, gambling emporia and fast food chains covered its facades. Bottom image taken in 2004

6.5   Another iconic workers' club, Zueva, with its famous glazed circulation tower designed
by Ilya Golosov in 1927. Still in use today as a cinema and for community activities

dilemma that was to haunt the activities of the avant-garde. How was it possible to manage the spectacular complexities of urban revolution that was being captured by painters, writers and filmmakers, without destroying it through a toxic mix of instrumental reason and vulgar realism? How could the architect and urban planner provide rational responses to the problems of the metropolis without resorting to an economic and technological determinism that would sweep away diversity and complexity and sacrifice individual liberty for some abstract notion of the collective will? In short, if the revolution had been successfully accomplished how might it be possible to represent socialist democracy spatially without recourse to the bulldozer of the Cartesian imagination and the architectural programme of an absolutist state?

The future beckoned. This was not a time for hesitation and scepticism. The philosopher's critique of the violent and destructive consequences of politically engineered rationalism and the first dystopian novel had yet to be written. The cult of science and machine aesthetics still seemed innocent and benign, and the distortion and elevation of scientific materialism to a status previously reserved for notions of God, had yet to consolidate its grip and wreak its havoc on idealism and subjectivity.[20] If scientific and technological development had been uncoupled from capital accumulation and class power, then building production and urban planning could surely develop in a manner that was qualitatively different from that found in capitalist societies. There appeared to be no particular reason then for the architects and novelists of the Soviet avant-garde to criticise the adaptation of the scientific and technological accomplishments of capitalism. The working class would seize control of the means of production, and the tyrannical machine that Marx had so eloquently described, would be tamed and used beneficially in the interests of the whole of society.

Forward march. The machinery of progress must be set to work with great haste. But what kind of machine would it be? What kind of thinking would set it in motion, and what kind of city would it create? Architects, planners and novelists went to work with unbridled enthusiasm to give this new world a shape and form. The old Petersburg and Moscow would soon be unrecognisable.

FETISH

Science, Technology and Instrumental Reason

Generators hummed and sparked. Objects flew, signals crossed the Atlantic, x-rays illuminated bones, elevators soared into the sky, space-time warped, everything was accelerating, and a whole new universe of formal and structural possibilities had been revealed. It was both natural and a social obligation for architects and planners to throw themselves into the orbit of new mathematics, material science and mechanised production, and to search for new forms of knowledge with which to organise building production with objectivity and precision. New landscapes of production, infrastructure and ways of living were modelled and draughted. Employing all the wizardry of new forms of transport and communication systems, enthusiastic talk of disurbanism, decentralised networks of settlements, workers clubs,

6.6 By 1989 something approaching 90 per cent of all new housing construction in the Soviet Union was being prefabricated out of concrete panels. The goal was to organise building production as a fully integrated and automated system in which there was a continual feedback loop from inception to completion. At its height it employed 13,000,000 workers. Photos taken in 1988

communes, participative public art projects and spontaneous street festivals dominated the conversations in bars and journals.[21] In theory at least, theirs was to be a new dialectical form of urbanism in which individual liberty would be balanced with the need for collective solidarity and social cohesion. The contradictions between town and country would be resolved, science and technology would deliver automated homes, and the idea of a capital city and the socio-spatial inequalities of the capitalist city would become distant memories of a pre-communist past.

On the margins of the stratosphere, Krutikov drew flying ring cities that hovered above the earth. Meanwhile the Constructivist's grappled with the real-time possibilities of building science, investigated prefabrication and new tectonic structures and dreamt of a formula that could express 'the rhythmic pulsation of the cosmos'. Krasilnikov tried to work out a design method based on mathematical principles. Bogdanov, predicting later research in automated design and information systems, imagined a creativity 'that understands itself', whilst Nikolaev, adapting the theories of Frederick Taylor and his Russian counterpart, Gastev, on the scientific organisation of labour, endeavoured to scientifically organise everyday life in a commune.

Not to be outdone by the architects' plans, novelists steeped in the visions of writers like the mystic philosopher Fëdorov, Chernyshevsky, Jules Verne and H.G. Wells, were similarly intoxicated by the belief in the limitless potential of Soviet society. Equally vast quantities of ink were devoted to excavating the future shape of a socialist society and city, and in an extraordinary outpouring of millenarian fever, it is estimated that anything up to 200 hundred science fiction novels were written in the decade that followed the revolution.[22] In Vivian Itin's *Land of Ginguri*, work has become a festival and the city an assemblage of 'public squares of mirrored glass, continuous gardens and palaces of dreams'. Whilst Nikolsky, *In a Thousand Years,* creates a landscape that mimics the Disurbanist's decentralised networks. In this utopia there are no real cities as such, rather a world made up of huge green forests, that give way 'periodically to buildings, glassed-in communities, museums and theatres'.[23] Even Trotsky joined the fray imagining that the old cities of the capitalist and feudal past would eventually give way to 'titanic constructions of city-villages'.[24]

However, in marked contrast to such optimistic views of the future, other modern writers gazed at the images of idealised modern Phalansteries, machine landscapes, orthogonal grids and gleaming towers and instead of a vista overflowing with opportunity and scientific progress, saw a city bereft of adjectives, inhabited by numbered individuals in precarious technological landscapes. This was a world in which the logic of science and technology hadn't led to the liberation of human beings from need, as dreamt of by the architect and utopian novelist, but had become instead an instrument of domination.

INTEGRATION

Yevgeny Zamyatin and the Flattened Universe

Before Orwell and Huxley, it was Yevgeny Zamyatin who addressed these themes in the iconic novel *We*. Like *Petersburg, We* plays with compositional techniques

6.7   For all the promise of the avant-garde and the monumentalism of the Stalinist city, the twentieth-century history of Russian architecture really belongs to the industrialisation of the building industry and the development of the *mikrorayon*. These two are both on the outskirts of Moscow, taken in 1989[25]

and concepts of time. If *Petersburg* cuts and orchestrates a fragmented temporally splintered landscape, in *We*, time beats with an unassailable metronomic logic as Zamyatin takes us on a journey into the technological utopia of One State, where the dreadful contradictions and conflicts that characterise *Petersburg* and human history have been magically resolved. Fear, worry, and despondency are no longer part of the fabric of the city or the human mind and the novel starts with a promise that soon it will be possible, with the aid of the extraordinary ellipsoid glass machine, the Integral, 'to integrate completely the colossal equation of the universe, to unbend the wild curve, to straighten it tangentially, and to flatten it into an undeviating line.'[26] It is a city that resembles the streamlined factory-made landscapes of modernist architects in which 'everything is crystalline, steadfast, everlasting.'[27]

There are none of the belching chimneys, caryatids and shaggy Manchurian hats pouring onto the streets that haunt Bely's Petersburg. Neither do we encounter Zamyatin's 'dragon city', in which he depicts a Petersburg that 'screeched and rushed into the unknown, out of the human world.'[28] No, there is none of this old-fashioned uncertainty and doubt. We find instead a city in which order has triumphed, a city of utter mathematical precision and geometric purity, bereft of even a whiff of the chaff of barley. It is a city that has been gripped by insanity, in which science has been transformed into a violent scientific rationalism applied to the human body and nature. Music is forged in factories. Liturgical rituals that celebrate the victory of scientific and technological reason punctuate daily life. In One State all the proletarians have been liberated from the unseemly clutter of unnecessary desires, emotions and names and willingly submit to surgery designed to 'extirpate the imagination'. Any lingering doubts that D-503 might harbour are held at bay by an obligation to rid the world of the messy garbage of pre-utopian life. To bolster his determination and to expel any romantic attachment for the past, D-503 visits the Ancient House, a 'godforsaken structure', where he gazes with horror at life before the Great War. 'We walked through a room containing small beds for children (children were also private property in that era). And there were more rooms; flashing mirrors, gloomy chests, sofas covered in unbearably clashing fabrics, huge fireplaces, and an immense mahogany bed. What we have now – our eternal splendid glass – could be seen nowhere except in their pathetic little rickety rectangular windows.'[29]

THE DANCING MACHINE

Zamyatin's Secret Love

As a naval architect and a teacher of engineering science, Zamyatin had a detailed knowledge of new developments in materials, structures and communications. He was a huge fan of H.G. Wells, and the almost affectionate descriptions of the colossal mechanical constructions in One State are reminiscent of 'the gigantic globes of cool white light' and 'mighty cantilevers' that Wells's character the Sleeper awakens to.[30] Zamyatin's invocation of the Integral is also a self-conscious literary

6.8   Top image from 1984, the glass and steel dome of the Yuri Gagarin Space Pavilion in what was once the Park of Economic Achievements – a Soviet-era theme park of pavilions celebrating the technological and economic development of Soviet society. Bottom: the old state supermarket GUM, now rebranded as an elite shopping arcade and architectural reference to the Crystal Palace of 1851 that enthralled continental Europe. A virtuoso display of the art of engineering and a literal plan of the world view of the Victorian bourgeoisie, it was derided by Dostoevsky as the structural creation of an immutable mathematical logic, that worst of all presaged a world of boredom.[31] In contrast and in keeping with the opinion of most visitors, it was celebrated and idealised by Chernyshevsky as a symbol of progress and modernity. In Vera's famous fourth dream in *What Is To Be Done?*, it is rescued from Dostoevsky and restored not only as a majestic assemblage of glass, iron, crystal, aluminium, platinum, air-conditioning and electricity, but as the architectural form in which her utopian society is realised.[32] Indeed, the ability of her dream palace to resolve all of humankind's problems is paralleled by the magical powers possessed by the Integral. Her vision of an ideal city in a bucolic rural setting was a common enough response to the perceived irredeemability of the nineteenth-century capitalist metropolis and it sits within a tradition that includes Fourier's Phalanstery, Howard's Garden City, and the linear cities and disurbanism of the early Soviet avant-garde, a lineage that Marshall Berman has described as a 'dream of modernisation without urbanism'.[33]

Closer to home, Zamyatin would have wandered through the old GUM – the iron and glass cathedral of consumption that rivalled any of the Parisian Passagem – and would have seen Lenin's favourite building, the Moscow Radio Tower. He might also have encountered the work of the early avant-garde such as the *Cité Industrielle* by Tony Garnier, the drawings of the Italian Futurists and the exploding geometries of Russian Suprematism. The super-industrialised landscapes of Chernikov and the glazed sphere and telegraph masts of Leonidov's Library were yet to be published, but Tatlin's Monument to the Third International in 1919 had been well publicised and the gasps of astonishment that greeted its unveiling, and which it still provokes today, could easily be mistaken for D-503's description of the Integral. Like the Integral, Tatlin's tower was also a 'laboratory' in which the problems of human history and the mechanics of universal bodies would be resolved. Just as generations of architecture students have gazed in awe at Tatlin's revolving metal structure, so D-503 arrives ecstatic at the 'grandiose mechanical ballet' of twirling regulator globes, balance beams and musical routers. It is a scene that he finds beautiful. Why? 'Because it is non-free movement, because all the fundamental significance of the dance lies precisely in its aesthetic subjugation, its ideal non-freedom.'[34]

In an essay published a year after *We* in 1923 called *Literature, Revolution and Entropy*, Zamyatin commented that: 'Some day, an exact formula for the law of revolution will be established. And in this formula, nations, classes, stars and books will be expressed as numerical qualities.'[35] Given that Zamyatin wrote *We* before the inauguration of the first five-year plan, there is something prophetic about his vision of a society in which the quality of everyday life is measured in terms of quantities. In truth, of course, he was paraphrasing an older fear – Dostoevsky's deeply held scepticism of the perfectibility of the ideal man and city that he explores in *Notes from Underground*. There he projects a future 'in which everything will be so precisely calculated and designated that there will no longer be any actions or adventures in the world.' With the power and rigour of logic and logarithm 'all possible questions will vanish in an instant.'[36] Then, and only then, will the Crystal Palace, the Integral, and the All Proletarian Home be built.

6.9   The architecture of an absolutist state. Hostile towards modernism, the Soviet bureaucracy of Stalin's era preferred something rather more solid: two of the seven Stalin towers. Top image: a housing complex on the Moscow River designed by Chechulin and Rostovsky, 1952. Bottom image: Moscow State University, MGU

ANTI-UTOPIA

Form is an Unknown X[37]

We is conventionally thought of as the godfather of twentieth-century dystopias. Frederic Jameson, however, suggests that it is better understood as a 'true anti-utopia in which the utopian impulse is still at work.'[38] After all, D-503 leaves us with the ambiguous statement: '...I'm certain we'll win. Because reason has to win.'[39] In other words, amidst the automaton fear of a self-reproducing bureaucracy in which scientific reason has revealed its nemesis and utopia its dystopian underbelly, there still flickers the possibility that truth will out and right will be discovered. The same tensions stalk the narrative of Andrei Platonov's *Foundation Pit*. If Zamyatin plays with a fetishised scientific language to reinforce his message, Platonov, who was also an engineer (as, indeed was Dostoevsky), is equally adventurous in the unconventional way he uses language. Dislocated, strangulated, grotesque and sometimes absurd expressions emerge from character's mouths as if they are speaking by remote control. Cliché-ridden shibboleths and degraded revolutionary rhetoric tumble across the pages in a manner that was symptomatic of the ideological distortion of language that belonged to the Stalinist regime and which was to culminate in the 'realism of social deception', otherwise known as Socialist Realism.[40]

Most critics and literary historians see the *Foundation Pit* as a lyrical condemnation of the course the revolution had taken, a novel in which Platonov expresses his disillusionment with the Party bureaucracy and his horror at the violence that underpinned the process of collectivisation and industrialisation. Accordingly, the pit is not a foundation for the future, but an immense grave, and the book ends with the peasantry collectively digging themselves into an abyss.[41] This is all true. But it is not quite the whole story. After all, there was still the rhetoric, and even if words like progress, freedom, emancipation, and happiness had been largely emptied of meaning, they were still connected by a fragile umbilical chord with an ideal that was once worth fighting for. It is a contradiction that is exemplified by the 'All Proletarian Home', a project that is simultaneously futile but necessary.

ENTROPY

The Construction of Happiness

A sibling or close relative of Apollon Apollonovich and D-503, it is Andrey Platonov's engineer Prushevsky's task to set out the foundations for the new proletarian home. But it was to be no ordinary building. It was to be an incubator of new social relations, a platform for a new way of life, an extraordinary construction, the likes of which no one had ever seen before. Like Vera's Palace and the Integral, it too would integrate the Universe. Prushevsky speculates that 'in a year's time the entire local class of the proletariat would leave the petty-proprietorial town and take possession for life of this monumental new home. And after ten or 20 years, another engineer would construct a tower in the middle of the world, and the labourers of the entire terrestrial globe would be settled there for a happy eternity.'[42]

6.10   All dreams of proletarian homes have long gone and been replaced by the architecture of finance capital and private condominium. Top: retro Stalin housing block in the Sokol area. Bottom: new Moscow international business district

The All Proletarian Home would guarantee not just mechanical protection against harsh winters, but it would engineer 'the peace and stability of the future…' Having completed all of his necessary calculations, Prushevsky had 'ensured the indestructibility of the future all-proletarian dwelling and felt comforted by the sureness of the materials destined to protect people who had until then lived on the outside.'[43]

Prushevsky is not just an engineer. He is driven by what he thinks is in humanity's best interests. He is possessed by dreams of planting into a 'fresh abyss an eternal stone root of indestructible architecture'[44] But he is also stricken by an expectation of his imminent death, doubt, and foreboding. In a daydream he sees 'some peaceful white buildings that shone with more light than there was in the air around them.'[45] He doesn't know their name or their purpose but they have a 'precise tenderness', they exude peace, colour and beauty that meant they could only have been built on a remote star, for it is an architecture of 'faith and freedom', the like of which seemed alien to the 'gray colour of his motherland'. In his bones he knows that at some point there will be a future, but it is opaque and far away, and only one thing is certain, 'there is a long way to the end.'[46]

It is tantamount to an epitaph for the already lost world of the avant-garde that is retreating as Platonov is writing the novel. For Prushevsky is not laying the foundations for an elegant Dom Narkomfina or a kinetic Tatlins's tower. No, it is something else entirely, an indestructible stone monument that would never be big enough and would never be built. Even as the perimeter for 'the womb matrix for the house of future life' is completed, the village's 'chief revolutionary' decides that it must be immediately expanded, not by a factor of four but by a factor of six. Platonov can only be referring to one thing – the plans for the Palace of the Soviets first announced at the Congress of Soviets in 1922. I can only guess, but I am sure that Platonov must have glimpsed Boris Iofan's winning scheme, for the parallels are poignant. For it too was like an abyss, a monstrous pit into which the dreams of the avant-garde, the literary endeavours of modernists and so much else was poured, such that instead of Prushevsky's All Proletarian Home, there arose a colossal bureaucratic edifice that would negate and swallow everything in its path whilst singing joyful songs of statistical certainty.

EPILOGUE

Passing Memory

In the *Queen of Spades*,[47] Pushkin tells of Hermann, who is intent on finding out the secret formula with which an old countess used to win at cards without fail. On her deathbed she plays a trick by giving him only a partially correct code. To begin with, he amasses considerable wealth, seemingly unassailable at the table. Supremely confident, he gambles his whole fortune on a single game, convinced that he has the right hand. Of course, it proves to be wrong and he loses everything, including his mind and is committed to an asylum where, to the end of his days, he mutters with unerring rapidity 'Trey, seven, ace! Trey, seven, Queen'.

6.11 The hoarding hides the spot where the Hotel Rossiya once stood. With its 3,000 rooms, it was one of the largest in the world and boasted what was then one of the most ambitious electronic surveillance systems. The frieze provides an illustrated history of the last 20 years of turbo capitalist kitsch architecture that has mushroomed across the city. Bottom image: Cherry Casino night club

My only hope is that some of the plutocrats and mediaeval-style suzerains rebuilding Moscow will similarly find themselves as mumbling inmates of the mad house. Some of them have already been put away. Others stay in power. Better still would be to see them scream with horror as they wake in the morning to find their noses had embarked on a Gogolian walkabout, leaving them with a flattened face and an inability to sniff out new business ventures. Gogol also wrote about speaking dogs. So did Bulgakov, and his articulate canines had mastered the power of human speech with a rich vocabulary of expletives. Maybe this is what drove a famous Russian model to murder. She objected so strongly to her coiffured hound being barked at by a popular stray mongrel called Malchick that she proceeded to pull a knife from her Prada handbag, and in front of tearful children, ferociously stabbed him six times in the neck.

…Out of curiosity I decided to visit the museum of the revolution, which an elderly red track-suited woman reminded me was round the corner.

'Ah yes of course, just up there on the left, the old maroon pastel coloured building. But it's not called that any more, no, now it's the Museum of Recent History.' The City authorities had called time on time itself. Capitalist boomtowns do not possess such embarrassing relics. Now it's a dead and buried clutter of dimly-lit timber and glass cases surrounded by fading turquoise walls. The same grandmothers that had welcomed heroes in former days supervise it. Now they are there to usher visitors to the souvenir shop. None of it ever really happened you know…

NOTES

1   Sigizmund Krzhizhanovsky, *Memories of the Future* (New York: New York Review Books, 2009). See in particular the extraordinary short stories, 'Quadraturin' and 'The Bookmark', that both have wonderfully surreal architectural subtexts.

2   Back then there was relatively little available in English and it wasn't until the early 1980s, with the publication of the work of Catherine Cooke, Anatole Kopp and Khan Magomedov that a true picture of the depth and breadth of the early Soviet experiment began to emerge. The key early texts available in the UK were: Oleg Shvidovsky, *Building in the USSR* (London: Studio Vista, 1971), Catherine Cooke (ed.), *Russian Avant Garde-Art and Architecture* (London: Architectural Design, No. 53, 1983), Anatole Kopp, *Constructivist Architecture* (London: Academy Editions, 1985) and Selim Khan Magomedov's *Pioneers of Soviet Architecture* (London: Thames and Hudson, 1987). In addition, the English version of Mosei Ginsburg's *Style and Epoch* was published in 1982. Catherine Cooke went on to co-edit a number of books on Chernikov, Leonidov and others, culminating a decade later in *Russian Avant-Garde: Theories of Art, Architecture and the City* (London: Academy Editions, 1995).

3   Bogdanov depicts a glass and osmium spaceship – the 'Etheroneph' – that lands in Moscow in 1926 to whisk Leonid away to socialist paradise on Mars. Alexander Bogdanov, *Red Star – The First Bolshevik Utopia* (Bloomington, IN: Indiana University Press, 1984), p. 39.

4   As opposed to its more conventional use as a synonym for newness or innovation.

5   Mikhail Bakhtin, 'Forms of Time and Chronotope in the Novel', in *The Dialogic Imagination* (Austin: University of Texas Press, 1981), p. 84.

6   Mikhail Bakhtin, *Speech Genres and Other Late Essays* (Austin: University of Texas Press, 2010), p49. See also Franco F. Moretti, *Atlas of the European Novel 1800–1900* (London: Verso, 2009), p. 35ff, who, in a similar vein, argues that 'without a certain kind of space, a certain kind of story is simply impossible'.

7   Bakhtin uses the term *raznorechiye*, normally translated as 'heteroglossia', to capture the complexity and diversity of speech types that make up language.

8   Bakhtin, Mikhail, 'Forms of Time', p. 263.

9   Ibid., p. 271.

10   However, although the impetus given by the Bolshevik Revolution propelled Russian modernism in a different direction from that in the West, the chronotopic shift in the nature of both modern architecture and literature was a universal phenomenon.

11   Fyodor Dostoevsky, *Crime and Punishment* (Moscow: Raduga Publishers 1985).

12   Andrei Bely, *Petersburg* (London: Penguin, 1978), p. 157.

13   Ibid., p. 93.

14   The text is elusive and elliptical, jumping around in a manner that defies conventional notions of a linear narrative. There is an almost disturbing, haunting quality to the novel. Images of the spectral, the ephemeral, the shadowy and the cosmic, scatter the text and plunge us further into a city that appears to be stumbling wildly and madly like a drunken spinning top. The result is an almost supernatural kaleidoscopic landscape, where fiction, non-fiction, reality and illusion compete with each other. Marshall Berman comments that the novel consists almost 'entirely of broken and jagged fragments.' See Marshall Berman, *All That is Solid Melts into Air – The Experience of Modernity* (London: Verso, 1989), p. 256.

15   Bely, *Petersburg*, p. 12.

16   Ibid., p. 225.

17   Ibid., p. 21.

18   Ibid., p. 11.

19   Ibid. , p. 232.

20   Even now, the mantras of orthodox Marxism, the *Diamat*, are stuck in the corner of my mind in the same way as religious catechisms; 'the negation of the negation, the unity of opposites and the transformation of quantity into quality'.

21   Paradoxically the ideas and concepts of the avant-garde to do with decentralisation, mobility, networks and event architecture didn't vanish with its defeat but migrated to the West and were revisited in the radical architectural programmes of the 1960s. The urban visions of the Situationists, the work of Cedric Price and, to an extent, the ideas of Arcigram and Superstudio, can all be traced back to the work of the Soviet avant-garde. In their different ways they, too, grappled with the crisis of the capitalist city and explored notions of mobile and flexible infrastructure, of uncertainty, of the 'event', thus re-energising an architectural debate that ironically in a quite different political context has remerged in the twenty-first century as a critical response to the globalisation of capital.

22   See the fantastic survey of early Soviet ideas on the future in Richard Stites, *Revolutionary Dreams: Utopian Vision and Experimental Life in the Russian Revolution*, (Oxford: Oxford University Press, 1989). These notes come from the chapter 'Utopia in Time: Futurology and Science Fiction', pp. 168–85.

23   Ibid., pp. 174–7.

24   Leon Trotsky, Literature and Revolution, (University of Michigan Press: 1971), p. 249

25   These were satellite suburbs of concrete panel towers, the largest of which were home to 250,000 inhabitants. Now, of course, surpassed by the urbanisation in China. See Charley, 'The Concrete History of Modernity' in Hermannsen and Hvattum (eds), *Tracing Modernity* (London: Routledge, 2004).

26   Yevgeny Zamyatin, *We* (London: Penguin, 1993), p. 1.

27   Ibid., p. 45.

28   Yevgeny Zamyatin, *The Dragon and Other Stories* (London: Penguin, 1983), pp. 81–2.

29   Zamyatin, *We*, p. 28.

30   Herbert G. Wells, *The Sleeper Awakes*,(London: Penguin, 2005), p. 42.

31   Fyodor Dostoevsky, *Notes from Underground* (London: Vintage, 1993), p. 25.

32   Nikolai Chernyshevsky, *What is to be Done?* (New York: Cornell University Press, 1989), p. 370.

33   Berman, *All That Is Solid*, p. 44.

34   Zamyatin, *We*, pp. 5–6.

35   See essay called 'Literature, Revolution and Entropy' in Yevgeny Zamyatin, *Soviet Heretic* (London: Quartet Books, 1991), p. 108.

36   Dostoevsky, *Notes from Underground*, pp. 24–5.

37   See 'Constructivism as a Method of Laboratory and Teaching Work', *SA*, No. 6, 1927, pp. 160 and 166. Published in English in Cooke, *Russian Avant-Garde* (1995).

38   Frederic Jameson, *Archaeologies of the Future – The Desire called Utopia and Other Science Fictions* (London: Verso, 2007), p. 202.

39   Zamyatin, *We*, p. 225.

40   For an early essay on these themes see Jonathan Charley, 'The Making of an Imperial City', in the *Journal of Architecture*, Vol. 1, No. 1, RIBA (London: Chapman and Hall, 1996).

41   Andrey Platonov, *The Foundation Pit* (London: Vintage, 2009), p. 148.

42   Platonov, ibid., p. 19.

43   Ibid., p. 27.

44   Ibid., p. 43.

45   Ibid., p. 60.

46   Ibid., p 61.

47   Alexander Pushkin, 'The Queen of Spades' in *Collected Works* (New York: Everyman's Library, 1999), pp. 258–87.

7

Sketches of War II: The Graveyards of Historical Memory

INTRODUCTION

Our extraordinary ability to destroy buildings and cities, the industrialisation and mass production of armaments and building components, the impact of the 'culture of fear' on urban and architectural design, the ubiquitous presence of military technology in the civilian world, and the 'soft' militarisation of everyday life in advanced capitalist societies. These are just some of the themes that inevitably arise in any discussion about the relationship between war and architecture. 'Sketches of War' reflects upon these issues and is narrated in the form of a journey to the 'graveyards of historical memory'. Narrated in a series of short fragments, it visits places as diverse as the military remains of the Cold War along the coastlines of Scotland, a slave fort in Brazil, Franco's mausoleum, a bombed maternity hospital in Belgrade and the Oradour memorial village in France. Of the many questions posed, there is one in particular that 'Sketches of War' seeks to address: is it possible in any meaningful sense to objectify the memory of war and tragedy? This chapter is an extended version of a paper given at a conference in Cork in 2010 called 'Ordnance: War, Architecture and Space'.

7.1   Entrance
plaque to the
memorial village
Oradour-sur-
Glane, France

7.1   Entrance plaque to the memorial village Oradour-sur-Glane, France

TRYING TO REMEMBER

The need to objectify the memory of war and tragedy is a survival mechanism by which we distance the overwhelming reality that the history of civilisation is shadowed by barbarism. We feel obliged to build memorials, erect plaques and preserve the remains of brutal episodes in which the act of remembrance is also a desire to forget. To be haunted on a daily basis by the knowledge that the history of capitalism is a history of conquest, enslavement, robbery and murder is psychologically ruinous.[1] Equally traumatic is the antithetical history of architecture as a *Natural History of Destruction*.[2]

One of my earliest architectural memories is of my family's hometown of Plymouth. To the east of the bright new city centre planned by Abercrombie is located the Charles Church. It was left in ruins after 1945 as a permanent reminder of the 59 bombing raids that virtually destroyed the city. This physical expression of the relationship between 'hope in the future' and the 'memory of tragedy' was confusing as a child and remains difficult to resolve. Which is why, faced with the prospect of total historical amnesia, philosophers asked three questions: Can there be poetry after Auschwitz? How do we address the fact that the 'curse of irresistible progress is irresistible regression?'[3] And how do we deal with the knowledge that the state of emergency in which we live is not the exception but the rule?[4]

Two decades before, in 1918, Kropp and Müller are talking in the German trenches. 'Albert, what would you do if all of a sudden it was peacetime?' 'There's no such thing as peacetime', replies Albert curtly.[5]

7.2   Gun shop in central Bucharest

WORD WAR

Albert was, of course, correct. I decided to construct a literary war machine to help me understand how this came to pass. The result was a formidable army. In the historical and theoretical frontline, I positioned Marx, Mandel, de Landa, Deleuze, Guattari, Virillio, Baudrillard and Davis, who were equipped with powerful narrative weapons on everything from the permanent arms economy to the intelligent war machine, nomadology, and urban class war. The novels of Sebald, Mailer, Vonnegut, Heller, and Levi were evenly distributed to add polish, finesse and a different sort of gravitas so that like soldiers and ordnance prior to conflict, the final assembly was spic, span, and ready for a photo shoot. I think about firing an opening salvo of anti-war poems by Sassoon and Owen, but instead I load the literary war machine with its first missile, Eisenhower's valedictory speech in 1961. 'My fellow Americans, we are compelled to create a permanent armaments industry of vast proportions.'

The cumulative power of such writings underline what we, like Albert, already know. Far from being an aberration or an exception, war in all of its transferable configurations is ubiquitous. It permeates our everyday lives and built environment. Conquest breeds the privatisation of urban space; technological exchange permits the mass production of bombs and buildings; reconnaissance merges with civilian surveillance; and the fortress is reborn as the fortified condominium. If anything, a non-militarised society at peace with itself and others, and the corollary, a peacetime city, would be the greatest departure from the social and economic reality of capitalist societies. In 1949, to commemorate this state of affairs, the Ministry of Truth declared that War was in fact Peace, and that cinemas should only show films of dismembered enemies.[6]

7.3
Commemorative
bullet holes
in Berlin

ANECDOTAL WAR DATES

In 1945, the Corporation of the City of Glasgow published a planning report.[7] Armed with benevolent zealotry, Robert Bruce (a complete historical coincidence) described his plan to consign urban poverty, cholera and unsanitary dwellings to history. The remedy was as simple as severing a gangrenous leg: the demolition of 95 per cent of the Victorian city. Away with the marbled interiors of the City chamber. Away with Greek Thomson and Macintosh. Away with it all, done in the name of the people. Out of the grimy ruins of the nineteenth century would rise a glittering collage of the Ville Radieuse, Broadacre and other modern utopias. A cynic could be heard muttering on the backbench of the debating chamber.

'You see, what the Luftwaffe began, the urban planners will now complete'. A timely trick of fate of which Napoleon's Baron von Haussmann would have been proud. Bulldoze the past as Aldous Huxley recommends, and in so doing conveniently relocate a potentially insurgent population to the periphery. 'Job done', as they say. 'Job done'.

In 1909, the Figaro published the 'Futurist Manifesto' for a new art and architecture. 'War is the world's only hygiene' Marinetti screamed.[8] In his rabid imagination the Futurist city would be forged out of a toxic cocktail of militarism, patriotism and misogyny. Nothing was sacred, and if plans required the destruction of museums, academies and libraries, then so be it. 'Take up your pickaxes, your axes and hammers and wreck, wreck the venerable city, pitilessly.'[9]

In 1872, a year after the defeat of the Paris Commune, Zola published the *Kill*. Saccard is looking out over Haussmann's boulevards and explaining to his wife Angele the way in which necessary infrastructural improvement could help prevent proletarian insurrection. 'There it is laid out before us. Nothing could be simpler. "Paris slashed with sabre cuts, its veins opened, providing a living for a 100,000 navvies and bricklayers, traversed by splendid military roads which will bring forts into the heart of the old neighbourhoods."'[10]

7.4 Abandoned croft on the Ardnamurchan peninsula, Scotland

Somewhere, no doubt in a dusty cellar, an archivist catalogues the historical evidence of urbicide. He has been at it for centuries, but today his head is throbbing in an alarming manner as he finds it increasingly difficult to distinguish between the destructive tendencies of capitalist urban development and the retribution meted out by vengeful armies.

ACCUMULATION BY DISPOSSESSION

At the turn of the sixteenth century, after the departure of the last emir from Granada, pyromaniac ancestors of the Italian Futurists like Ferdinand II and the Grand Inquisitor Francisco de Cisneros, were still lighting ritual bonfires of Arabic texts in an effort to purify Spain and remove the traces of the scholarly traditions of the once great Islamic libraries. Meanwhile, European philosophers and scientists were preparing an economic and philosophical revolution in which democratic reason would be merged with primitive capital accumulation. Rooted in the violent dispossession of others, maps became more valuable than gold, and in a stroke of malevolent cartographic genius, the conquistadors and bandits of rival empires simply wrote, 'terra incognita' and 'terra inhabitus'.

Court and ecclesiastical historians of the ancient world confirmed that these new lands bore no trace of civilisation. A few centuries later, the Frankfurt School assured us that since enlightenment had relinquished its own realisation and knowledge had abandoned truth, such prejudices would multiply and remain a permanent feature of everyday life.[11] Long before that, Goethe's Gabriel warned us; 'paradisal brightness must swap with dreadful night'. So it was that African miners' heads were shaved lest gold nestled in their hair. And so it was that the immortal sentiments 'Liberté, Egalité and Fraternité', etched into institutions devoted to law and money from Brussels to Paris, did not extend to the black Jacobin revolutionaries on St Domingue, whose leader Toussaint L'Ouverture died in the Fort de Joux Prison.

And so it is that a ruined croft nestles into the west coast of Scotland and a mildewed stone fort perches on the coast of Brazil. They sit unhappily in landscapes whose picturesque qualities belie the fact that they have born witness to too much violence and hunger. Remotely located, there is only the occasional walker who stumbles by and momentarily glances at the fading structures, unaware that they can be read as memorials to the violent expropriation of the agricultural producer from the soil. At least that is what I saw. Piles of innocent stones that can tell a story if you let them about the unleashing of a class and racial warfare that destroyed the last traces of the ancient commune and turned the Highland and African farmer into landless wage labourers and slaves.

Cleared from the glens by mercenaries wielding guns and fictitious legal documents and maps – tactics developed during the enclosure of common lands in England and perfected in imperial land grabs – for many highlanders there was only one option, emigration. Voyages away on the other side of the Atlantic, whilst walking up the coast of Bahia, I remembered a documentary about slaving forts on the West African coast. It struck me as I looked back up the hill from the beach towards the arched doorway of a slave fort that if you drew a line east from the entrance, it would connect directly with the corridor of 'no return' at the Fort Elmina in Ghana – a tunnel of unimaginable misery that led straight out into the ocean.

Taking photographs in such places feels reprehensible, a little like posing for a fashion shot amongst the broken headstones of the Jewish cemetery in Budapest. But that is what we do in order that moments of tragedy become postcards of our time, pretty pictures of flickering palmed sun and elegiac moor. Something for the *flâneur* to send home.

ERASURE

We left L'Escorial behind and trudged up the winding mountain road through the remorseless drizzle. As we approached the summit, the mist momentarily cleared to reveal a colossal granite cross.

> What is the meaning of this? I will tell you, it is really quite simple, to the victor goes the spoils, one of which is the right to write history, or in this case build it. For those that won, this tomb is a national act of atonement, a symbol of civilization. But for those that lost it is a monument to barbarism.[12]

Blessed by the Pope as a basilica, the violence that the mausoleum represents should have come as no surprise. After all, I have digested the architecture of the Third Reich and Stalin's Russia. I have read guidebooks for Belgrade that make no mention of Tito. I have wandered alone through the megalomaniac maze of Ceausescu's palace, which should never have been reoccupied as seat of political power. I have travelled across landscapes that scream of the violent dispossession of others and unknowingly trod along a picturesque street in the docks of Rio whose

7.5 Franco's
Mausoleum,
El Vallee de
los Caídos

cobbles hide an African graveyard. I have crossed borders that no longer exist
and others conjured up out of nothing. I have studied maps in which, armed with
scissors, glue and set square, cartographers at the behest of their political masters
have created and then erased whole nations. Who now remembers Woodrow
Wilson's map, sealed with the stamps of authority that clearly shows Armenia,
Kurdistan and Palestine existing in real space and time?[13] Who remembers the
ethno-linguistic map of Africa that marks the territory of the hundreds of distinct
nations that existed before colonial conquest?

Within this grisly catalogue of erasure and amnesia that unfolds like a geological
fault line through the history of architecture and geography, there is a special place
reserved for Franco's mausoleum. On a clear day the 150-metre cross can be seen
for 50 kilometres and rises above a stone terrace and monumental colonnade that
trigger images of the Zeppelin fields at Nuremburg. From the central arch hang
giant timber doors that open onto a darkened vestibule whose gloom gives no
warning of what lies beyond – a 200-meter vaulted nave quarried into the side
of the mountain by thousands of republican prisoners. Bathed in a sepulchral
orange and yellow light, it is flanked by the empty stares of eyeless granite warriors
glowering from under medieval stone hoods.

At its head the nave is crossed by a transept over which sits the main cupola
decorated with friezes that ostensibly commemorate victims and martyrs from
both sides that fell during the civil war. In reality it is homage to one man whose
name is engraved in the marble floor near the altar. His fascist lieutenant, Antonio
Primo de Riviera, is also mentioned, but the juxtaposition of the inscription 'Franco'
with Castilian flags, Catholic saints and crucified conquistadors leaves little to the
imagination. The message is transparent: Franco was the saviour of Spain who led
his people to a promised land, free from Reds, rebels and the damnable atheists
who had repeatedly destroyed the house of God.[14]

The guidebooks describe the architecture of the mausoleum as something out of a Hollywood movie set. Somehow playful in a gothic kitsch kind of way. But there is nothing picturesque about an architecture born out of the aesthetic conceits of totalitarian dictatorship and Spanish imperialism. Like the Sacré Coeur, it is an act of vainglorious vengeance, every square meter of which speaks of drunken power. It is as if its construction was driven by the obsession of burying forever the memory of the Popular Front government and, most of all, the Barcelona Commune of 1936. For this is what the mausoleum is quite unambiguously declaring – a permanent state of war on the 'alternative moral geography' of the barris, which maintained their fierce anti-clerical and anti-statist stance right up until the end.[15]

One can only wonder, as is the case with the Paris Commune, what kind of architecture and city would have emerged, had the Barcelona Commune survived. In the time honoured traditions of architectural class war, it had started to rebuild schools in confiscated buildings, occupied factories, located hospitals in the homes of the rich, made their libraries public property, changed street names and toppled statues of generals and holy figures.[16] With this in mind, the question arises what should be done with this monstrosity where, until the law on historical memory was passed in 2004, Franco's supporters still met to honour his memory? Seal it shut? Reduce it to rubble? Secularise it like the Pantheon? Wallpaper the interiors with copies of Abad de Santillan's blueprint for libertarian communism?[17] Perhaps it would be best to let nature take its course, to erect warning signs on the approach road and to distribute speakers all over the surrounding landscape that at regular intervals broadcast excerpts from anarchist and libertarian manifestos: '...power corrupts those who exercise it and those over whom it is exercised', even 'those who think they can conquer the state in order to destroy it are unaware that the state overcomes all its conquerors'.[18]

MILITARY VERNACULAR

We visit the camps, the cemeteries, the cells and the war museums. We try to get a grip on how it is that the human brain can inflict misery and suffering with such imagination, and how it is that the scientific and architectural history of war, violence and punishment is as rich and ingenious as its antithesis. By reflex, the camera shutter snaps the macabre landscapes, the painful machinery and the hostile buildings. This type of photography is therapeutic protection. Objectified in image form, the historical event is distanced, somehow easier to handle. It is a dangerous game. Without an historical caption, the surgery in Sachsenhausen concentration camp looks like any other white ceramic tiled laboratory. Without a caption, the strange geometric turfed hillocks around Garelochead could be mistaken for the sculpted byngs of a closed coal pit rather than the roofs of weapons silos. Other structures from the history of human conflict are easier to deal with, particularly those that technological

7.6 Type 4
Second World
War bunker,
Fife, Scotland

revolutions in weaponry have rendered useless and transformed into photogenic monuments. A favourite for the 'war' tourist are the 'Expressionist' bunkers of the Atlantic Wall built by the Nazis that Virilio documented with the care of an archaeologist and which Ballard imagined as cryptic space-age cathedrals designed to last 1,000 years.[19]

Not surprisingly, as an island nation, the British coastline is a treasure trove for the military rambler. You can begin a tour with a visit to the Martello towers – the Napoleonic era fortifications that dot the coastline from Suffolk to Sussex and look like giant up-turned buckets. Some lie in ruins but others have been converted into homes and arts centres. Then there are the 28,000 World War Two pillboxes which, like the Martello towers, have a website that maps them as a series of walks. On a tour of the military architecture of Fife in East Scotland, I calculated that there were four generic types. Type one nestles on the beachhead. It is the first line of defence and is of the troglodyte variety. Carved straight into the cliff face, the front wall is built out of stone. Type two sits amongst rocks on the headland. Constructed with stone walls and a reinforced concrete roof, it cannot make up its mind whether it should be hidden or exposed. Type three is resolutely aggressive. Situated on top of the cliff and built out of reinforced concrete cast *in situ*, it is resilient enough to withstand incoming gun fire but not soil erosion. Type four made of pink fletton brick capped with a concrete roof lies inland. Slowly enveloped by greenery, in time it will become indistinguishable from a funereal cairn. In the meantime, the pillbox doubles up as animal pen, homeless shelter, birdwatcher's hut and teenage hangout.

7.7 Housing
estate, east Berlin

THE MACHINIC PHYLUM

Four thousand miles east on the same latitude as Glasgow, 56 degrees north, I spent weeks on end wandering through Moscow's concrete panelled housing estates that increase in density, height and territorial size as you move outwards from the centre to the periphery. In the rain-soaked autumnal skies they stand erect like the totemic stones of long gone Neolithic societies. In brilliant sunshine they resemble a legion of alien machines. In reality the prefabrication of such vast quantities of housing is a monument to the victory of an economic and technological determinism that gripped the imagination of planners in both East and West. In the Soviet Union, giant house-building combines (*domo-stroitelniyi kombinati*) were to be the engine of this urban revolution that stretched from Berlin to Vladivostok. Staffed by anything up to 20,000 employees, workers were organised in cadres and brigades, largely replicating the centralised and concentrated power hierarchies of old school military structures. For nearly 40 years, without a pause, the DSK churned out concrete panels at the same speed as arms.

Soviet military planners and architect-engineers, like their counterparts in the West, had shared dreams. Employing similar materials, resources and machinery, the technocratic imagination aspired to produce both weapons and buildings in automated processes that dispensed with human labour. Fast moving assembly lines would solve the housing crisis and transform building workers from 'manual combatants' to 'thinker creators'. Meanwhile, in towns without grid references, scientists and engineers dreamt of the robotic production of smart weapons that eliminated the need for humans in both the factory and the battlefield. Any chance to minimise risk and uncertainty associated with combat–industrial labour must be grabbed. Work tools, weapons and the factory and military discipline of labour would become slowly indistinguishable from each other, as if the same machinic phylum traversed both.[20]

7.8 Seventieth anniversary of the Russian Revolution, Moscow

The factory that produces canons can also fabricate steel lintels. The first tanks and trams shared engines and tracks. The light bulb is pointed down to illuminate the street and up to spot aircraft. In 1906, Etienne Jules Marey invented the chrono-photographic rifle by merging the mechanics of 'repeater guns and repeater photography'.[21] Meanwhile on the building site, pneumatic drills and riveting guns gave birth to the Hilti Gun, laser-guided drills and saws. There is, in fact, a constant traffic and transfer of materials, mechanical and 'dromological' technologies from one sphere of production into another. Speed of assembly, accuracy, efficiency, increasing lightness and mobility are of critical importance to both military and construction planners. The graphite bomb replaces the megaton bomb. The lightweight interactive façade replaces the heavy concrete panel.

PERMANENT ARMS ECONOMY IN MOSCOW

But new technology is useless without the right kind of organisation and planning. Tactics, strategy and logistics are employed in both the war machine and the construction industry to extract some semblance of order out of the chaos and irrationality of both armed combat and building production, regardless of whether they are driven by the profit targets of capitalist firms or the plan targets of the state.[22] It is a vain exercise. One of the lessons from Mailer's *Naked and the Dead* is that the only thing that could be organised with any real military precision were the folded tent-flaps, duckboards and officers mess, none of which survived the first heavy rains. Similarly, for all the attempts to control what Marx and Engels called the 'anarchy' of capitalist production and Schumpeter, the 'perennial gale of creative destruction', the construction industry can no more escape economic crisis than General Cummings the unpredictable outcomes of jungle warfare.[23]

So it was on returning from photographing the concrete panels of 24-storey tower blocks that I stood on a city centre Moscow street watching the SS20 missiles trundle past in celebration of the seventieth anniversary of the 1917 Revolution. Spectators applauded with the same enthusiasm that they had once reserved for the miracle of hot water and modern domestic plumbing. By the early 1970s, armament and military expenditure had become a permanent feature of the economic and political life of advanced industrial societies.[24] It was a military industrial alliance in which the mass production of the means of production and consumer goods was joined at the hip to the mass production of the means of destruction; a merging of the Welfare and Warfare State in which an administered population enjoyed improved living standards under the threat of annihilation.[25] At the very moment when the British Prime Minister Harold Wilson was announcing that future prosperity would lie in the white heat of a scientific and technological revolution, it is estimated that the production of weapons 'amounted to nearly a half of gross investments the world over.'[26] By 1989, at the zenith of the 'total' industrialisation of the Soviet building industry, military expenditure stood at almost a third of GDP. It was the permanent arms economy par excellence that in two years had collapsed.

SECRET BUNKERS

It is probably difficult for people born after 1980 to understand the intense fear that periodically gripped the popular imagination after the bombing of Hiroshima and Nagasaki and the division of Europe into rival armed economies. I was three during the Cuban missile crisis and grew up in a generation for whom nuclear annihilation was not so much a distant possibility as a distinct probability. It was a culture of fear that spawned a mutant architecture devoted to secret weapons development and underground seats of government, such that in the event of a mushroom cloud, some semblance of warrior life would continue. W.G. Sebald described visiting an example of the former – the pagoda ruins on the isolated pebble beach at Orfordness that resembled a far eastern penal colony and where boffins dabbled in unspeakable forms of murder.[27] I went to an example of the latter madness, the Secret Control Bunker in Scotland built in the 1950s deep in the bowels of the earth, where retaliatory orders would be given and martial law organised.

For some reason I imagined it as a facsimile of a rural village, a quaint reminder of a lost idyll that would help survivors cope with their underground incarceration. Accordingly, I expected a cobbled street, a pub, a village church, post office, tartan wallpaper and maybe even a Macintosh tearoom. At ground level there is nothing to tell you about what lies underneath the grazing cows that wander around what looks like a farmhouse. But inside, the gift shop at the

7.9   Access corridor, Secret Bunker, Fife, Scotland

front door, a lift and then a steeply descending corridor take you down into a cavernous concrete mausoleum. The stench of unventilated claustrophobia hits the senses hard and reminded me of crawling along the passage to the inner chamber of the Great Pyramid of Khufu. In the event of nuclear war you might have acclimatised to the petrified atmosphere. But you would have remained lost in time and space, an increasingly rickety survival prisoner in permanent solitary confinement, trying to smile in a spartan interior of insipid institutional paint that stinks of boiled cabbage.

Two floors, two corridors with rooms of varying sizes to either side, barrack bunk bedrooms, closets jammed with communications gadgetry, a decrepit theatre of operations which had none of the panache of Spectre's control centre, a pathetic box chapel – the one concession to the spiritual world – and the one concession to peace, a sad CND exhibition. We can be sure that our rulers are still planning for a subterranean escape in the event of Armageddon. They have always invested heavily in tunnels, hidden cellars and camouflaged escape routes. The difference nowadays is that so can we. For a few thousand quid you too can build yourself a bunker and stockpile cans of food and toilet chemicals. It is tempting to think that this abject fear of annihilation is misplaced. Equally, it is tempting to think of the Secret Bunker as a dead world of dead time, a stuffed dummy reinforced by antiquated computer technology and the spectres of Woodbine-smoking grey-blue uniforms. Like most historical theme parks, it presents the past as a crazed curiosity shop. The reality, however, is that the ideological conflict that generated such paranoid architecture has not disappeared; it has simply been transformed and retargeted. This is not a place to dwell and I am glad that I would have been incinerated in the first seconds.

7.10   The 'high
street' in Oradour-
sur-Glane, France

PICTURESQUE WARS IN MECHELEN AND ORADOUR

I was participating in a workshop in Belgium on architectural memorials. Screwed to the yellow brick of the former Dossin barracks in Mechelen there is a plaque that commemorates the 24,461 Jews who were deported from here to the German camps. In the basement of the four-storey block there is a museum founded in 1995 that documents some of the atrocities. It features harrowingly familiar black and white photographs of smiling victims snapped on summer days before the end. Alongside hang images of messianic Belgian Nazis, convinced that they were acting according to the laws of nature and history.[28] Inside the street level courtyard where prisoners were assembled, there is a garden with rose bushes, flowerbeds and trees. But this is not a garden of remembrance; it is a park for the residents who bought flats when the barracks were converted into accommodation, and who clearly do not believe in history's ghosts. Nothing, I fear, could be built or constructed to alter that. Maybe the barracks should have been left as a ruin, given over to nature and left to sleep. My only thought was to leave a placard on a piece of wood with the words, 'Nobody lives here'.

In contrast, the preserved in aspic village of Oradour-sur-Glane is uninhabited by the living. This is where the SS division 'Der Führer' used a church as an oven to cook all the women and children. I had a horrible feeling that I was looking through the camera viewfinder at a film set composed of ruined yellow stonewalls, wired 1940s telegraph poles, abandoned cars and swaying sycamores. Birdsong was the only thing to break the silence. Kurt reminds me that this is to be expected. He says 'everything is supposed to be very quiet after a massacre, and it always is, except for the birds'.[29] I looked at the groups of bored school children being marched around and told stories of unspeakable horror. I wondered what they made of it. Did they think they were extras in a war film?

7.11   Entrance
to Breedonk
Fort, Belgium

THEATRICAL OPERATIONS AT BREEDONK

I took a bus to Breedonk Fort that functioned as a prison and interrogation centre for Jews, political prisoners and resistance fighters. It was a brilliant winter day, perfect for taking voyeuristic photographs of the traces of monsters that capture little but the rather kitsch and theatrical character of such places. Reality is suspended. Breedonk becomes a twisted theme park or a ready stage set for warped thespians. After all, they speak of the theatre of operations and the theatre of war. This was on my mind as I walked past the mannequin entrance guards standing in glass cases and the polished SS insignia in the mess room. The feeling of the inappropriate nature of this type of 'atrocity exhibition' deepened as I walked along the labyrinthine corridors, stopping to smell a musty cell, to stare at the butcher's hook from which prisoners were suspended, and to gawp at fetishised artefacts that masquerade as art installations.

No amount of facsimile can convey the reality of terror. The most frightening thing in the Stasi headquarters in Berlin is not the rubber-water torture chamber. It is the thoroughly mundane interview rooms that in their bureaucratic ordinariness reinforce Hannah Arendt's argument about the banality of evil.[30] Like Walter Sebald, I trod around the perimeter of Breedonk trying to grasp exactly what part of the human imagination could have conceived, planned and built such a '… monstrous incarnation of ugliness and blind violence…'. A structure that seems disconnected from 'anything shaped by human civilisation, or even the silent relics of our prehistory'.[31]

But Breedonk is not exceptional. It is a footnote to the modern history of carceral architecture. This begins with the Panopticon and continues to the ugly and disconnected warehouse prisons, barbed refuge centres and labour camps of the twenty-first century. It represents an unbroken linear history of the human

imagination hard at work adapting the accumulated knowledge of how to instil
terror. I remembered Goldstein who seemed to speak not just for Jews, but for
everyone.

> No sacrifices were paid, no lessons were learned. It was all thrown away, all
> statistics in the cruel wastes of history. All the ghettoes, all the soul cripplings, all
> the massacres and pogroms, the gas chambers, lime kilns – all of it touched no
> one, all of it was lost…There was nothing in him at the moment, nothing but a
> vague anger, a deep resentment, and the origins of vast hopelessness.[32]

CLEAN WARS IN BELGRADE

> All of a sudden, between one and two in the morning, an almighty explosion
> shook Belgrade's houses to their very foundations so that every window in
> every house from Dorcol to Cubura was obliterated. A terrible panic gripped the
> civilians of Belgrade who had no idea what had happened.[33]

It was in fact a Serbian commander blowing up a bridge across the Sava to halt
the advance of the Austrians who, undeterred, launched an artillery attack on the
centre of Belgrade. That was in 1914, but it was similar to the stories I had heard of
the NATO bombardment that had started with incomprehension as to how they
could be attacking a central European capital.

In a German prisoner of war camp, Edgar Derby imagines a letter written to his
wife. 'We are leaving for Dresden today. Don't worry it will never be bombed.'[34] So
thought Sasha and Mika on their way home through central Belgrade. The sirens
are wailing, but they surely wouldn't dare, and if they did well, perhaps it won't be
so bad. After all, computer video propaganda shows that the era of indiscriminate

carpet bombing has ended and a new type of warfare has begun – war in which 'strategic targets' can be bombed with spectacular accuracy.

The order was given and missiles slammed into the Ministry of Internal Affairs, the Ministry of Justice and the Yugoslav Army HQ on Kneza Milosa. It was part of a ferocious NATO aerial attack across the country that killed hundreds of civilians. In Belgrade alone, school buildings were damaged, a hospital hit, and fires burned in a gynaecological clinic and psychological hospital. But the NATO press office had nothing to worry about for they have at their disposal a rich linguistic arsenal with which to camouflage such 'unfortunate incidents': collateral damage; peacekeeping; friendly fire; operational security; legitimate target; false allegation…

The information war had been launched with full force. It was after all a 'clean' war, even though the idea of clean war – like that of a clean bomb or an intelligent missile – is a sure sign of madness.[35] Which is why the media resort to fables and just as in the mythological manned mission to Mars of Capricorn One, 'the day there is a real war you will not be able to tell the difference.'[36]

There was no mainstream news of the curious lightning balls and exploding BLU-114/B graphite bombs that spread extremely fine carbon wires over electrical components. Seventy per cent of Serbia's power grid short-circuited. Amnesty subsequently found evidence of highly toxic and carcinogenic residues that could only have come from 'imaginary' depleted uranium ordnance. In the 'hysterical trompe l'oeil' of carefully selected images pumped out by Western media there were no pictures of this dirty war or the environmental catastrophe at Pancevo, 17 kilometres outside Belgrade, where the petro-chemical plant was destroyed.

For days the smoking buildings emitted black and white clouds of a highly toxic mixture of ammonia, crude oil, liquid chlorine, hydrochloric acid and mercury that settled on the town and the surrounding fields and induced bursts of black rain. The costs to civilians of these poisonous winds and precipitation are incalculable.

In contrast, the reconstruction loans organised by the IMF and the World Bank to help the country back on its feet were easy to work out. As in previous military conflicts such as Vietnam and Iraq, these loans were tagged to highly lucrative financial contracts with construction firms from approved NATO countries, amongst them Brown and Root, a specialist in the construction of infrastructure and a subsidiary of ex-Vice President Dick Cheney's Halliburton Group.

TOTAL WAR ON CIVILIANS

Twenty-five years ago I was stopped and questioned by police for walking along the pavements in Beverley Hills. Perhaps because there was noone else walking. Perhaps because I was taking photographs of signs normally reserved for covert military installations that had been domesticated on the front gates of a Tudor mansion. 'Warning, Approach with Caution. Armed Response'. Since then, the city of fear has been exported worldwide.[37] As dangerous as any contagious illness,

7.13   City centre communications tower, Bucharest

the middle class in particular has been gripped by a form of siege psychosis. If it were a B-movie it would be listed as 'The Return of the City State – a paranoid fantasy in which your darkest fears of barbarian proletarians scaling the city walls and battering the gates come horribly true.'

All sense of perspective is lost in a very old fashioned way – a real and tangible fear of any 'other'. They can't head for the hills, so they head for real estate supplements that advertise gulag luxury towers in sparkling technicolour. In Moscow they want to build a totally sealed dome to protect inhabitants from all possible encounters with aliens. Ballard promises civil war. In Brazil they go straight for the heart. 'Come live in liberty', the slogan says, 'Peace of mind for you and your family'. Helipads, crenulated walls, spiked fences, searchlights, cameras and private security forces keep the home under observation. As well they might, since many of the towers are nestled between *favelas*, in which a different form of armed combat takes place – gangster against gangster, gangster against the police, gangsters armed not just with guns but with hand-held missile launchers with telescopic lenses and digital film recorders.

Everything is held in camera by both sides. This reflects the fact that the science and techniques of both cinema and war – optics, cameras, screens, lights, tracking, mapping, reconnaissance and shifting fields of perception and representation – are now fully employed in the contemporary city.[38] The merging of the audio-visual technologies and tactics of the modern war machine with urban life has helped create a 'martial landscape', a 'softly' militarised city that speaks of the arch-semiotics of class war.[39] This is a price we seem willing to pay for the illusion of peace and security. And it is an illusion in which ideological deception and the mangling of a coherent sense of reality by the weapons of mass communication is essential to mask the reality of war and to convince us that living in a civilian maximum-security jail will conquer fear.[40]

NOTES

1   Marx writes in his essay 'So-called Primitive Accumulation' the following: 'In actual history, it is a notorious fact that conquest, enslavement, robbery, murder, in short force plays the greatest part.' Karl Marx, *Capital*, Vol. I, (London: Penguin, 1976), p. 874.

2   This is a reference to Walter Sebald, *On The Natural History of Destruction* (Penguin: London, 2004). Dealing with the controversies that arose in the latter half of the twentieth century in the manner in which historians had dealt with both the actions of the Third Reich and the allied bombing of Dresden and Hamburg, he writes in relation to memory and forgetting: 'Rather, it is as if a diffuse ability to forget goes hand-in-hand with the recurrent resurgence of images which cannot be banished from the memory, and which remain effective as agencies of an almost pathological hypermnesia in a past otherwise emptied of content.' p. 153.

3   See Theodore Adorno and Max Horkheimer, *The Dialectic of the Enlightenment* (London: Verso, 1989), p. 36 (1944).

4   Writing in the context of the struggle against fascism, Walter Benjamin, in his famous 'Theses on History' comments that: 'The tradition of the oppressed teaches us that the "state of emergency" in which we live is not the exception but the rule. We must attain to a conception of history that is in keeping with this insight. It seems to me to be equally apposite to our contemporary condition.' Walter Benjamin, *Illuminations* (New York: Schocken, 1969), pp. 256–7.

5   Taken from one of the most influential novels about war – Erich M. Remarque, *All Quiet on the Western Front* (London: Vintage, 1996) (1929).

6   This is, of course, a reference to Orwell's novel, *1984*, and his depiction of a society permanently at war governed by the omnipotent Ministry of Truth that declares 'War is Peace, freedom is slavery, ignorance is strength.'

7   Robert Bruce, *First Planning Report to the Highways and Planning Committee of the Corporation of Glasgow*, Second Edition (Glasgow, October 1947).

8   Felippo Marinetti, 'The Foundation and Manifesto of Futurism' in C. Harrison and P. Wood (eds), *Art in Theory, 1900–1990: An Anthology of Changing Ideas* (Oxford: Blackwell, 1993), pp. 145–9.

9   Marinetti, *The Foundation*, ibid., p. 147.

10   Emile Zola, *The Kill (La Curee)* (Oxford: Oxford University Press, 2008), p. 69.

11   For the theorists of the Frankfurt School, notably Adorno, Horkheimer and Marcuse, the fusion of rationality with the priorities of a capitalist commodity economy had transformed reason, or rather 'rational thought', into a form of essentially violent instrumental rationality, such that: 'With the abandonment of thought, which in its reified form of mathematics, machine and organisation avenges itself on the men who have forgotten it, enlightenment has relinquished its own realisation.' Adorno and Horkheimer, *Dialectic of Enlightenment*, p. 41.

12   This is, of, course a paraphrase of two well-known statements: 'The ideas of the ruling class are in every epoch the ruling ideas, i.e. the class which is the ruling material force of society is at the same time its ruling intellectual force.' Karl Marx and Friedrich Engels, *The German Ideology* (London: Lawrence and Wishart, 1985), p. 64, and 'There is no document of civilisation which is not at the same time a document of barbarism.' Walter Benjamin, 'Theses on History' in *Illuminations*, p. 256.

13   For a good survey of the political geography of Turkey, Armenia and the middle east, see Robert Fisk, *The Great War for Civilisation* (London: Harper Perennial, 2006).

On Turkey's relationship with Armenia, see Taner Akcam, *A Shameful Act – The Armenian Genocide and the Question of Turkish Responsibility* (London: Constable, 2007).

14   The attack on ecclesiastical property was a feature of all three French revolutions (see Chapter 6 in this volume), the two Russian revolutions (see Chapter 7), and had been a regular feature of workers' uprisings in the Iberian peninsular, not just in 1936, but previously in the insurrection of 1909.

15   Chris Ealham, *Anarchism and the City – Revolution and Counter-Revolution in Barcelona, 1898–1937* (Edinburgh: AK Press, 2010), p. 86. An excellent and highly detailed account of the extraordinary working-class resistance in the city's barris.

16   For details of the revolutionary festival that was famously visited by George Orwell, see Ealham, *Anarchism,* pp. 170–91. Another account notes how, occupying one of the most modern buildings in Barcelona, the Casa de Cambo, as their headquarters, the anarchists began to organise the collectivisation of urban public services. Clubs, neighbourhood committees and graffiti mushroomed throughout the city as banks were seized, rents decreased and a policy for the socialisation of agriculture were announced. See Robert Kern, *Red Years Black Years: A Political History of Spanish Anarchism, 1911–1937* (Philadelphia: Institute for the Study of Human Issues, 1978), pp. 163–9.

17   Minister of the Economy in the Generalidad in Catalonia was Abad de Santillan, the author of a 'Libertarian Planning Blueprint', a series of notes on the organisation of labour from the factory councils to the Council of the Economy. See Daniel Guérin, *No Gods No Masters: An Anthology of Anarchism*, Book Two (Edinburgh: AK Press, 1998), pp. 100–103.

18   Quote in Peter Marshall, *Demanding the Impossible, A History of Anarchism* (London: Fontana, 1993), p. 456.

19   See for instance James G. Ballard, *The Atrocity Exhibition* (London: Harper Perennial, 2006), p. 14, Paul Hirst, 'Defence of Places from Sieges to Silos', in *Space and Power: Politics, War and Architecture* (Cambridge: Polity, 2005), p. 211, and not forgetting Paul Virilio, *Bunker Archaeology* (New York: Princeton University Press, 1994).

20   This refers to the convertible relationship between tools and weapons that sometimes make it quite difficult to distinguish between the two. 'Some have spoken of an "eco-system", not only situated at the origin, in which work tools and weapons of war exchange their determinations: it seems that the same machinic phylum traverses both.' See Gilles Deleuze and Felix Guattari, *A Thousand Plateaus: Capitalism and Schizophrenia* (University of Minnesota: Athlone Press, 1996), p. 395.

21   See Paul Virilio, *War and Cinema: The Logistics of Perception* (London: Verso, 1989), p. 96ff.

22   For de Landa the machinic phylum runs through out natural and human history and refers to any process in which order emerges out of disorder. The war machine understood as the historical accumulation of military knowledge and practice strives to produce order and discipline out of chaos. Manuel de Landa, *War in the Age of Intelligent Machines* (New York: Zone Books, 2001), p. 20ff.

23   Friedrich Engels, *Anti-Dühring* (Moscow: Progress Publishers, 1978), pp. 331–9 and Joseph A. Schumpeter, *Capitalism, Socialism, and Democracy* (London: Routledge, 2010) (1943), p. 70ff.

24   Ernest Mandel in his chapter, 'The Permanent Arms Economy and Late Capitalism', argued that Marx's schema – Department One, the production of means of production and Department Two, the production of consumer goods – should be extended to

include a third department, the production of means of destruction. Ernest Mandel, *Late Capitalism* (London: Verso,1999) (1972), p. 274.

25   'The society of total mobilisation, which takes shape in the most advanced areas of industrial civilisation, combines the productive union of the features of the Welfare State and the Warfare State.' Herbert Marcuse, *One-Dimensional Man: Studies in the Ideology of Advanced Industrial Society* (London: RKP, 1986) (1964), p. 19.

26   Mandel, *Late Capitalism*, p. 275.

27   Walter Sebald, *The Rings of Saturn* (London: Vintage, 2002), p. 233.

28   In her discussion on ideology and terror in totalitarian dictatorships, Arendt comments that: 'The rulers themselves do not claim to be just or wise, but only to execute historical and natural laws; they do not apply laws but execute a movement in accordance with its inherent law. Terror is lawfulness, if law is the law of the movement of some suprahuman force, Nature or History.' See Hannah Arendt, *The Origins of Totalitarianism, Ideology and Terror* (New York: Harvest, 1976) (1948), p. 464.

29   Kurt Vonnegut, *Slaughterhouse 5* (London: Vintage, 2000) (1969), p. 14.

30   Taken from the title of Arendt's meticulous dissection of the moral and political dimensions of Eichmann's trial. Hannah Arendt, *Eichmann in Jerusalem: A Report on the Banality of Evil* (London: Faber and Faber, 1963).

31   Walter Sebald, *Austerlitz* (London: Penguin Books, 2001), p. 25.

32   Norman Mailer, *The Naked and the Dead* (London: Harper Perennial, 2006) (1949), p. 679.

33   Misha Glenny, *The Balkans: Nationalism, War and the Great Powers, 1804–1999* (London: Penguin Books, 1999), p. 312.

34   Vonnegut, *Slaughterhouse*, p. 107.

35   Jean Baudrillard, *The Gulf War Did Not Take Place* (Sydney: Power Publications, 2009) (1991), p. 43.

36   Baudrillard, *The Gulf War*, p. 59.

37   Paul Virilio, *City of Panic* (Oxford: Berg, 2005), p. 91.

38   Virilio, *War and Cinema*, p. 86.

39   Mike Davis, *City of Quartz: Excavating the Future in Los Angeles* (London: Verso, 1990), p. 223.

40   'Full-scale annihilation of the sense of reality in which the weapon of mass communication is strategically superior to the weapon of mass destruction, whether atomic, chemical or bacteriological.' Virilio, *City of Panic*, p. 34.

8

The Shadow of Economic History II: The Architecture of Boom, Slump and Crisis

INTRODUCTION

We gazed with earnest hope for signs of recovery and longed for the airwaves to tell us that 'the worst is past, economic Armageddon has been averted, and house prices are rising again.'

Back in 2004, I wrote a short essay called 'Boom and Slump on the Clyde and Liffey', in which I expressed my astonishment that the Irish economy and housing market hadn't crashed.[1] For the situation in Dublin was quite unprecedented in economic history. At the height of the Soviet industrialisation of the building industry, the construction sector accounted for 13 per cent of GDP. But in Ireland by the end of 2004, it had reached 22 per cent, prompting the Bank of Ireland to admit in early 2005 that the construction industry's role in the Irish economy was 'above equilibrium'. The boom, fuelled by a massive increase in speculative housing, was clearly unsteady, and with over 40 per cent of new flats unsold and unlet, one didn't have to be an economist to work out that something had to give. However, it is characteristic of all such gold rushes that in the race to capitalise on investments the normal laws of reason are suspended. 'The Shadows of Economic History' picks up on this debate and places the recent crisis in the architectural and building industry in an historical context.[2] It argues that it was simply irrational for architects and contractors to behave as if the boom would go on forever. Capitalist development has always been marked by periodic crises, and building production has always exhibited cycles of expansion and contraction. So what caused the economic recession and where on earth did the profoundly mistaken belief come from that we could cheat history? This essay was first published in the *Architectural Research Quarterly* (*ARQ*) in 2010. This version has been both re-edited and added to.

8.1   The cranes
of boundless
prosperity, Liffey
River, Dublin

A YEAR TO REMEMBER

In the autumn of 1929 the mightiest of Americans were, for a brief time, revealed as human beings. Like most humans, most of the time they did some very foolish things. On the whole the greater the earlier reputation for omniscience, the more serene the previous idiocy, the greater the foolishness now exposed. Things that in other times were concealed by a heavy façade of dignity now stood exposed, for the panic suddenly, almost obscenely, snatched this façade away.[3]

(*J.K. Galbraith,* The Great Crash 1929*)*

The construction boom that spanned the advent of the new millennium was seductive and intoxicating. Super profits on land development, the availability of cheap credit, booming house prices, showcase urban regeneration projects and relentless advertising promises seemed to confirm the 'new common sense' that we had entered an era of boundless prosperity and crisis-free economic growth. It was an ideological consensus that reached its apogee in Gordon Brown's notorious declaration that the era of boom and bust was over. Then, almost overnight, the door slammed shut. Oblivious to the warning sirens, economists and bankers expressed concern and then terror as the global financial system went into meltdown. It quickly dawned that what had started as a local financial and banking crisis connected to the trade in mortgage debt in the United States had assumed global dimensions and was potentially as destructive as the great crash of the 1920s. Worse still, talk was not just of a serious recession, but of a crisis that focused a spotlight on the legitimacy of the political class that had allowed neo-liberal speculation and unregulated financial engineering to traverse the boundaries of economic science.

The impact on building production and the housing market in the United Kingdom was instantaneous as panic struck, cranes came to a halt, and architectural firms laid off staff. Light years away from the dream of managed equilibrium, or even a temporary downturn in the trade cycle, the construction sector faced the most ruthless slump in its fortunes that anyone could remember.[4] Construction output stagnated, new orders were frozen and, by the end of 2009, an estimated 60 per cent of contractors had made staff redundant. No sector of the industry was immune. Giants like Balfour Beatty and Bovis, plant hire and engineering firms, materials producers, scaffolders and countless architectural practices all announced redundancies. It was estimated that in the construction industry alone, anywhere between 250,000 and 400,000 workers had lost their jobs by the start of 2010.[5] Worse still, the house building industry had reached its lowest peacetime level of activity since 1921; a predicament compounded by a 50 per cent increase in home repossessions.

If the threat of economic disintegration wasn't bad enough, the construction industry remained highly dangerous – a situation greatly exacerbated by the casualisation of employment. The construction union UCATT reported that the annual death toll on building sites had exceeded 70, with hundreds of serious injuries.[6] If we were to add to this the environmental degradation and social destructiveness of three decades of neo-liberal economic policy, in which the vocabulary belonging to a social agenda in architecture was virtually forgotten, the word catastrophe, loaded as it is with drama and tragedy, for once seemed appropriate.

VISIONS OF HOPE AND OPTIMISM

> The bankers were also a source of encouragement to those who wished to believe in the permanence of a boom. A great many of them abandoned their historic role as the guardians of the nation's fiscal pessimism and enjoyed a brief respite of optimism.[7]
>
> (Galbraith, The Great Crash 1929)

The deep shock that gripped the building industry resulted not just from the rapidity with which property markets and the banking system collapsed, but also because it contradicted what had become the received wisdom of neo-liberal ideology. This maintained that capitalism was 'the eternal and natural form of economy', and that a crisis-free capitalist system was both imaginable and realisable.[8] It proposed that 'human well-being' could 'best be advanced by liberating individual entrepreneurial freedoms and skills within an institutional framework characterised by strong private property rights, free markets and free trade'.[9] But it had other ambitions beyond this.

The neo-liberals' long-term objective was to extend the operation of competitive market relations into all areas of our lives and to transform profoundly the social and cultural landscape of Britain by institutionalising a 'business ontology' that supported the view that it was 'simply obvious that everything in society, including health care and education, should be run as a business'.[10] As for the built environment, the same sort of logic painted a landscape in which the building

8.2   Juggernauts
full of prosperity

industry was overwhelmingly privately owned and the power of the state and public authorities to regulate what got built was severely restricted. Ideologically, the advocates of neo-liberalism equated individual liberty with home-ownership and insisted that the best way of meeting our collective and individual needs in the built environment was through the operation of a 'self regulating free market' in land and building services, which, if left unfettered, would allow a state of 'perfect competition' to prevail between firms and individuals.[11]

Although this vision of social freedom – based on the sanctity of private property and free markets – was profoundly utopian, for many, including the majority of large building contractors, property speculators and landowners, the neo-liberal world-view was alluring and irresistible. Like a fundamentalist religion it demanded loyalty but promised wealth and salvation. But whilst the blind faith of its disciples was undoubtedly instrumental in causing the crisis, it is a little too easy to blame neo-liberalism for single-handedly wrecking the economy and construction sector; not least because neo-liberalism itself came of age in response to another crisis that occurred at the end of the 1970s. This suggests that the underlying causes of crises perhaps lie elsewhere. Here it is important to remember that 40 years ago, before the rise of neo-liberalism in the US and UK, there was a broad consensus of a different kind. It was based on Keynes's proposition that with intelligent state regulation, the capitalist economy and the building industry could be planned in coordination with the market in an efficient and equitable manner; a proposition that triumphed in Britain in the urban and architectural programme of the welfare state.[12]

Such was the ideological consensus that in 1970, Arthur Okun, the former Chair of the Council of Economic Advisers, declared that, 'with the neoclassical Keynesian synthesis now in the hands of every enlightened government, recessions like airplane crashes were preventable, and business fluctuations as a threat to the smooth operation of the modern economy were obsolete'.[13]

The mood that surrounded what appeared to be the 'discovery' of the secret formula of stable economic growth was as contagious as that accompanying the neo-liberal programme that was to replace it and encouraged economists and politicians to announce triumphantly that: 'The miracle of the market, superintended by the state, could now virtually guarantee perpetual growth.'[14]

What was so extraordinary about this utopian euphoria was that it came at the very moment when the post-war boom was coming to an end. The uprisings of the late 1960s, a falling rate of profit, the intensification of the Cold War, the conflicts in southeast Asia, the oil crisis, uncontrolled speculation and the subsequent crash in the global property market heralded the onset of a crisis that hit the UK construction sector particularly badly. Office space lay empty, construction on new projects was suspended and output crashed in both public and private building activity.[15] It was a slump that prompted curiously familiar headlines. In the first four months of 1977, *The Times* and *The Architects' Journal* ran cover stories that read: 'Worst Outlook for Builders', 'Unacceptable Level of Building Sector Unemployment', 'Damaging Long-Term Effects of Fall in Construction Industry', 'Construction Sector Faces More Jobless and Permanent Damage', and '2,000 Architects Laid Off'.[16] It was estimated that at the height of the crisis one in three architects had been made redundant and that in the construction industry as a whole, 400,000 jobs were lost.[17]

By 1979, the economy and the building industry were on the brink of ruin. What happened next has become the stuff of economic legend as a newly elected Conservative Party unrolled a programme to dismantle heavy industry, to peel back the welfare state, privatise the public sector and extend the operation of market forces into areas previously insulated from commercial pressure. The Keynesian consensus was dispatched to economic history and by the end of the 1980s, the political and social landscape of Britain had been transformed. The organised labour movement that had fought to protect jobs emerged from battle battered and in disarray, whilst the power of the capitalist class that had declined over the previous three decades was significantly restored.[18]

The construction industry, in which Conservative Party members like Keith Joseph, Cecil Parkinson and the treasurer McAlpine, all had interests, was one of the first sectors to be targeted. Headed by Michael Heseltine, another senior Tory, an employers' campaign was launched to discredit public sector building and architects' departments and to confront left wing demands for the nationalisation of land and the building industry.[19] As attacks on the public sector increased, the labour movement mobilised and launched campaigns to tackle homelessness, to halt the sale of UK council housing, to regulate the activities of labour-only subcontractors and to prevent urban development authorised against the public interest such as Canary Wharf.[20] But despite these and other struggles, by the mid 1980s, the ideological hegemony of deregulation, free markets and fast money had gripped not just the imagination of powerful construction firms and speculative developers, but of large swathes of the population.

Between 1969 and 1989, as a proportion of new UK house building, the public sector share declined from 51 per cent to 13 per cent. New orders for all types of building work in the public sector fell from 48 per cent to 23 per cent. And by 1990, 92 per cent of total national building output and 98 per cent of new public housing was produced by the private sector.[21] Direct labour departments and local authority architects' departments had virtually vanished in the space of two decades, and the trade union organisation of building workers had reached a new low. Ideologically at least, the neo-liberal project appeared to have been accomplished.

In reality however, the situation was far more fragile and precarious. By the middle of 1990, *The Architects' Journal* began to run alarming headlines including 'Gloomy Outlook For Practices' and 'Oblivion Beckons As Slump Bites', while the Department of the Environment revealed an 18 per cent fall in total construction orders during the second quarter of 1989 – 'the most dramatic decline for a quarter of a century'.[22] A year later, it still looked bad. An estimated 56 per cent of new commissions in London had been abandoned or postponed and, nationally, 52 per cent of practices experienced a fall in workload.[23] As the recession bit harder, *The Times* predicted that a recovery in the building industry had been ruled out until at least 1994.[24] In all, it was estimated that a massive 40 per cent of architects and technicians were made redundant between 1990 and 1993.[25]

However, far from rebuilding the public sector or questioning free-market orthodoxies, the remedy for the recession in the early 1990s was to extend the operation of the free market; to prise open new opportunities for private sector-led land and building development; and to consolidate a model of a post-industrial economy in which the services sector, tourism and retail outstripped what was left of the manufacturing sector as a proportion of GDP.[26] The beleaguered public sector was attacked once more with, for example, 44 per cent of staff in the Building Services Department at London's Haringey Council being made redundant.[27] If things had gone temporarily wrong, it was not the fault of neo-liberal economic theory or the new mathematics and latest insights of the Chicago School of Economics; it was that these theories and policies had not been driven far enough. Undeterred – and buoyed by the collapse of the Soviet Union – in the mid 1990s, the political right would once again claim that the combination of liberal parliamentary democracy and free-market capitalism had proven to be the best way of organising human society. Economic crises were not caused by any implicit flaw in the process of capital accumulation but were the results of unforeseen events and accidents.

THE ARCHITECTURE OF BAROQUE FINANCE

> In all great speculative orgies devices have appeared to enable the speculator so to concentrate on his business…The machinery by which Wall Street separates the opportunity to speculate from the unwanted returns and burdens of ownership is ingenious, precise and almost beautiful.[28]
>
> (Galbraith, The Great Crash 1929)

Neo-liberalism was no overnight sensation. Although it can trace its ideological roots back to the early nineteenth century, its re-emergence after the Second World War as a critique of socialism, state planning and collective property was largely down to the work of Hayek and Friedman, whose ideas found a natural

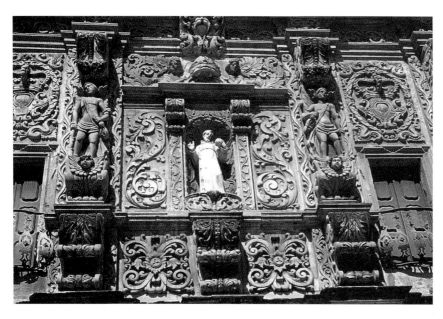

8.3   Dripping in gold leaf, the architecture of baroque finance

home in conservative think tanks in the UK such as the Institute of Economic Affairs (founded in 1955), the Centre for Policy Studies (1974) and the Adam Smith Institute (1976).[29] Neo-liberalism was successful in creating a smoke screen in which the real and tangible nature of political and economic change was camouflaged. Indeed, in its audacious claims on future history, the pronouncements of neo-liberals can be compared with some of the outlandish declarations of the Soviet bureaucracy on the 'global victory of socialism', in which the reality of economic stagnation was masked by the rhetoric of limitless progress. Neo-liberals engaged in a very similar game of make-believe despite Joseph Schumpeter's warning, as far back as 1946, that the proposition that free trade and a perfectly competitive system would prevail and that it represented the optimal way of distributing resources, was essentially mythological.[30]

Architecture played a significant role in supporting and creating such myths. Whereas the architectural community after the Second World War had seen itself as a handmaiden of progressive social change with nearly half the profession working for the public sector,[31] it had, by the end of the twentieth century, embraced the virtues of neo-liberalism. In many respects it had little choice but to go where the money was. Ideologically, the idea of the city as a democratically governed polity was transformed into 'City Ltd Inc.', a seemingly limitless and lucrative real estate opportunity driven by business and self-interest, whose glittering skyline was no longer punctured by the spires and pediments of ecclesiastical and state power, but by the prefabricated shells of luxury flats, shopping cathedrals and financial nerve centres.

This was more than just an illusion. It was symptomatic of the rupturing of architecture and urban development into two distinct realities. In one universe lay the ruined landscape of working-class industrial Britain – the abandoned factories; the crumbling housing estates; the scarred landscapes and boarded-up high streets.

In the other lay the world represented by the desperate competition between cities and regions to attract capital investment by turning themselves into theme parks, by winning the right to host prestigious sporting or cultural events, or by releasing land to build glitzy waterfront developments and 'freedom through luxury living' apartment blocks. Given that the 'law' of uneven development represents the geographical history of capitalism, such acute socio-spatial inequalities in wealth and opportunity shouldn't really surprise us; neither should the fact that the architect has been deeply embroiled in the construction of such a split reality. For in truth, the architectural profession has always tended to be fairly amoral about whom it serves, regardless of any ethical contradictions that might arise.

Alongside the representation of state power, for 300 years it has been more than happy to perform a vital ideological role in legitimising and celebrating capital. In the nineteenth-century city, as a testament to its new found political power, the bourgeoisie prided itself on building prestigious banks and stock exchanges that, like law courts, not only occupied strategic locations in the city but in the case of the Paris Bourse, were spectacular neo-classical monuments that occupied an entire urban block.[32] One hundred and fifty years later, the ascendancy of finance capital during the neo-liberal era represented a new opportunity for architecture to continue this tradition. As if to underline Simmel's observation about our compulsion to 'weigh, measure and re-numerate' the qualitative aspects of things in money terms,[33] institutions devoted to the making of money and the circulation of capital like the Lloyd's Building, Canary Wharf and the Gherkin in London have become famous as tourist icons and landmarks. The picturesque mansion Château de la Muette, the birthplace of French monarchs, was reborn as the home of the OECD, and wealthy institutions such as HSBC and the Frankfurt European Central Bank employed signature architects such as Fosters and Coop Himmelbau to illustrate their financial power with displays of structural gymnastics. Meanwhile in Moscow, keen to catch up in the global race to become an economic powerhouse, a new international business district is threatening the stratosphere.

And as the glittering towers of finance capital burst the clouds in one city after another, we find ourselves in the bizarre predicament of looking admiringly at the architectural bravado of institutions that have been instrumental in causing the current crisis and so much misery. It is as if we are lost in a parody of Marx's essay on the fetishism of the commodities. For the architecture of finance capital is truly a fetish world, a phantasmagoria in which, as Marx put it, we understand the relationship between people and each other's labour in the 'fantastic form of a relation between things'.[34] It is stranger still when we consider that, stripped of the symbolic capital loaded into the structure and entrance lobby, most of the office buildings that make up a city's financial services district, and which house the institutions that form what economists have called a 'global financial architecture', are designed to maximise 'exchange value' through the provision of as much rentable floor space as possible.

This kind of ideological dislocation is reflected in the pseudo-scientific linguistic fog developed by the financial system, a semantic code that makes the operations of money markets as difficult to understand as the Latin names of obscure plant life.

Indeed, the ubiquitous glass and steel headquarters of finance capital can easily be imagined as an alien botanic garden, in which strange species of life known as hedge funds, derivatives and all manner of debt and equity securities grow alongside genetically engineered flora and fauna known by mysterious abbreviations such as CDOs, CMBSs, RMBSs and ABXs.[35] Such 'financial instruments' were the nuts and bolts of what has been called a 'baroque' financial system, designed to siphon off vast profits through the overvaluation of private sector assets and to camouflage the reality of greater volumes of debt.[36] It was a particularly apposite analogy, given that the baroque is an architecture so laden with extravagant motifs and surfaces that the simplicity of space and structure is often obscured. And there was no greater illusion of prosperity than that created by the spiralling out of control of 'fictitious' capital and credit. The pyrotechnic display of readily available money had not only fuelled one of the biggest consumer booms in memory but had helped to forge a grotesque scenario, in which the house and home had come to function as an ATM; that is, as a ready source of credit that could be borrowed against.[37] By the end of 2010, the consequences of casino capitalism were pervasive. Our cities were littered with empty apartment blocks and call centres with hastily concealed 'To Let' signs. They were scarred by crumbling social infrastructure and public transport systems and inhabited by a population shocked at the manner and speed with which the utopian promises of neo-liberalism had disintegrated, and increasingly angry at the renewed attack on the public sector.

IGNORING THE WARNINGS

> It is another feature of a speculative mood that, as time passes, the tendency to look beyond the simple fact of increasing values to the reason on which it depends greatly diminishes. And there is no reason why anyone should do so as long as the supply of people who buy with the expectation of selling at a profit continues to be augmented at a sufficiently rapid rate to keep prices rising.[38]
>
> (Galbraith, The Great Crash 1929)

Casting his verdict on the reign of Baron Haussmann, Marx famously commented that it amounted to a series of 'colossal robberies committed upon the city of Paris by the great financial companies and contractors.'[39] The same could be said about the relationship between finance capital and cities like London and New York over the last three decades. Indeed, reading David Harvey's brilliant account of the political economy of the reconstruction of Paris in the aftermath of the 1848 Revolution is a little like reading the urban history of the recent past only with different names and actors. The differences are significant but the similarities are extraordinary. Haussmann's strategy was simple, mobilise the power of the state alongside private companies of builders, developers and architects, so as to create a 'well organised monopolistic form of competition with him at the top of the hierarchy.'[40]

To complete his imperial utopia, Haussmann required massive injections of new capital and with Napoleon's blessing, he turned to the bankers and, in particular,

the Pereire brothers. The ancestors of late twentieth-century bankers and financiers, the Pereires were like experimental architects in their ability to imagine elaborate structures and vertically integrated financial systems whose principal goal was 'grand unashamed speculation in future development.'[41]

In the same fashion that neo-liberal ideology encouraged individuals to believe that boom time would last forever, so in nineteenth-century Paris the lure of wealth through speculative urban development beguiled many a sane investor into believing that a crash would never happen. For any student of economic history, then, the shock that accompanied the recent crash is somewhat bizarre. However, such amnesia is symptomatic of a wider malaise, in which one of the most striking aspects about the current economic recession has been the rupture between the empirical proof of cyclical trends and periodic crises in the economy and the persistent belief that it is nevertheless possible to control capitalist production in a sustainable manner.[42]

To a large extent, this reflected the adoption by international economic organisations of neo-liberal doctrine about which there was no widespread agreement.[43] For more than 300 years, all the evidence underlines the fact that the economic history of capitalism and, therefore, architectural and building production, has been precarious and unstable. It has been a history marked by recurrent crises of both an economic and political nature, in which the output and profitability of architectural and construction firms has been bound up with the fate of capital accumulation and the direction of economic growth.[44] As Harvey again reminds us, there have been hundreds of financial crises around the world since 1973 and 'a good number of them have been property or urban development led.'[45]

Marx and Engels were in no doubt as to the underlying volatility of capitalism and as long ago as 1848 they commented that: 'Constant revolutionising of production, uninterrupted disturbance of all social conditions, everlasting uncertainty and agitation distinguish the bourgeois epoch from all earlier ones.'[46] Capitalist economic and urban development was revolutionary, extraordinarily inventive, but simultaneously violently destructive. It was a flaw they encapsulated in the term 'anarchy of production' that described the contradiction between the enormous creative social power unleashed by capitalist production and the fact that the means to control and profit from it lay in private hands.[47] It was an 'anarchy' expressed in such phenomena as cycles of boom and slump, overproduction, wastage, the periodic destruction and replacement of one form of technology by another, designed obsolescence and inter-capitalist competition – features that resonate powerfully in the construction industry. But Marx argued something else: that capitalism hid a crippling weakness. Although the history of capital accumulation might indicate a growing absolute mass of profit in the economy as a whole, the rate of profit over historical time, despite technological and organisational innovations, had a tendency to fall and it was this that lay behind the continual crises that have afflicted the history of capitalism.[48]

This is a complicated and controversial argument both theoretically and empirically.[49] However, in a recent review of the performance of the world economy, Brenner has argued that the net profit rates of US, German and Japanese manufacturing dropped by 40 per cent between 1950 and 1990 and that, between 1973 and 1998, average rates of profit, productivity and real wages in leading capitalist economies consistently fell, while the average rate of unemployment doubled.[50] It seems reasonable to suggest since construction statistics are often embedded within those for manufacturing (the cycles of which it broadly mimics), that while construction output and the 'total mass of profit' in the industry might have risen over time during periods of intensive urbanisation and architectural activity, profit rates as a whole across the construction sector have also been declining. If we were to draw a graph of the historical trajectory of output and profitability in the British construction industry, it would resemble the summits and ravines of a craggy mountain range rather than the even and predictable slopes of an artificial ski-run. It would show periods of intense construction activity and sustained growth followed by downturns and periods of stagnation.

What we do know is that the imperative for capitalists is to use whatever means are necessary to maintain their profitability. Here the 'law of the tendency of the rate of profit to fall' becomes even more problematic, since Marx himself detected a whole number of measures employed during crises to arrest falling rates of profit that he called 'counteracting tendencies'.[51] Firm takeovers, the depression of construction and architectural workers' wages, the worsening of working conditions, securing technological superiority over competitors, the organisational restructuring of management systems, diversifying into new areas of building activity, shifting capital to areas where labour power is cheaper, are all ways in which construction firms have tried to ride out recessions and kick-start construction into a new round of accumulation.[52]

While Marx's account of how technological and organisational change produces a tendency for the rate of profit to fall can be questioned, 'his essential insight that such changes have a key role in destabilising everything and thereby producing crises of one sort or another is indubitably correct'.[53] It is, however, one of the curious features of the economic history of capitalism that, at the moment when a crisis appears to threaten its very survival, 'geographical switches' and technological and organisational innovations emerge that create opportunities for renewed economic growth. In this sense Harvey suggests, crises can be thought of as 'the irrational rationalisers of an always unstable capitalism'.[54]

For Schumpeter, this cyclical process of destruction and creation, of economic decline and growth, was the 'essential fact' about capitalist economic history. Like it or not, firms could not avoid what he labelled the 'perennial gale of creative destruction'. In a passage clearly indebted to Marx, Schumpeter talked of 'the secular sabotage perpetrated by the bourgeoisie', in which economic structures are constantly being destroyed and recreated.[55] Here, alongside the obvious story of urban restructuring, one only has to reflect on technological innovation in the construction industry and how, at each stage in the transition from craft production to the factory production of building components, old forms of technology and labour organisation were swept away or subsumed by new forms. In other words, temporary devaluations of capital and recessions were unavoidable. The task for Schumpeter was not about visualising how capitalism administers existing structures, including that of the city, but about understanding how it creates and destroys them.[56]

Beyond the broad metaphorical description of economic history as 'creative destruction', discerning whether there is any pattern to cycles of economic growth and decline – and, therefore, of construction activity and urbanisation – has been contentious ever since Kondratieff suggested that the performance of the main industrial economies over the nineteenth century could be represented as a sinusoidal graph of 50-year long cycles of growth and decline. Taking a longer historical view of this process of 'uninterrupted disturbance', Giovanni Arrighi argued that the economic history of capitalism could be modelled as a sequence of four overlapping 'systemic cycles of accumulation'. These, he suggested, stretched back to 1500 and could be imagined as 'long centuries' made up of recurrent phases of stable growth alternating with 'phases of crisis, restructuring and turbulence'.[57] Importantly, each of Arrighi's historic cycles had a specific geographical dimension that related to the leading role that the Genoese, Dutch, British and Americans played in the development of the global capitalist economy; a shifting balance of power that was naturally reflected in intensive urbanisation and spectacular architectural developments. However, as Arrighi points out, such hegemonic positions do not last and as US control over global economic development has faltered and capital has flowed into newly emerging markets such as China and east Asia, it is not surprising to find that spectacular examples of new urbanisation and architectural excess are occurring in cities like Shanghai and Singapore.

Ernest Mandel also took cyclical theory as his starting point and argued that not only was it possible to distinguish between business cycles, partial and full economic crises, but that if the trajectory of the average rate of profit was plotted over time, there were clearly observable periods of long waves of expansion and depression which corresponded with distinct historical periods.[58] Mandel's model is compelling, not least because the expansionary and depressive waves match key phases in the process of urbanisation. He suggests that between 1780 and 1970, there were four distinct periods when the average rate of profit in the capitalist economy rose. The first up to the 1820s corresponded with the industrial revolution and the explosion of construction activity that provided the fixed capital and infrastructure necessary for capital accumulation. The mechanisation of building construction accelerated as new class relations were established. The modern contractor is born, and a class of 'free' waged building workers enters a labour market and a contracting system characterised by a 'restless and competitive anarchy'.[59]

The second and third waves paralleled the rise of finance capital and the heyday of imperialism in the second half of the nineteenth century. The process of urbanisation intensified. Domestic house building expanded, the construction of the key institutions of state and capital became ever more ambitious and new cities in the colonies were consolidated. Mandel's last 'expansionary wave' corresponded to the period between 1945 and 1970. Capital accumulation and the process of (sub)urbanisation were fully integrated, the mass production of consumer goods reached new heights, profitability was restored among firms involved in the industrialisation of the building industry, and there was massive investment in the construction programme of the welfare state. However, sandwiched between these periods of growth were downturns in the average rate of profit, in which a combination of trade recessions, speculative bubbles, the overproduction and devaluation of capital, increased unemployment and political unrest could threaten to destabilise economic development and social cohesion. Most significantly of all, Mandel argues, such phenomena, if left unresolved, can spark revolutions and global depressions; as the events of 1848, 1917, 1929 and 1936 demonstrated all too clearly.

WHAT CAN WE DO TO PREVENT ECONOMIC CRISES?

> *No one, wise or unwise, knew or now knows when depressions are due or overdue. Rather, it was simply that a roaring boom was in progress in the stock market and, like all booms, it had to end.*[60]
>
> (Galbraith, The Great Crash 1929)

Implicit in the ideas of authors like Mandel, Arrighi, Schumpeter, Marx and Harvey is the possibility for constructing a quite different periodisation of modern architecture based on the cycles and crises that characterise capital accumulation. This narrative would attempt to show how, despite the history of anti-capitalist struggle, the strategic decisions taken about where and what to build have been driven by the political and economic priorities of the capitalist class. It would also seek to illustrate that the dream of a sustained and socially equitable programme, for capitalist economic development is profoundly utopian and in reality impossible. If this is the case, then what is the alternative? It might well be that any attempt to develop a socialist programme for architecture and construction would encounter the same problems associated with the technological determinism, bureaucratic centralisation and political repression that characterised the development of the

8.5   What goes up must come down: tower block demolition, Gorbals, Glasgow, 2009

building industry in the Soviet Union. But it is worth trying to rescue from the twentieth century some of the ideals that a renewed socialist programme for urban development might aspire to.

The city is recast as an experimental laboratory testing different infrastructural networks and construction technologies according to their social usefulness, ecological footprint and temporal adaptability. The city no longer exhibits the acute social and spatial inequalities that have hitherto characterised urban development. The disestablishment of centralised state power makes the headquarters of economic and political bureaucracies redundant. The strategic headquarters of finance capital are turned over to civilian use. Architectural form is liberated from the judgmental tastes of those who wield political and economic power. Democratically elected councils, in accordance with the wishes of individuals and communities, plan the important collective aspects of the built environment, education, housing, transport and healthcare. Land and the principal means of building production are socially owned and controlled, and workers' collectives run all large building and architects' firms. Markets continue to operate as they have throughout human history. The important question is who regulates them and in whose interests. How to attain such ideals, even if they are considered desirable, is clearly predicated on the success of a broad-based anti-capitalist alliance. However, alternatives do exist, and we have at our disposal a rich history of experiments in how cities can be made and used in ways which are not defined by capitalist imperatives.[61]

What is remarkable is that, despite the increased frequency and depth with which financial and monetary crises have occurred since the 1970s, there has been no widespread rejection of the neo-liberal programme for economic development by the political elites of the world.[62] So far, we have witnessed the bail-out of banks with public money, the promise of a little 'light' regulation of the financial system and cuts to public services. Indeed, it appeared at the time of writing in the summer of 2010 to be 'business as usual; no admittance unless on business'. What is likely is that construction and architectural firms will look at the lessons of previous crises and recessions. They can sack staff, adopt new techniques of production, intensify the rate of exploitation, take over weaker companies, find new markets and exploit the few remaining branches of land and building construction that have hitherto escaped or evaded the full impact of capitalist commodity production.

It is probable that, through a combination of these techniques, the capitalist building industry will recover from its present crisis and estate agents and contractors will celebrate the birth of another boom. But, if so, it seems certain that the period of renewed prosperity will be followed at some point by another slump and a crisis whose proportions may be even greater. When we consider that many of the rapid urbanisation programmes currently underway in China, the middle east, India and Latin America are debt-financed, this possibility starts to look like a probability.[63] As Marx warned: 'From time to time the conflict of antagonistic agencies finds vent in crises. The crises are always but momentary and forcible solutions of the existing contradictions. They are violent eruptions, which for a time restore the disturbed equilibrium.'[64]

NOTES

1   For an earlier sketch of this article see Jonathan Charley, 'Boom and Slump on the Clyde and Liffey', in *Building Material* (Dublin: Architectural Association of Ireland), Winter 2005, pp. 8–12.

2   In particular it draws upon the immense contribution of David Harvey, who has done more than anyone else to develop a Marxist critique of the capitalist built environment in which economic analysis is placed at the forefront. It has also benefitted from the comments of Csaba Deak.

3   Joseph. K. Galbraith, *The Great Crash 1929* (London: Penguin, 1992), p. 26.

4   See the online archives for the *Financial Times*, *The Guardian*, *The Architects' Journal* and *Building Magazine*. For statistics see *Housing and Construction Statistics Quarterly* published by the National Statistics Office at www.nso.gov.uk [accessed 11 June 2010].

5   That is approximately 20 per cent of the construction workforce. See the report in www.masonryfirst.com [accessed 11 June 2009] and the report in www. contractjournal.com for a list of the full extent of job losses and redundancies in the construction industry.

6   See 'Oxford Vigil for Worker Killed by Girder' and 'TUC Congress – Delegates Support UCATT Call for Guilty Directors to Face Jail Term' in the journal *Building Worker* published by UCATT (Union of Construction, Allied Trades and Technicians), Autumn 2008, http://www.ucatt.info [accessed 25 November 2010].

7   Galbraith, *The Great Crash 1929*, p. 96.

8   Isaac Ilyich Rubin, *A History of Economic Thought* (London: Pluto Press, 1989), pp. 335–41. First published 1929.

9   David Harvey, *A Brief History of Neoliberalism* (Oxford: Oxford University Press, 2009).

10   Mark Fisher, *Capitalist Realism: Is There No Alternative?* (Winchester: Zero Books, 2009), p. 17. In short, neo-liberalism aims to 'financialise everything'; Harvey, *A Brief History of Neoliberalism*, p. 33.

11   Economic history suggests the opposite; that successful and sustained growth has normally come about by 'the state planning, coordination and reorganisation of capital flows'. David Harvey, *The Enigma of Capital – And the Crises of Capitalism* (London: Profile, 2010), p. 69.

12   For a good survey of post-Second World War architecture see Nicholas Bullock, *Building the Post-War World: Modern Architecture and Reconstruction in Britain* (London: Routledge, 2002).

13   Quoted in Robert Brenner, 'The Economics of Global Turbulence: A Special Report on the World Economy 1950–1998' in *New Left Review*, No. 229, 1998, p. 1.

14   Brenner, 'The Economics of Global Turbulence', p. 2.

15   See Michael Ball, *Rebuilding Construction: Economic Change in the British Construction Industry* (London: Routledge, 1988), pp. 98–113.

16   Ronald Emler, 'Worst Outlook for Builders', *The Times*, 26 January 1977, p. 18; G.T. Bodkin, 'Unacceptable Level of Building Sector Unemployment', *The Times*, 8 February 1977, p. 20; Hugh Wilson, J.W. Baxter et al., 'Damaging Long-Term Effects of Fall in Construction Industry', *The Times*, 31 January 1977, p. 16; Malcolm Brown, 'Construction Sector Faces More Jobless and Permanent Damage', *The Times*, 3 March 1977, p. 18; Malcolm Brown, '2000 Architects Laid Off', *The Times*, 22 April 1977, p. 25.

17   Conference of Socialist Economists, *Building With Direct Labour – Local Authority Building and the Crisis in the Construction Industry* (Direct Labour Collective: London, 1978), p. 27.

18   Harvey argues that one of the distinguishing features of the neo-liberal project was the restoration of class power. See Harvey, *A Brief History of Neoliberalism*, p. 201.

19   See for instance an article in *The Times* by Stephen Goodwin: 'Nationalisation of Builders Urged', 3 September 1977, p. 15. On the campaign for building industry democracy and the employers' response, see the pamphlets by the Direct Labour Collective, 'Building With Direct Labour', (1978), mentioned previously and also 'Direct Labour Under Attack – The Rundown of Council Building and Housing' (Direct Labour Collective: London, 1980). For an analysis of the failures of capitalist economic development in the 1970s, see 'The Conference of Socialist Economists London Working Group', *The Alternative Economic Strategy: A Labour Movement Response to the Economic Crisis* (London, 1980).

20   For articles on the history of the labour process in the building industry see various entries in 'The Production of the Built in Environment', *The Proceedings of the Bartlett International Summer School*, 1979–1995, Volumes 1–17.

21   See *Housing and Construction Statistics Quarterly*, 1969–1979, 1978–1988, published by the National Statistics Office at www.nso.gov.uk [accessed 5 May 2010].

22   'Oblivion Beckons As Slump Bites', *Architects' Journal*, 5 September 1990, p. 9.

23   'Gloomy Outlook For Practices', *Architects' Journal*, 3 April 1991, p. 9.

24   'Building Recovery Ruled Out', *The Times*, 1 August 1992.

25   'New Figures Show Recession Deepening For Architects And Construction Industry', *Architects' Journal*, 3, February 1993, p. 8.

26   'Builders In Appeal To Major', *The Times*, 1 October 1991. In a bizarre historical echo
     of the 2009 rescue mission of the 'Get Britain Building' movement, the building
     firms appealed directly to the then Prime Minister John Major, arguing that without
     expansion in central and local government programmes the recession could cost
     industry 300,000 jobs and recovery would not start until 1993.

27   Implying as it does that the problem somehow lay in the continuing survival of
     vestiges of the public sector. See 'Public Sector Hit By Cash Cuts', *Architects' Journal*,
     13 March 1991, p. 9.

28   Joseph, K, Galbraith, *The Great Crash 1929*, pp. 46–7.

29   David Harvey, *A Brief History of Neoliberalism*, p. 57.

30   Joseph A. Schumpeter, *Capitalism, Socialism, and Democracy* (London: Routledge,
     2010), pp. 88–9. First published 1943.

31   Bullock, ibid., p. 219.

32   The Paris Bourse commissioned by Napoleon in 1808 is probably unrivalled in this
     sense. A neoclassical colossus, it occupies an entire urban block. But in another
     historical echo of the contemporary crash, it was also the headquarters of a finance
     aristocracy that ruined the French economy by systematically defrauding the state
     through speculation on loans and debts, an incestuous orgy of gambling in which
     'money, filth and blood commingle(d)'. Karl, Marx, *The Class Struggles in France 1848 to
     1850* (Moscow: Progress Publishers, 1972), pp. 30–31.

33   Inspired by Marx, Simmel wrote extensively about the relationship between the
     development of a modern money economy and daily life in the modern city. See
     George Simmel, 'The Metropolis and Mental Life' (1903), republished in N. Leach (ed.),
     Rethinking Architecture: A Reader in Cultural Theory (London: Routledge 1997),
     pp. 69–79.

34   K. Marx, 'The Fetishism of Commodities and the Secret Thereof' in *Capital*, Volume 1
     (London: Penguin, 1976), p. 163.

35   CDOs (collateralised debt obligations), CMBSs (commercial mortgage-backed
     securities), RMBSs (residential mortgage-backed securities) and ABXs (asset-backed
     securities). In the United States, where the first domino fell, George Soros depicted the
     mechanisms invented to lubricate the flow of credit as 'an alphabet soup of synthetic
     financial instruments'. See George Soros, 'The Crisis and What To Do About it', reprinted
     from *The New York Review of Books* in the *Guardian*, 22 November 2008.

36   That is, as an alternative to state borrowing and public debt. See R. Brenner,
     'Devastating Economic Crisis Unfolds', *Green Left Weekly*, 25 January 2008, http://www.
     greenleft.org.au [accessed 30 November 2010].

37   Effectively masking the economic reality of the fact in Brenner's words that: 'We have
     witnessed (in the past decade) the slowest growth in the US economy since World War
     Two and the greatest expansion of the financial or paper economy in US history'.
     R. Brenner, *The Economics of Global Turbulence* (London: Verso, 2006), p. 3.

38   Galbraith, *The Great Crash 1929*, p. 33.

39   Karl, Marx, *The Civil War in France* (Peking: Foreign Languages Press, 1970), p. 414.

40   See David Harvey, *Consciousness and the Urban Experience – Studies in the History and
     Theory of Capitalist Urbanisation* (Baltimore, MD: Johns Hopkins University Press, 1985),
     pp. 70–90, offers an excellent overview of the reconstruction of Paris. But the full story
     is told in D. Harvey, *Paris, Capital of Modernity* (London: Routledge, 2006).

41 Harvey, *Paris: Capital of Modernity*, p. 117.

42 As Ball notes, an earlier generation of economists had proved empirically the existence of long waves in building activity. Michael Ball, *Rebuilding Construction,* p. 98.

43 In effect, economic science had been replaced by an ideology principally aligned with the interests of the financial community. Joseph Stiglitz, *Globalisation and its Discontents* (London: Penguin, 2002), pp. 220–30.

44 This has prompted economists to model the capitalist economy, either to prove that stability and equilibrium is possible, or that capitalism is in a process of inexorable decline. Compiling statistics and graphs, they try to plot the historical patterns of productivity and profitability and the relationships between different industries. They ask whether the construction industry mimics the rest of the economy, drives it, or lags behind in its own peculiar world. They speculate on whether the peaks and troughs that dominate construction history are indicative of minor fluctuations, business cycles, or long waves of depression and expansion that point towards a crisis of greater magnitude. See for instance Marian Bowley, *The British Building Industry* (Cambridge: Cambridge University Press, 1966); Ball, *Rebuilding*, and for a whole number of critical essays on the history of the building industry, see the seventeen volumes of *The Proceedings of the Bartlett International Summer School*, 1979–1995.

45 Harvey, *Enigma*, p. 8.

46 This famously proceeds: 'All fixed, fast-frozen relations with their train of ancient and venerable prejudices and options are swept away, all new formed ones become antiquated before they can ossify. All that is solid melts into air, all that is holy is profaned, and man is at last compelled to face with sober senses, his real conditions of life, and his relations with his kind.' K. Marx and F. Engels, *The Communist Manifesto* (London: Penguin Classics, 1980), p. 83.

47 See for instance F. Engels, *Anti-Dühring* (Moscow: Progress Publishers, 1978), pp. 331–9.

48 See Karl Marx, 'The Law of the Tendency of the Rate of Profit to Fall' in *Capital*, Volume III, Part III (London: Lawrence and Wishart, 1984), pp. 211–31.

49 For a summary of the debate see Ben Fine and Laurence Harris, *Re-Reading Capital* (London: Macmillan, 1983).

50 Robert Brenner, 'The Economics of Global Turbulence', pp. 1–10.

51 Karl Marx, *Capital*, Volume III, pp. 232–40.

52 During the 1970s and 1980s, although the general rate of profit across the British economy as a whole was in 'secular decline', the big contractors such as Wimpey, Tarmac and Laing maintained their profits precisely by engaging in these sorts of activities. However, big firms might survive a recession but plenty of smaller ones do not, as the recessions of the 1970s and early 1990s showed.

53 David Harvey, *The Enigma of Capital*, p. 101.

54 Ibid., p. 71.

55 Schumpeter, *Capitalism, Socialism, and Democracy*, p. 73

56 Ibid., pp. 76–8.

57 Giovanni Arrighi, *The Long Twentieth Century: Money, Power and the Origins of Our Times* (London: Verso, 2010).

58 Ernest Mandel, *Long Waves of Capitalist Development* (London: Verso, 1995), pp. 1–27. First published 1980.

59   Richard Price, *Masters, Unions and Men* (Cambridge: Cambridge University Press, 1980), pp. 25–31.

60   Galbraith, *The Great Crash 1929*, p. 51.

61   See 'Glimmers of Another World', Chapter 5 in this volume. See also David Harvey's new book, *Rebel Cities* (Verso: London, 2012), that picks up on Lefebvre's work on the right to the city and the urban revolution and gives a snap-shot of aspects of contemporary resistance. For a survey and directory of alternative architectural practice see Nishat Awan, Tatjana Schneider and Jeremy Till, *Spatial Agency: Other Ways of Doing Architecture* (London: Routledge 2011).

62   Harvey, *The Enigma of Capital*, p. 54.

63   Harvey revisits his theory of crisis in Chapter 2 of *Rebel Cities*, 'The Urban Roots of Capitalist Crises'.

64   Marx, *Capital*, Volume III, p. 249.

9

Scares and Squares II: A Literary Journey into the Architectural Imaginary

INTRODUCTION

As Chapter 6 indicated, some of the most powerful literary evocations of architecture are to be found in literary texts where the city, rather than merely providing a setting, frames and propels the narrative. 'Scares and Squares II' explores this proposition further in a journey through the rather loosely defined genre of utopian and dystopian fiction that begins with Thomas More and ends with Saramago.[1] It started life as an idea for a fictional chat show, in which rival teams of writers and architects battle it out over the idea of the modern city.[2] On one side sat H.G. Wells, Zamyatin, Orwell and Huxley, on the other Tony Garnier, Corbusier, Hilbersheimer and Bruce. Through a series of at times hostile conversations, they explored the marked disjuncture between the way the architect and the writer depicted the early modern city.

Although for formal reasons I have removed all of the footnotes in order to present it very much as a story, 'Scares and Squares II' is the product of considerable research into what has become a popular theme and subculture in both literary and architectural studies. The full list of literary references is contained in a bibliography at the end. For those unfamiliar with some of the theoretical references, 'Scares and Squares II' plays with a number of recurrent themes that have been explored by many writers, but by two in particular: Darko Suvin in *The Metamorphosis of Science Fiction* and Frederick Jameson in *Archaeologies of the Future*.[3]

If I was to select one idea from these groundbreaking surveys, it is that such literature should never be confused with futurology or reduced to 'Boys' Own comic book' tales of fabulous new technologies and gizmos.[4] It was, after all, Philip K. Dick who argued that his tales were not so much about the future as about the *here and now*. Sure, his novels are weird and decidedly other-worldly, but there is always something familiar about the places and situations he describes. This is what is meant by 'cognitive estrangement'. It refers to the way in which such literary representations allow us to recognise their subject, at the same time as making them seem unfamiliar.[5] I have coined my own version to describe such tales that

I think of as narratives of an 'exaggerated present.' There is, of course, much more to be said about such a genre that at its best deals with all of the complex issues affecting the human condition, from our understanding of history, nature, reality and technology, to our very existence as a species. My main interest in this chapter is naturally enough with 'space' (!) and before we lift off, a few parting words from Jameson: 'We need to explore the proposition that the distinctiveness of Science Fiction as a genre has less to do with time (history, past, future) than with space.'[6]

NEITHER LULLABIES IN HEAVEN NOR NARCOTIC FANTASIES

I am sitting in a capsule about to take off on a limbo journey into alternative forms of social reality. I stack the books and drawings that picture the modern city on the console. Intended as guides to help me navigate the rival claims on paradise that I am likely to encounter on my journey, they have left me confused, and they are as contradictory as the views through the windows. On the left horizon of the launch pad sits the utopian universe of the early bourgeoisie. Its tourist brochure promises liberation through capital accumulation and private property. On the right flutters a crimson banner that declares that socialism 'only has to be discovered to conquer the world by virtue of its own power'. Two magic dreams that propel the history of the narrative utopia.

CHRONOTOPIC UNIONS AND BATTLEFIELDS OF ANTINOMIES

Capsule readouts and jabbering screens whisk me through a contested historical landscape of chronotopic confusion, in which the novelists' texts and architects' images seem to have merged. The city of the novel speaks like a character and the drawings masquerade as space–time literary adventures. Both are casualties of the Battle of Antinomy. The libertarian stands before the state. Reason battles superstition. Reality tackles myth. Technology is mastered and then made a servant of the war machine. Nothing is going to be that simple. Armed with a mythic technological elixir, I might well be catapulted to a fearless redemptive Utopia, or maybe to sin city and the seductive pleasures of the weird and the wired. Or then again, I might simply return to where I started, to the worst nightmare of them all, the neo-liberal dystopia that transformed the revolutionary pathos of the early bourgeois utopia into an ontological *novum* that maintained that the world and everything in it should be run as a business.

9.1   Stage I. On the journey from utopia to dystopia. Neither lullabies in heaven nor
narcotic fantasies but chronotopic unions and battlefields of antinomies

THE PRISON HOUSE OF HISTORY

Either way, I will find myself trapped within an historical analogy. The instruction manual makes it abundantly clear. It is impossible to imagine anything that does not have some foundation in the corporeal and material reality of the world the writer and architect inhabit. It is impossible to imagine anything completely and unutterably new. Each chapter in the history of the narrative utopia is built on those that preceded it. As I wait, I realise that this is why the human imagination is drawn to these stories. Not because they are exercises in futurology or nostalgic myth, but because they critically examine and *stretch* contemporary reality. As narratives of an *exaggerated present,* they express the tension between the writer's and architect's lived existence and the imaginative projection of that life into an 'unknown other', creating something that appears at least to engender something new of the world. It could not be otherwise. It is why I am here.

BEWARE OF *TABULA RASA* AND APPARITIONS OF THE *NOVUM*

As the countdown to *novum* begins, I contemplate stopping at the greatest *novum* of them all, Moscow, 1917. 'We shall build a new civilisation,' proclaimed the Bolsheviks, 'but it will be constructed on the achievements of the bourgeois era, even if that means Taylorism and Opera.' Avant-garde revolutionaries are angry and upset as the Commissar of the Enlightenment turns on them. 'No, Gospodin Aleksander Bogdanov, you can not build a *Proletkult* disconnected from history. A proletarian architecture? A proletarian literature? Ridiculous.' Distraught, Bogdanov left for where he hoped his anarcho-syndicalist utopia might exist, the revolutionary red planet itself: Mars. Like the golden sphere in Strugatsky's zone that promises miracles, the lure of the *novum* is irresistible, and the iconic texts and images of the literary and architectural avant-garde that are piled at my feet almost without exception posit a break in history, even if they know that history cannot be erased, even if it becomes bunk. 'Be prepared then,' the historian announces, 'for a deeply unsettling feeling of cognitive estrangement. Imagine looking at yourself in a mirror. You have been tarred and feathered. You will recognise the subject, but in a manner that makes it seem unfamiliar. Dematerialisation is the stuff of adolescent fantasy, but de-familiarisation, well that is another matter.'

WELL-TRODDEN PATHS

I have decided to travel through a wormhole that will transport me to the origins of the utopian city. I tap my coordinates as best as I can and the capsule advisory system issues an immediate warning. 'It is a truly cursed route with an unknown destination.' Maybe I will find the disciples who vanished in the stone circles, tribal communities and matriarchal communes of our distant prehistory. I have heard tales of mad returnees who speak of an incandescent glow, of a mysterious *iskra.*

9.2   Stage II. Stop in the prison house of history but beware of *tabula rasa* and apparitions of the *novum*

9.3   Stage III. Well-trodden paths lead to surveillance in heaven

Legend has it that it is the foundation spark of primitive communism, dreamt of by the elderly Marx and Engels, their parallel travellers Bakunin and Kropotkin, and by all who share in the collective desire to find evidence of that place before the Fall.

SURVEILLANCE IN HEAVEN

To journey too far back or forward is to risk incarceration in the dungeons of the Moorlocks or apes. So the clock of time is set for the sanctuary of Thomas More's Aircastle. But this city is not the bucolic haven as oft imagined. It is true that Godly and goodly Communists proclaim the principles of the equal distribution of goods and the abolition of money. And it is true that with its 6,000 families it is the same size as a model Soviet Sotsgorod. But there is something unsettling in Aircastle. Stalking brick and flint three-storey terraces, spying through the orange night-time windows, a malign presence controls the behaviour of its inhabitants. For More tells us that 'In Utopia everything is under state control. Everyone has his eye on you', not least from the watchtowers that punctuate the city walls. Worse still, there are no swaying signs promising ale-fuelled song. 'No sir, there are no wine taverns, no ale house, no brothels, no places of seduction, no secret meeting place.' And so, before the Panoptican speculations of Ledoux and Bentham, More turns out to be the godfather of a prison state with Stasi children. He prefigures the dialectic of the utopian imagination, and all the subsequent debates about liberty and discipline, freedom and order, anarchism and socialism.

TIME TRAVEL TO THE HOUSE OF WISDOM

The capsule arrives at Bacon's Bensalem, a city constructed from blue brick and translucent oiled windows. Situated at its centre are the ladder to heaven, the *scala coeli*, and the lanthorn, the fountain of all knowledge and intelligence. Welcome to Salomon's House, a vast repository of knowledge that brings together the entire world's sciences, arts, manufactures and inventions. Bacon had received a nocturnal visitation from a representative of the House of Wisdom dressed in the garb of ancient Persia. He spoke of a ghostly library of astronomical, mathematical and philosophical knowledge that had been assembled by Muslim scholars in Baghdad. He wept as he narrated how it had been torched by Mongols, reassembled in Andalusia and then razed to the ground again, this time by jealous Catholics. Bacon awoke. With the pleas of the itinerant sage in his head and with an alchemist's passion, he set about building a facsimile, a fully immersive sensory and scientific environment. He put pen to paper and sketched out plans for a pantheon bigger than any cathedral to God that would be devoted to the celebration of human discovery and invention. Observatories, laboratories, museums, and all manner of technological wizardry tumbled forth. Bacon sits back and admires his creation, a dazzling array of institutes devoted to the manipulation and demonstration of

9.4   Stage IV. Time travel to the house of wisdom and then on to the Phalansterie

smell, sound, light, sight, liquid, metals, mechanics, maths and motion. I would have liked to have stayed in this Fun Palace.

COMRADES, TO THE PHALANSTERIE

The time clock skips from AD 1625 to 1830. The light from Bensalem's pantheon is unable to illuminate the glazed galleries of Fourier's Phalansterie that is terrifying in its austere immensity. In his slumber Fourier dreamt of merging Versailles with L'Escorial, the palace of a sun god with the mausoleum of Castilian kings. The city is unredeemable, come hither men and women of the world, for here lies salvation; you shall live in majesty in the quiet of nature. Forget the ugliness, filth and chaos of your miserable tiny little houses, the Phalanx has constructed 'a building as perfect as the terrain permits', a place where nothing is left to chance. A rule-bound fusion of church, factory, dormitory, workshop, telegraph, temple and parade ground; it is a full one point two kilometres wide. Fourier is deeply earnest. This is humanity's final destination. I was told that the Phalansterie rehearsed many of the arguments that would come to dominate twentieth-century debates on new ways of living such as the German *Neue Sachlicheit* and the Russian *Noviye Byt*. The didactic information leaflet confirms this: 'We have resolved the contradictions between work and play, the country and the city, individual liberty and social duty. How you might ask? It is simple, by turning the town into a single building in which we can initiate the individual into new social rituals and build a new society.' The Phalansterie propaganda for a good life has an unforgiving edge. It has done away with the street, the alley and all those dark spaces where the unexpected happens. It is of its time, and in that time it was logic. But it is not a place I wish to dwell for long. It reminds me of the chilling advert that adorns the entrance to Saramago's fortified condominium built on top of Plato's cave. 'We prefer you to need what we have to sell.'

FROM MUSCOVY TO PYRAMIDS ON THE ASIAN STEPPE

Lurching through sluggish time, the data indicates a general flight from the city of capital. It cannot be resolved, not now, not ever. There is only one solution, and that is to take Fourier's blueprint and replicate it. I am reminded that later in the twentieth century, in the hands of various dictators, the flight from the city would take a malevolent turn. Driven by blood and soil, intellectuals were dragged to the fields to discover hardened callouses. Historical wires cross and fuse. But these are not rural prison camps that I see before me, they are Chernyshevsky's agricultural communes in which men and women are equal. They are dominated by enormous aluminium and glass structures that stand like pyramids of old 'amidst fields and meadows, orchards and groves'. They stretch as far and as wide as the eye can see 'three or four versts apart', such that the vast expanse of the Russian and Asian steppe has been transformed into a 'gigantic chessboard' on which giant chessmen

9.5   Stage V. From Muscovy to pyramids on the Asian steppe,
       after which, comrades, let's march to the dung store

parade. 'And why not stay here?' you might ask; because I would miss the noise and chaos of the city, and because despite the noblest of aspirations, a life in harmony with nature tending fields, picking fruit, is not for me. It is also rooted in a hopeless nostalgia for a mythological state of being before the fall of man and woman, and worse still for a pre-capitalist world, where lord and peasant lived in idyllic harmony. Computer, take me to the metropolis, and fast.

COMRADES, TO THE DUNG STORE

I was looking forward to my stay in Morris's post-revolutionary London. But it proved to be a bitter disappointment. It too was plagued by nostalgia sickness and was eerily reminiscent of the New Urbanism that has bugged the imagination of urban planners. They, of course, do not share Morris's critique of capitalism and his imagined transformation of industrial hard labour into art. Neither, I suspect, would they be impressed by his idea to turn the Houses of Parliament into a dung store, nor by the actions of English revolutionaries who, 200 years before transformed St Paul's into a market hall. But they would have adored his romantic facsimile of a mythological medieval London. No smog, cholera, or belching foundries, London is transformed into a collection of handsome, idyllic villages inhabited by vegan, felt-stitched artists living in red-brick homes. The pamphlet guide encourages visitors to join the singing citizens as they amble along streets resplendent with pretty gay little wooden structures. Enjoy a rest, it suggests, in the abundant orchards, where sweet-smelling flowers bloom luxuriantly and send delicious waves of summer scent over the eddying stream that is now the Thames. Just the thought of it all makes me feel nauseas. Morris's world may well have dispensed with evil capitalists and down-trodden workers, but also, so it would appear, electricity. He balances precariously. On one side of the Styx arises a vision of a politically progressive future, on the other a reactionary pre-modern myth.

LA VILLE DES SYNDICATS

In the same time and space it is only a short journey to Bellamy's nineteenth-century city. Eyes brighten. The social and spatial inequalities of the capitalist city have been resolved. Commanding the metropolis is a victorious industrial army of labour. It is a city in which syndicalist sentiment, then so popular in the workers' movement, finds a home. Iberian, Russian and French anarchists read poetry and act out the Lyon silk weavers' sweet world of labour. Workers and their families download music by telephone into their homes, which have been designed to suit all tastes and circumstances. Domestic servitude has come to an end and when it is time to eat, families trek to the palace of dining – or rather, a hotel of eating, in which each family rents a room. The state prison has vanished, and when it rains, the city is transformed into the city of arcades. But it is still made out of the same stuff – statues, squares, fountains, miles of broad streets and public buildings of colossal

9.6   Stage VI. Leave the la Ville des Syndicats and wake up in the new world

size and grandeur. It is meant to be Boston, but it could easily be nineteenth-century Paris, in which working class areas have been spared bulldozers and bullets and the Commune has survived beyond its six months.

WAKING UP IN THE NEW WORLD

The journey enters new territory in which the dream of the perfect society is beginning to crack. H.G. Wells speaks: 'Imagine the Crystal Palace built on Sydenham Hill in 1851, imagine it growing, twenty-fold, thirty-fold, a hundred-fold, beyond measurement, until it straddles the whole city. Imagine all of the great cities of the world, Paris, Berlin, Rome and Madrid similarly encapsulated in a glass and iron bubble. Fill these cities with mind boggling machines for recording and transmitting sound and image. Scatter the sky with flying monoplanes. Inhabit the dome with a vast army of labourers in identical outfits ruled over by a small elite. Imagine now if you will, that there are no longer any suburbs, that the villages in which our ancestors used to till the soil have been replaced by agricultural enterprises on a colossal industrial scale and you will begin to have an idea of how our future cities might appear.' The high priest speaks across the world through telegraphed bleeps. 'The machine is our future. In the machine we must place our trust. All hail the machine.'

THE FIRST SIGNS OF CATASTROPHE

The flight control system suggests a detour to Forsters' antithesis of the technological utopia, the first of many to come. Humanity's ability to transform nature has gone horribly wrong. Disease and the exploitation of resources have rendered the planet toxic. They flee the capital again, but this time underground. Engineers have constructed a vast network of subterranean cities in the form of a beehive. Facsimiles of natural light provide a soft radiance to automated hexagonally-shaped capsules where buttons and switches summon food, clothing and anything an individual might need. There are no musical instruments. Instead, rooms throb with 'melodious sound'. It is ingenious, a masterpiece of science and technology and the only connection with the surface are the vomitories that protrude into the ruins of former civilisations. The machine becomes the state and god. 'It is the friend of ideas and the enemy of superstition'. There are no nightmare scenarios of technological Armageddon, or so think the waxy population. The machine after all is 'omnipotent, eternal, blessed'. And then one day it stops.

GEOMETRIC REASON

Such possibilities are of no interest to the architect Tony Garnier. Unperturbed by tales of the capitalist city rampant, and visibly drunk on stories of iron, glass and world fairs, he sweats profusely with parallel motion and set square. Geometric

9.7   Stage VII. The first signs of catastrophe despite geometric reason

pattern books and manuals on industrial production are open on his desk. He has embraced whole-heartedly the scientific legacy of the enlightenment. 'I believe in logic and rational planning, not only to bring greater justice to a world stricken by dreadful inequality, but to build new cities that are physically and intellectually severed from the pestilence and corruption of the old. Cities in which there exists a harmony between where we work and live, and between our private and public lives. I believe the best way to achieve this is through the organisation of social life within the framework of a zoned grid.' We walk through the Cité Industrielle, a giant letter T planted into a natural landscape crisscrossed at rectangles like an elongated chequers board. Everything is neatly arranged in an orgy of the Cartesian imagination. The city as machine. Mothers with prams walk along well-planted streets and turn left or right through perfect 90-degree angles to carefully designed schools and medical clinics. Men catch trams to dock and factory at 7.25 precisely. It is so brilliantly well ordered and laid out that chance vanishes from the vocabulary. I recognise the grand intentions, but can't help feeling that I am looking over the edge into the abyss.

THE UNIVERSE INTEGRATED

A temporal stone's throw away, D-503 recalls his arrival in the city of light and glass. He has been tasked with building a machine, a combination of the Tower of Babel and the theory of relativity that will integrate the colossal equation of the universe, unbend its wild curve and flatten it into an undeviating line. 'I saw again, as though right then for the first time in my life. I saw everything: the unalterably straight streets, the sparkling glass of the sidewalks, and the divine parallelepipeds of the transparent dwellings of the squared harmony of our grey-blue ranks.' The engineer–novelist Yevgeny Zamyatin cautions. 'It is not reason, science, or mathematics that is the problem, but the merging of the technocratic imagination and scientific reason with political power. Such a marriage can only lead towards despotism, a veritable mathematical dystopia of epic proportions in which there is no need for adjectives or love, a world in which urban and social lives are surrendered to technological and economic determinism.' But there is little chance of respite. Time and space are accelerating at terrifying speed.

CITY OF MATHEMATICAL ORDER

In Paris a strange round, spectacled man speaks. 'These writers write. I build. They do not understand the pressing problems of urban planning and the necessity of social engineering. What would they have us do? Leave the future of the city to romantic literary tropes or childish nightmares? Render our fragile futures to the predilections of insurgent proletarians or try and practically deal with urban construction?' Extraordinary three-dimensional perspectives and axonometrics raise the visions out of the ground. Spectral bodies are sketched over the top.

9.8   Stage VIII. The universe once integrated dreams of a city of mathematical order

The images are peppered with cars, trains, planes and zeppelins. Architects and planners with religious conviction herald the dawn of a new sensibility. 'Above all, the modern age is made up of geometry. After a century of analysis, modern arts and thought are seeking something beyond the random fact and geometry leads them towards a mathematical order. The set square is the necessary and sufficient tool for action, because it serves to determine space with absolute unambiguity.' I am convinced that Aldous Huxley wants to kill him, even though they have consumed the same opiates.

THE REVOLUTION IS A NUMERICAL QUANTITY

The clock dial starts to turn spasmodically. Moving back and forth, fast and slow, whirring with a spatio-temporal sickness. It clatters to a halt a mere six years forward. I am beginning to display signs of schizophrenia. Mindful of the dialectic of the Enlightenment, I clutch desperately at the desire and hope that another world is possible. But this is film noir and another over-coated 'other world' being is hanging on the street corner, beckoning downwards into the dark, in which the joys of high science and the structural gymnastics of new technology are descending into their violent instrumental other. I stagger through Hilbersheimer's orange and black cells pierced by a tape loop that bleats sheeplike. It would be altogether more rational to flatten the crumbling stone city and replace it with standardised housing blocks arranged around fast moving transport links. Architectonic form must be reduced to a single formal law limited to geometrical cubic forms. We must repress diversity and obliterate nuance. Let measurement impose itself as the master. 'Chaos is forced to take form: logic, clarity, mathematics, law.' Zamyatin gasps from afar. 'My friends, when I said that some day, an exact formula for the law of revolution will be established. And in this formula, nations, classes, stars-and books-will be expressed as numerical qualities, I was joking.'

CITY OF DREADFUL NIGHT

I am consumed by a violent travel sickness as the clock lurches to 1936. Little has been reconciled. The city is familiar but not. Known but cognitively estranged. It is *novum*, but somehow very old. I am convinced my descent is heading into Dantean deepening circles, to the wrathful and the sullen, to the tombs of the Epicureans. There hangs a placard that reads: 'No-one ever said that Utopia existed, let alone was real or pleasant.' The downward spiral continues. I exit into the city of Huxley's *Brave New World* and slide along the glittering vitrified surfaces. All the museums have been closed and historical monuments detonated. Literature has been shredded, as always happens in such situations. There is no need for the past. On the edge of the city before the parkland that separates the satellite suburbs, the windows of the 20-storey high Factory of Internal and External secretions are constantly illuminated with a fierce brilliance. It is working around the clock to ensure that fertility and biological reproduction proceeds without interruption. Three times

9.9   Stage IX. The revolution is a numerical quantity that creates a city of dreadful night

higher and looming over the centre of the city is the giant tower of the Bureau of Propaganda and the College of Emotional Engineering. Its 60 storeys cast a shadow over the silver-blue houses inhabited by Alphas and Betas. As has been customary throughout urban history from the Roman *latifunda* to the urban improvements acts of the nineteenth century, the armies of the lower castes occupy barracks physically removed to the periphery. 'It is how things should be,' says the minister 'everyone knows their place in the hierarchy, and if they have any doubt or indeed any delusions, then let me remind them of our city's other landmark, the "majestic buildings of the Slough crematorium…its four tall chimneys…flood-lighted and tipped with crimson danger signals".'

NOTHING BUT RUIN

Pausing for breath, aware of the forbidden zone on the other side of the wall that preserves the memory of humanity, I plummet still further to the utterly miserable ruins of Orwell's London. In Huxley's city technology works and the home of Lenina provides a lifetime of automated bliss with babies in bottles. Now, the lifts don't function. The street-level landscape is filled with vista after vista of leaky patched-up nineteenth-century houses, 'their sides shored up with baulks of timber, their corrugated windows patched with cardboard and their roofs with corrugated iron, their crazy garden walls sagging in all directions.' It is the polar opposite of the plans for victorious reconstruction that are splattered across the magazines and journals of architects and planners. A man called Abercrombie plans noble new civic centres on the bombed-out remains of cities. The Ville Radieuse makes a comeback. There, at least, the utopianism of new town construction and social engineering is alive and well. But not in the terminal gloom of Orwell's London. The plaster flakes from the walls, pipes burst, the street reeks permanently of cabbage and bad lavatories and the battered little doorways are 'reminiscent of rat-holes'. They will say later that it is a satire on the Soviet Union, but the Soviet city was far more robust and well-built than this place. For this isn't bomb damage, it is a permanent state of being, like being locked in the torment of a feudal fiefdom that has no past and no future and has simply always been. The only thing that rises above the destitution and misery are four impossibly large ministries that dwarf the rest of the city. White and pyramidal, the Ministry of Truth houses 3,000 rooms above ground and the same below, and its myriad windows are as 'grim as the loopholes of a fortress'. Winston's heart quails. 'It was too strong, it could not be stormed. A thousand rocket bombs would not batter it down.' There is only one solution for the Party, which is to relentlessly proselytise through organised spectacles their ideal of a 'world of concrete and steel' so as to mask the decaying and dingy city. My head is getting cloudy and mixed-up. Kaleidoscopic visions of tuberculosis cities that have been crushed by Stalin's wedding cakes, nineteenth-century law courts and the fortresses of finance capital induce vomiting.

9.10   Stage X. Nothing but ruins and psychosis cities

PSYCHOSIS CITY

I look at myself from all angles in the reflective surfaces of the capsule interior. I am, I think, showing the advanced signs of fear-induced psychosis. Three hundred and fifty years after Aircastle and I am stumbling along the oily night-time streets of Nabakov's Padukgrad. They are deserted, as usually happens in the gaps of history, in the *terrains vagues* of time. Monolithic granite blocks and parapets puncture clouds. Illiterate armed guards appear out of mists either side of the no man's land bridge. Eu-topia is a faded footprint. But at least for the time being, there is still history in the palimpsestic layers of the city where every stone 'holds as many old memories as there are motes of dust…'. I flip back in time to seek legal advice in Kafka's lawyers' rooms. But they are dangerous, situated in claustrophobic attics with Matta Clark-holey floors through which legs get stuck. They are almost dark, increasing the possibility of accidents, lit by a small skylight so high up that smoke from a chimney enters nostrils and blackens faces. There appears to be little redemption. So I shift time from central European dictator towns and return to Britain. But it's no good, either. The lift is jammed in the eco-catastrophe class war tower block where none of the new technology works. Like Ballard's protagonist, I too, feel peculiarly exhilarated at the possibility of complete social disintegration. Attracted like a car crash voyeur to the 'growing atmosphere of collision and hostility', I gaze at spectacularly horrific Alcatraz towers that stretch to infinity.

SCAVENGING FOR THE REMAINS OF COMMODITIES

The extravagant futurology of Skylon Britain is long forgotten. The white heat of technological revolution has gone rot-sour. There is to be no liberation from need or hard labour. The 1960s archigrammers, metabolists and super-studios turn the dialectic of the Enlightenment into a comic opera. Architects begin to flee from the responsibility of believing that they can change the world for the better. Fault lines are beginning to appear in their visions of utopia. They investigate the romance of non-capitalised spectacles, of Situationist drifts and detournéments that evoke a city of mobility, chance and shifting atmospheres. But the city of play that they write about as if it were a novel at some point has to be drawn. This is the curse of the architect who, like an addict with drugs, cannot resist the lure of the mega-structure. However mindful of the critique of rationalism, however desirous of kinetics and ergonomic human responsiveness, and however determined they are to avoid determination, vast mechanical structures like fantastic beasts of burden trample across the land. But at least they tried. Writers have a feast day, and I am spoilt for choice as I choose a destination. Social disintegration, ecological catastrophe, drugged hallucinations, mysterious epidemics and omnipresent war have consigned the literature of utopia to the distant shelves of Borges's library. It is bitter but compulsive reading. The console is now permanently illuminated with warning signs not to enter. But I must, to try and see if anything can be salvaged. Some of the landscapes have merged as if time was slipping or rather space was overlapping. I found myself in Flat 18a of a municipal block of flats somewhere

9.11   Stage XI. Scavenging for the remains of commodities, I became lost in a linguistic urban prison in a post-Second World War concrete town. The date and location monitor reads Burgessgorod, 1962. Through the windows to the west, a group of droogs stalk the estates and ancient domies to relieve their ancient boredom with indiscriminate violence. I descend in the lift, but step out into somewhere else entirely. It is still 1962, but I have left 'new town gone wrong' and instead am afloat on a *Drowned Earth*. The threat of ecological catastrophe has been realised. Politicians eventually decide to act, but it was too late, far too late. Nations migrated north and south to the Polar regions as the former inhabitable and temperate zones were overrun by Triassic nature. The mammals died. Humans stopped reproducing. Giant gymnosperms, iguanas, and mosquitoes the size of fists claimed the metropolis of European civilisation, 'and only the steel-supported buildings of the central commercial and financial areas' survived the encroaching floodwaters. As for 'the brick houses and single-storey factories of the suburbs', they 'had disappeared completely below the drifting tides of silt'. Here and there, human scavengers explored the ghost cities, foraging for the fetish remains of commodity culture and museums to remind those that survived of a life once had. I demand of the computer some relief and beg for a few pages of redemption, even a paragraph or two in which hope springs. It is naïve at best.

LOST IN A LINGUISTIC URBAN PRISON

I lurch eight years forward to 1970. It really is bonanza time for the twisted mind. I feel drawn by a relentless curiosity to the literary imaginings of far-away places that are as near as the end of my nose. It is a morbid compulsion, and against my better judgment, I leap into sensory deprivation and follow in the footsteps of the acclaimed polyglot linguist who visits Karinthy's *Metropole*. It is very eastern European of a certain era, a collage of Warsaw, Prague, Budapest, Berlin, Bucharest and Moscow, and it 'spread over a plain into distances further than the eye could see'. It is not yet the Asimovan city planet of Trantor, whose surface is completely covered in hard grey steel, but in whatever direction I turned, it disappeared into an infinity of every building typology that industrial culture had invented over the previous 200 years; factories, apartment blocks, prisons and slaughterhouses – a seething mass of brick and concrete regularly punctuated by chimneys that proliferate across the landscape like desiccated trees in the aftermath of battle. There is a hemispherical domed fort that is carved from 'raw unshaped stone' and exudes a 'chilly utilitarianism', such as that of a Roman stockade or medieval watchtower. Maybe it's Moorish in origin. But try as I might, I can't pin it down. I scan his notebooks to see what I can glean from his immense knowledge of languages that included Sanskrit Swahili and Mandarin, but to no avail. I, like him simply can't work out where I am. Despite this I experiment with various ingenious strategies in my endeavour to be understood. It should have been easy if it had been a normal city. But there seemed to be no railway station, no post office, in fact no visible means of communication or transport that I could use to geographically locate myself. I am incarcerated in a hotel room, staring at a skyscraper that day by day rises in inverse proportion to my descent into hopelessness. All the forgotten

9.12   Stage XII. Firemen rule in suburbia and there is great danger in effective dreaming

essays by Hegel and Marx on alienation and estrangement begin to make sense. The city and its inhabitants remain indecipherable, nowhere more so than in the stadium, where an incomprehensible game starts with 15 teams and eight balls, the point of which is to escape over the fence. As for the possibility of my liberation, I look out for the stream that he found. Logically in any conventionally understood universe, this should lead to the sea and to home.

FIREMEN RULE IN SUBURBIA

It is a short space hop to another suburban tract ripped to pieces and reassembled as a dictatorship. The dictatorship of the suburbs looms large in the literary imagination. Bradbury's 451 is famous because the firemen don't put out blazes, they start them with ceremonial funeral pyres of books and anything that smacks of independent thinking and knowledge. Ferociously, they hunt transgressors with vicious and lethal mechanical hounds. Locked in antiseptic homes, the wives feed themselves on aspirin and piped seashell music. Oddly, the neat houses don't have porches or lawns. An uncle says, 'they didn't want people sitting like that, doing nothing, rocking, talking; that was the wrong kind of social life. People talked too much. And they had time to think. So they ran off with the porches. And the gardens too.' Apart from that, nothing seems that out of the ordinary and the inhabitants shoot from home to work on the jet-black subway, thoughtless and content. Beatty explains the logic of such peace and harmony. 'More sports for everyone, group spirit, fun, and you don't have to think, eh? Organise and organise and super organise super super sports. More cartoons in books. More pictures. The mind drinks less and less.' The only problem is that like the rebel Montag I too can't resist books and so it doesn't take long for me to wreak vengeance. In this I needed little encouragement since I had long ago declared war on suburbia and throw myself wholeheartedly into a splendid frenzy of destruction, I attack the neat home. I burn the bedroom walls and the cosmetics chest, the chairs, the tables, and in the dining room the silverware and plastic dishes, everything that suggested that a life without knowledge and text could be beautiful and content.. My vendetta complete I follow in Montag's footsteps and flee to join the sanctuary of the forest people, where I like everyone else am assigned the job of memorising a book. It is unclear how successful this enterprise will be because a mushroom cloud looms in the distance.

THE DANGERS OF EFFECTIVE DREAMING

Grey-white dust from ugly clouds that blot out the sun settle on head and shoulders. Dreaming seems to be the only way of escaping radioactive veneer. If I wanted, I could volunteer for Ursula le Guin's psychiatrist's chair. But it is a false dawn. I realise that Frederick Jameson was right about George Orr. Neither he nor anyone else will ever successfully imagine Utopia. I watch from a distance, for who knows what Orr might dream. This is highly dangerous territory. Every time he thinks of a solution to the problems of the modern city, it has unforeseen consequences, setting in motion a chain of events that causes towers to vanish, others to appear that had never been built, and suburbs to dissolve 'like smoke on the wind'. He dreams of an end to racism but only succeeds in transforming the world into a uniform grey. The more effective his dreams, the more grotesque the results. Obsessed by Malthus, he wipes six billion people off the planet in a wild fire of carcinomic plague. He tries to rebuild his home city of Portland, but just as it is nearing completion, 'the handsome cubes of stone and glass interspersed with measured doses of green, the fortresses of Government – Research and Development, Communications, Industry, Economic Planning, Environmental Control' begin to dematerialise and melt. In a state of limbo, the city is 'half wrecked and half transformed, a jumble and mess of grandiose plans and incomplete memories'. Utopia has been murdered again as 'fires and insanities ran from house to house'.

'MAN, I AM TRULY WIRED, IN ALL SENSES OF THE WORD.'

All the exaggerated presents hurtle down the freeway in the shape of Philip K. Dick. He wrote the script. 'No, say no, and no again. This is not the future it is now.' Neo-liberalism has yet to take its toll, but world capitalism is battling against mortal enemies, not the crumbling fortress of the Soviet bloc but against non-believers on its home turf and ungrateful natives who have spurned the idea of Western civilisation. I stumble through entropic ruins, dosed to the gills on hallucinatory drugs, encountering at every step, ruination, urban decay and successive crises of identity. The prospects for tranquility and peace are remote. Darko Suvin proffers the possibility of the 'de-alienation of human kind', but it has never seemed so far away. Smart technology is no use in these pages. Neither the machines for manipulating time, empathy boxes, nor the vid phones and hover cars. They just heighten the unresolved terror of antonymic warfare, in which the real and imaginary, the human and robotic, safety and fear, war and peace, individual liberty and invasive surveillance, clash and splinter into a million fragments. The capsule spins in 360-degree circuits looking for a way out. I meet Isidore in a 'deteriorating, blind building of a thousand uninhabited apartments, which like all its counterparts, fell, day by day, into greater entropic ruin'. Then I am lost in tumbled miles of cheap hotels and broken-down tenements, bacterial crystals and radiation tabs. Scarcely have I recovered before I am propelled into the detritus of yet another terrifying suburban America, a seamless homogenised and endless succession of McDonalds, bugs, malls and bungalows.

INFECTED IN THE ZONE

Is that all that is left?, I wonder. I stop in the Strugatsky brothers' zone. Someone or something has been here before. The computer assures me that it is Earth, but a spot that is part of a galactic network of picnic parks. It has been quarantined.

9.13   Stage XIII. 'Man, I am truly wired, in all senses of the word.' I fear that I am infected

I dress accordingly. The visitors left their rubbish behind, ignoring the 'dispose of carefully' signs. But it wasn't polystyrene or plastic wrappers but some kind of radioactive plasma that has rendered the land and the city forbidden. Peering through goggles, I can make out what look like plague quarters. The asphalt is cracked and filled with grass. I think it must once have been an industrial town that limped towards termination. For there is still 'yellow ore piled up in cone-shaped mounds, blast furnaces gleaming in the sun, rails, rails and more rails, a locomotive with flatcars on the rails'. But it is spectral, and empty, and 'there were no people. Neither living nor dead.' A solitary stalker flits furtively amongst the rusting hulks. He is heading out where no man should go. If he returns he will only bring disaster, but he is compelled. He tells me that out in the zone there is a magic orb. It is a 'copper colour, reddish, and completely smoot' and it will fulfill whatever you ask of it. I remember the psychiatrist's chair in the *Lathe of Heaven*. I imagine it as a genie's lamp or the word of God. As I listen, a million odours descend, 'sharp, metallic, gentle, dangerous ones, as crude as cobblestones, as delicate and complex as watch mechanisms, as huge as a house and as tiny as a duct particle.' I struggled for breath and felt the filter on the mask clogging up as the air became hard, 'developed edges, surfaces, and corners, like space was filled with huge stiff balloons, slippery pyramids, gigantic prickly crystals.' He informs me that unless I leave immediately, I will become permanently infected and a danger to others like a friend of his who, after journeying in the zone, went to live in Detroit. Poor old Detroit. It was reduced to rubble long before the car plant closed. His friend opened a barber's shop and 'all hell broke loose'. It was awful. 'Over 90 per cent of his clients die during a year: they die in car crashes, fall out of windows, are cut down by gangsters or muggers, drown in shallow waters, and so on and so forth.' As the carnage continued unabated, the city and its suburbs were enveloped by natural disasters, typhoons and tornadoes. 'And that's what happens,' he tells me, 'such cataclysmic events take place in any city, any area where an emigrant from the zone settles.' I wish him well in his hunt for what might be the grail but might equally be a Pandora's box, more awesome in its power than ever before imagined.

SURVIVORS GO GREEN OR FERAL

Doris Lessing provides some *Memoirs*. This city is stalked by 'it', an undefined other that comes in many forms, 'a consciousness of something ending', be it pestilence, war or any of the tyrannies 'that twist men's minds'. In the distance I can see convoys of people. It dawns on me that the city is emptying. Infrastructure has broken. Food supplies have been cut. Normal civic life hovers over the descent into barbarous primitivism. An elderly lady explained, 'There was no single reason for people leaving. We knew that all public services had stopped to the south and to the east, and that this state of affairs was heading our way.' Realising that it wasn't a pack of wolves that had appeared out of cracks in the ground but feral children, I hid. The streets were theirs. They communicated through signs and guttural sounds and had largely lost the power of language. A handmade missing person note had been pinned to the door of a block of flats. The children were none-too choosy where the flesh they consumed came from.

9.14   Stage XIV. Survivors go green or feral. Others return to traditional values

'The building, as a machine, was dead.' Nobody mourned. Squatters banded together and occupied vacant properties, turning them into urban farms. But this was only ever going to be a temporary measure. Everyone had agreed that the solution to the crisis of humanity and the modern city was to flee once more into agricultural nirvana where there were reports of Babylonian 'gardens beneath gardens, gardens above gardens' that had trebled the food growing-surfaces of the Earth. The option button illuminates on the console. 'Would you like to visit another of her creations on *Shikasta*?' I read the profile. A perfectly round garden city that has been cloned from Ebenezer Howard. It is all cupolas and pastel shades and trees and gardens and markets and stalls and curved streets, so ideal, so perfect that the whole ensemble emits the sound of a platonic solid that holds the population and the animals on the verge of ecstasy. Not this, please not this. The clock threatens to spin backwards to Fourier, Morris, Chernyeshevsky and all the other illusions of being at one with nature. I plead with my machine to go forward, to seek out new urban life. Bubonic plague might end life as we know it but bucolic ideals render it tedious and dull to the point of madness.

THE RETURN TO TRADITIONAL VALUES

It is 1985, and this is the solution. Only the old school still retain belief in meta-narratives. The majority of architects has simply abandoned all hope and retreated into an infantile game of history plays in which nothing is true. Utopia is discredited, at least those associated with an alternative to the capitalist city. This is, of course, an illusion. In fact, architects remain as betrothed to ideology as before; it just so happens that it is the ideology of their political masters who have triumphantly declared the end of history. This time, I have awoken in something like a compound, which, judging by the word on top of the high-red brick wall, is called Gilead. The landscape is cut from the pages of a house and garden magazine with perfectly trimmed lawns, and clean, recently-printed façades smothered in folk art. The main street is 'like a museum, or a street in a model town constructed to show the way people used to live'. It is Epcot, New Urbanism, the new Arcadia, Stepford, all rolled into one, the perfect town with perfect people, but then, it is not. There are no children. A Soul Scroll shop on the corner pumps out prayers that dutiful women pick up on their way to the one modern building in town that has a 'huge banner draped over its door – 'Women's Prayvaganza Today'. It is quiet – too quiet. A nunnery-line of women draped in red cloaks files past. A black van with 'the white-winged eye on the side', cruises down the street taking note and looking for deviant behaviour. Bodies hang from hooks on a wall near the town hall. Of all the nightmares I have visited, this is one of the scariest. It is a devil's brew, in which religious fundamentalism meets crypto-fascist misogyny, rolled out in an endless routine of suburban discipline and punishment. And there is no respite. Warnings remind citizens that on the other side of the surrounding wall, atomic power plants have exploded and a 'mutant strain of syphilis' has wreaked havoc. I make a note to check the advertising supplements and real estate sections of homemaker magazines and journals, for I am positive I have seen apartments for sale in just such a place.

9.15   Stage XV. The escape chute isn't working. It leads only to Dantean ice

THE ESCAPE CHUTE ISN'T WORKING

It is too late to turn back now. Where would I go? It has become abundantly clear to me that all these accumulated utopias and dystopias aren't somewhere else, they are just facets, aspects and features of the place where I started my journey. I approached what looked like Lisbon. But it was not the city that I knew, 'it was a great mass of pitch which, on cooling, had hardened in the shape of buildings, rooftops, chimneys, all dead, all faded'. The Stalker's prophecy had come true. I carried a virus. It must be my fault. It had begun with a few individuals who were taken to a dilapidated old mental hospital and locked up in isolation wards. They had been stricken by a mysterious and highly contagious form of blindness. All that any of the victims could see was an impenetrable white light. No shadows and tones or brightness or contrast, just an immense milky fog, dense and consistent. To begin with the government refused to call it an epidemic. 'Rest assured citizens it is no more than an unfortunate temporary concurrence of circumstances.' Of course it was not my fault. The virus could not have preceded my arrival but since I am in a permanent state of temporal and spatial confusion, I can no longer tell what is forward and what is back, or what is future and what is past. It appeared that all was under control but as the number of inmates swelled, the mental hospital filled to bursting point. Potential escapees were shot by guards, who themselves went blind, as so, bit by bit, did the rest of the civilian population. The speed with which normal civil order, codes of conduct and social mores disintegrated was shocking. Bodily hygiene became impossible as the mental hospital descended into barbarism. Lavatories and bathrooms 'were soon reduced to fetid caverns such as the gutters in hell full of condemned souls'. The courtyard where, under former regimes, the insane would be allowed to breath fresh air was covered with a thick layer of faeces and rotting human flesh. Ballard described *Lord of the Flies* in a tower block. This was the same, only in the wings and corridors of an institution designed to keep its inmates under surveillance. Banks collapsed as fearing Armageddon, citizens withdrew all of their money, many going blind before they could spend it or hoard it in a safe place. Reason was abandoned as old superstitions and magic replaced logic. Self appointed seers 'proclaimed the end of the world, redemption through penitence, the visions of the seventh day, the advent of the angel, cosmic collisions', and the death of the sun. I knew that one day it would come to this. There were too many people already all over the world preparing for the end. Survival communities had already buried themselves in the Appalachian Mountains. Fanatics claimed that dinosaurs and humans walked the Earth together. At long last, two plus two equalled five. White-robed priestlings circulated the television tower in Brasilia, waiting for the imminent arrival of the space ship. Incipient madness gripped not just individuals but whole nations. The descent into mysticism didn't surprise me. Many just sat, immobile, and ate, trusting in the daily horoscope to sort out their fate. My head throbbed with the ear-splitting torrent of mumbo jumbo. All the scientific and technological marvels of human progress became useless over night. Within weeks, the city was dead.

DANTEAN ICE

There are many more stops on this journey. I wrack my brains for a happy ending, but find none. It somehow seems implausible. The fuel rods that drive the utopian impulse seem spent. I pause to ask myself, how could all of this have come to pass? The answer I know full well. Capital fuses with science. Knowledge capitulates to profit. Utopia has landed in Dante's Ninth Circle, where traitors against their benefactors are fully covered by ice. Vonnegut's Bokonon stares out at a frozen world and writes the last line of his treatise. 'If I were a younger man, I would write a history of human stupidity.'

Journey interrupted.

NOTES

1   It was first read at the conference 'Haunted Houses and Imaginary Cities' in Lisbon, October 2010. This is a considerably expanded version.

2   'Scares and Squares I' was presented at the conference 'Architexture: Textual and Architectural Spaces', hosted jointly by the Department of Architecture and Literary Studies at the University of Strathclyde in May 2008. It led to a book co-edited with Sarah Edwards called *Writing the Modern City: Literature, Architecture and Modernity* (London: Routledge, 2011).

3   Probably the two best surveys of the field are: Darko Suvin, *Metamorphoses of Science Fiction* (New Haven and London: Yale University Press, 1979), and Frederic Jameson, *Archaeologies of the Future – The Desire Called Utopia and Other Science Fictions* (London: Verso, 2005). See also Keith, M. Booker, *The Dystopian Impulse in Modern Literature: Fiction as Social Criticism* (Westport CT: Greenwood Press, 1994), Krishan Kumar, *Utopia and Anti-Utopia in Modern Times* (Oxford: Basil Blackwell, 1987), and Philip, E. Wegner, *Imaginary Communities – Utopia, The Nation, and the Spatial Histories of Modernity* (Berkeley, CA: University of California Press, 2002).

4   Suvin reminds us that it is impossible to imagine anything completely and unutterably new. He argues that science fiction does not depend so much on the *novum* or on the particular scientific rationale in any tale, rather it depends on the fact that 'the reality that it displaces, and thereby interprets, is interpretable only within the scientific or cognitive horizon.' Suvin, *Metamorphoses of Science Fiction*, pp. 66–7.

5   Inheriting the idea from Brecht, Suvin suggests that Utopia is always predicated 'on a certain theory of human nature. It takes up and refunctions the ancient topos of mundus inversus: utopia is a formal inversion of significant and salient aspects of the author's world which has as its purpose or telos the recognition that the author (and reader) truly lived in an axiological inverted world.' Suvin, ibid., p. 54. The same, of course could be said about the majority of all dystopian and science fiction work. In a similar vein, Jameson argues that 'Science Fiction enables a structurally unique method for apprehending the present as history, and this is so irrespective of the pessimism or optimism of the imaginary future world which is the pretext for defamiliarisation.' Jameson, *Archaeologies of the Future*, p. 288.

6   Jameson, ibid., p. 313.

Bibliography

Adorno, Theodore, and Max Horkheimer, *The Dialectic of the Enlightenment* (London: Verso, 1989).

Allan, John, *Berthold Lubetkin: Architecture and the Tradition of Progress* (London: Black Dog Publishing, 2011).

Anderson, Perry, *Passages from Antiquity to Feudalism* (London: Verso, 1974).

Arendt, Hannah, *Eichmann in Jerusalem: A Report on the Banality of Evil* (London: Faber and Faber, 1963).

——, *The Origins of Totalitarianism, Ideology and Terror* (London: Harvest, 1976).

Arrighi, Giovanni, *The Long Twentieth Century: Money, Power and the Origins of our Times* (London: Verso, 2010).

Arshinov, Peter, *History of the Makhnovist Movement* (London: Freedom Press, 1987).

Asimov, Isaac, *Foundation* (London: Harper Collins, 1995) (1953).

Atwood, Margaret, *The Handmaid's Tale* (London: Everyman's Library, 2006) (1985).

Awan, N., T. Schneider and J. Till, *Spatial Agency: Other Ways of Doing Architecture* (London: Routledge, 2011).

Bacon, Francis, 'New Atlantis', in *The Major Works* (Oxford University Press, 2002) (1625).

Bakhtin, Mikhail, *The Dialogic Imagination* (Austin: University of Texas Press, 1981).

——, *Speech Genres and Other Late Essays* (Austin: University of Texas, 2010).

Bakunin, M., 'The Revolution of February 1848, as Seen by Bakunin', in Guérin, D., *No Gods, No Masters: An Anthology of Anarchism*, Book 1 (Edinburgh: AK Press, 1998).

Baldrick, R., *The Siege of Paris* (London: History Book Club, 1964).

Ball, Michael, *Rebuilding Construction: Economic Change in the British Construction Industry* (London: Routledge, 1988).

Ballard, James G., *Drowned World* (London: Harper Perennial, 2006) (1962).

——, *High-Rise* (London: Harper Perennial, 2006) (1975).

——, *The Atrocity Exhibition* (London: Harper Perennial, 2006).

Barsukov, A. and A. Kristalnie, *Khozraschot na stroike* (Moscow: Gosfinizdat SSSP, 1932).

Baudrillard, J., *The Gulf War Did Not Take Place* (Sydney: Power Publications, 2009).

Beckles, Hilary, and Verene Sheperd (eds), *Caribbean Slave Society and Economy* (Jamaica: Randall Publishers, 1991).

Bellamy, Edward, *Looking Backward 2000–1887* (Oxford: Oxford University Press 2007) (1888).

Bely, Andrei, *Petersburg* (London: Penguin, 1978).

Benjamin, Walter, 'Hashish in Marseille' in *Reflections* (New York: Schocken Books, 1978).

——, *Illuminations* (New York: Schocken, 1986).

——, *Reflections* (New York: Schocken, 1986).

——, *The Arcades Project* (Cambridge, MA: Harvard University Press, 2002).

Bensaid, Daniel, 'Class Struggles in France, Neo-Liberal Reform and Popular Rebellion', *New Left Review*, No. 215, January 1996.

Berman, Marshall, *All That is Solid Melts into Air: The Experience of Modernity* (London: Verso, 1989).

Bettelheim, Charles, *Class Struggles in the USSR, First Period, 1917–1923,* and *Second Period 1923–1930* (Brighton: Harvester Press, 1978).

Bevan, Robert, *The Destruction of Memory: Architecture at War* (London: Reaktion, 2006).

Blackburn, Robin, *The Making of New World Slavery: From the Baroque to the Modern, 1492–1800* (London: Verso, 1998).

Boev, B., *Stroiteli v revolutzia* – in *'50 let' -Slavnie iubeli Sovietskik profsoyuz* (Moscow, Profsoyuzdat,1958).

Bogdanov, Alexander, *Red Star: The First Bolshevik Utopia* (Bloomington, IN: Indiana University Press, 1984) (1908).

Bogdanov, Nikolai P., *Kratkaya Istoria Soyuz Stroiteli* (Moscow: TK VSSR, 1927).

——, *Puti voroshdenia stroitelestvo i nashi zadachi* (Moscow: TK VSSR, 1925).

——, *Organisatsia Strotlenik Rabochik Rossii i Drugik Stran*, (Moscow: TK VSSR, 1919).

Bonnell, Victoria, *Roots of Rebellion: Workers' Politics and Organizations in St. Petersburg and Moscow, 1900–1914* (Berkeley, CA: University of California Press, 1983).

Bookchin, M., *The Third Revolution – Popular Movements in the Revolutionary Era*, Vol. 1 (London: Cassell, 1996).

——, *The Third Revolution*, Vol. 2 (London: Cassell, 1998).

——, *The Spanish Anarchists. The Heroic Years 1868–1936* (Edinburgh: AK Press, 1998).

——, *The Third Revolution*, Vol. 2 (London: Cassell, 1998).

Booker, Keith M., *The Dystopian Impulse in Modern Literature: Fiction as Social Criticism* (Westport CT: Greenwood Press, 1994).

Boulanger, Zalio et al., *Portraits d'Industrie, Collections du Musee d'histoire de Marseille* (Marseille: Edition Parenthèses, 2003).

Bové, José, 'Farmers Against Food Chains', in *New Left Review*, Second Series, No. 12, 2001.

Bowley, Marian, *The British Building Industry* (Cambridge: Cambridge University Press, 1966).

Bowlt, John, *Russian Art of the Avant-Garde: Theory and Criticism, 1902–1934* (New York: Viking Press, 1976).

Bradbury, Ray, *Fahrenheit 451* (London: Harper Collins, 2008) (1976).

Braudel, Ferdinand, *The Perspective of the World: Civilization and Capitalism, 15th–18th Century* (Berkeley, CA: University of California Press, 1992).

Brenner, Robert, 'The Economics of Global Turbulence: A Special Report on the World Economy 1950–1998' in *New Left Review*, No. 229, 1998.

——, 'Devastating Economic Crisis Unfolds', in *Green Left Weekly*, 25 January 2008, http://www.greenleft.org.au.

Brown, Kenneth, and Michel Peraldi et al., *Mediterraneans*, No. 13, *Marseille: Derrière Les Façades* (Paris: L'Association Méditerranéenes, 2002).

Bruce, Robert, *First Planning Report to the Highways and Planning Committee of the Corporation of Glasgow*, Second Edition (Glasgow, 1947).

Bullock, Nicholas, *Building the Post-War World: Modern Architecture and Reconstruction in Britain* (London: Routledge, 2002).

Burgess, Anthony, *A Clockwork Orange* (London: Heinemann, 2008) (1962).

Cameron, Gail, and Sam Cooke, *Liverpool: Capital of the Slave Trade* (Liverpool: Birkenhead Press, 1992).

Cassen, Bernard, 'Inventing ATTAC' in *New Left Review*, Second Series, No. 19, 2003.

Castells, Manuel, *The City and The Grass Roots: A Cross-Cultural Theory of Urban Social Movements* (London: Edward Arnold, 1983).

Charley, Jonathan, 'The Making of an Imperial City', *Journal of Architecture*, Vol. 1, No. 1, RIBA (London: Chapman and Hall, 1996).

——, 'The Concrete History of Modernity', in Hermannsen and Hvattum (eds), *Tracing Modernity* (Routledge: London, 2004).

——, 'Boom and Slump on the Clyde and Liffey', *Building Material* (Dublin: Architectural Association of Ireland, Winter 2005).

——, 'Global Iron – From Possil to Calcutta' in *Six Thousand Miles* (Glasgow: The Lighthouse, 2005).

Chernyshevsky, Nikolai, *What Is To Be Done?* (New York: Cornell University Press, 1989).

Coe, Peter, and Malcolm Reading, *Lubetkin and Tecton – Architecture and Social Commitment* (London: Arts Council of Britain, 1981).

Cohen, J.-L., P. Bourlier, C. Orillard et al., *GAUDI Programme, Making the City by the Sea: Forum and Workshop. Marseille 2001* (Amsterdam: Berlage Institute, 2001).

Conference of Socialist Economists London Working Group, *The Alternative Economic Strategy: A Labour Movement Response to the Economic Crisis* (London: Blackrose Press, 1980).

Conference of Socialist Economists, *Direct Labour Under Attack – The Rundown of Council Building and Housing* (London: Direct Labour Collective, 1980).

Conference of Socialist Economists, *Building With Direct Labour – Local Authority Building and the Crisis in the Construction Industry* (London: Direct Labour Collective, 1978).

Conrad, Joseph, *Heart of Darkness* (Oxford: Oxford University Press, 2002).

Cooke, Catherine, *Russian Avant-Garde – Art and Architecture* (London: Architectural Design, No. 53, 1983).

——, *Russian Avant-Garde: Theories of Art, Architecture and the City* (Academy Editions: London, 1995).

Dabydeen, D., J. Gilmore and C. Jones (eds), *The Oxford Companion to Black British History* (Oxford: Oxford University Press, 2008).

Daumalin, Xavier, and Marcel Courdurié, *Banques et utopias au XIXe Siecle* (Marseille: Chambre de Commerce et de l'Industrie Marseille-Provence, 2000).

Davis, Mike, *City of Quartz: Excavating the Future in Los Angeles* (London: Verso, 1990).

De Landa, M., *War in the Age of Intelligent Machines* (New York: Zone Books, 2001).

Debord, Guy, A. Kotányi and R. Vaneigem, 'Theses on the Paris Commune' in *The Situationist International Anthology*, ed. and trans. K. Knabb (California: Bureau of Public Secrets, 1981).

Deleuze, Gilles, and Felix Guattari, *A Thousand Plateaus: Capitalism and Schizophrenia* (University of Minnesota: Athlone Press, 1996).

Devine, Tom, *The Scottish Nation, 1700–2000* (London: Penguin, 2000).

——, *Scotland's Empire, 1600–1815* (London: Penguin, 2003).

Dick, Philip K., *A Scanner Darkly* (London: Gollancz, 1999) (1977).

——, *Do Androids Dream of Electric Sheep?* (London: Gollancz, 2001) (1968).

——, *Minority Report* (Orion: London, 2005) (1956).

Dostoevsky, Fyodor, *Crime and Punishment* (Moscow: Raduga Publishers, 1985).

——, *Notes from Underground* (London: Vintage, 1993).

Douglas, C., 'Barricades and Boulevards: Material Transformations of Paris', 1795–1871', in *Interstices*, New Zealand, No. 8.

Duncan, R., and A. McIvor (eds), *Militant Workers, Labour and Class Conflict on the Clyde, 1900–1950* (Edinburgh: John Arnold, 1992).

Ealham, Chris, *Anarchism and the City: Revolution and Counter-Revolution in Barcelona, 1898–1937* (Edinburgh: AK Press, 2010).

Edwards, Sarah, and Jonathan Charley (eds), *Writing the Modern City: Literature, Architecture and Modernity* (London: Routledge, 2011).

Engels, Frederick, *Anti-Dühring* (Moscow: Progress Publishers, 1978).

——, *The Origin of the Family, Private Property, and the State* (London: Lawrence and Wishart, 1981).

Fedorov, V.D., *Formirovanie rabochik kadrov na novostroikax pervoi piatiletki* (Ph.D diss., Gorkovsky University, 1966). Avotreferat, p. 15.

Driver, Felix, and David Gilbert (eds), *Imperial Cities* (Manchester University Press, 1999).

Duncan, Robert, and Arthur McIvor (eds), *Militant Workers, Labour and Class Conflict on the Clyde, 1900–1950* (Edinburgh: John Arnold, 1992).

Filtzer, Donald, *Soviet Workers and Stalinist Industrialization* (London: Pluto, 1986).

Fine, Ben, and Laurence Harris, *Re-Reading Capital* (London: Macmillan, 1983).

Fisher, Mark, *Capitalist Realism: Is There No Alternative?* (Winchester: Zero Books, 2009).

Fourier, Charles, *The Utopian Vision of Charles Fourier* edited by J. Beecher and R. Bienvenu (London: Jonathan Cape, 1972) (1851–1858).

Galbraith, Joseph. K., *The Great Crash 1929* (London: Penguin, 1992).

Gastev, A.K., *Kak Nado Rabotat, Prakticheski Vvdenie N.O.T,* (Moscow: Ekonomika,1972).

Ginzburg, Mosei, *Style and Epoch* (Cambridge, MA: The MIT Press, 1983).

Glendinning, M., R. McInnes and A. MacKenchie, *A History of Scottish Architecture* (Edinburgh: Edinburgh University Press, 1996).

Glenny, M., *The Balkans: Nationalism, War and the Great Powers, 1804–1999* (London: Penguin Books, 1999).

Guérin, Daniel, *No Gods, No Masters: An Anthology of Anarchism,* Vol. 1 (Edinburgh: AK Press, 1998).

——, *No Gods, No Masters: An Anthology of Anarchism,* Vol. II (Edinburgh: AK Press, 1998).

Hall, Peter, *Cities in Civilization: Culture, Innovation and Urban Order* (London: Phoenix, 1999).

Harrison, C., and P. Wood (eds), *Art in Theory 1900–1990: An Anthology of Changing Ideas* (Oxford: Blackwell, 1993).

Harvey, David, *Consciousness and the Urban Experience* (Baltimore, MD: Johns Hopkins University Press, 1985).

——, *Paris, Capital of Modernity* (London: Routledge, 2006).

——, *A Brief History of Neoliberalism* (Oxford: Oxford University Press, 2009).

——, *The Enigma of Capital – And the Crises of Capitalism* (London: Profile, 2010).

——, *Rebel Cities* (London: Verso, 2012).

Hazan, Eric, *The Invention of Paris* (London: Verso, 2011).

Hegel, Georg W.F., *Philosophy of Right* (Oxford: Oxford University Press, 1967).

——, *The Phenomenology of Spirit* (Oxford: Oxford University Press, 1977).

Heller, J., *Catch 22,* (London: Vintage, 1994).

Hirst, Paul, *Space and Power: Politics, War and Architecture* (Cambridge: Polity, 2005).

Hobsbawm, Eric, *Age of Empire* (London: Abacus, 1987).

——, *The Age of Capital* (London: Cardinal, 1988).

——, *Age of Revolution* (London: Abacus, 1997).

Hochschild, Adam, *King Leopold's Ghost. A Story of Greed, Terror, and Heroism in Colonial Africa* (London: Macmillan, 1998).

Hussey, A., *Paris: The Secret History* (London: Penguin, 2007).

Huxley, Aldous, *Brave New World* (London: Vintage, 2004) (1932).

Jameson, Frederic, *Archaeologies of the Future: The Desire Called Utopia and Other Science Fictions* (London: Verso, 2005).

Kafka, Franz, *The Trial* (London: Modern Voices, 2005) (1925).

Karinthy, Ferenc, *Metropole* (London: Telegram Books, 2008). Originally published in Hungarian as *Epepe,* 1970.Kenfick, William and Arthur McIvor (eds), *The Roots of Red Clydeside 1900–1914* (Edinburgh: John Donald, 1996).

Kenfick, William, and Arthur McIvor (eds), *The Roots of Red Clydeside 1900–1914* (Edinburgh: John Donald, 1996).

Koenker, Diane, *Moscow Workers and the 1917 Revolution* (Princeton, NJ: Princeton University Press, 1981).

Kollontai, Alexandra, 'The Workers' Opposition', in *Selected Writings of Alexandra Kollontai* (Westport, CT: Lawrence Hill, 1977).

Kopp, Anatole, *Constructivist Architecture* (London: Academy Edition, 1985).

Khan Magomedov, Selim, *Pioneers of Soviet Architecture* (London: Thames and Hudson, 1987).

Korolchuk, E.A., *Rabochiye Dvisheniye v 1870–90-x Godov* (Moscow, 1939).

——, *Kronika Revolutzionovo Rabochevo Dvisheniya v Petersburg, 1870–1904,* (Leningrad: Lenizdat, 1940).

Kropotkin, Peter, *The Great French Revolution 1789–1793* (London: Heinemann, 1909).

——, 'The Commune of Paris', in Schulkind, E. (ed.), *The Paris Commune of 1871: The View From the Left* (London: Jonathan Cape, 1972).

——, *The Conquest of Bread and Other Writings* (Cambridge: Cambridge University Press, 1995).

——, 'Western Europe', in *Conquest of Bread and Other Writings* (Cambridge: Cambridge University Press, 1995).

Krzhizhanovsky, Sigizmund, *Memories of the Future* (New York: New York Review Books, 2009).

Kumar, Krishan, *Utopia and Anti-Utopia in Modern Times* (Oxford: Basil Blackwell, 1987).

Le Guin, Ursula, *The Lathe of Heaven* (London: Gollancz SF Masterworks, 2001) (1971).

Lefebvre, Henri, *Critique of Everyday Life* (London: Verso, 1991).

——, *The Production of Space* (Oxford: Blackwell, 1991).

——, *Writings on Cities* (Oxford: Blackwell: 1996).

——, *The Urban Revolution* (Minneapolis, MN: University of Minnesota Press, 2003).

Lenin, Vladimir Ilyich, *Selected Works* (Moscow: Progress, 1977).

——, *Lenin: Volume Three. The Revolution Besieged,* edited by Tony Cliff (London: Pluto Press, 1978).

Lissagary, Oliver, *History of the Paris Commune of 1871* (St Petersburg, Florida: Red and Black, 2007).

Lissitzky, El, *Russia: An Architecture for World Revolution* (London: Lund Humphries, 1970).

Luxemburg, Rosa, *The Russian Revolution* (Ann Arbor, MI: University of Michigan Press, 1961).

MacLehose, J., *Memoirs and Portraits of 100 Glasgow Men* (Glasgow, 1886). See Glasgow Digital Library, http://gdl.cdlr.strath.ac.uk/mlemen/mlemen101.html.

Mailer, Norman, *The Naked and the Dead* (London: Harper Perennial, 2006).

Mandel, Ernest, *Long Waves of Capitalist Development* (London: Verso, 1995).

——, *Late Capitalism* (London: Verso, 1999).

Marchal, Jules, *Lord Leverhulme's Ghosts – Colonial Exploitation in the Congo* (London: Verso, 2008).

Marcus, G., *Lipstick Traces – A Secret History of the Twentieth Century* (Cambridge, MA: Harvard University Press, 1989).

Marcuse, H., *One-Dimensional Man: Studies in the Ideology of Advanced Industrial Society* (London: RKP, 1986) (1964).

Marshall, Peter, *Demanding the Impossible: The History of Anarchism* (London: Fontana, 1993).

Marx, Karl, *The Civil War in France* (Peking: Foreign Languages Press, 1970).

——, *The Class Struggles in France 1848 to 1850* (Moscow: Progress Publishers, 1972).

——, *Capital*, Volume I (London: Penguin, 1976).

——, *Pre-Capitalist Economic Formations* (London: Lawrence and Wishart, 1978).

——, *A Contribution to the Critique of Political Economy* (London: Lawrence and Wishart, 1981).

——, *Economic and Philosophic Manuscripts of 1844* (London: Lawrence and Wishart, 1981).

——, *Capital*, Volume III (London: Lawrence and Wishart, 1984).

——, *The Eighteenth Brumaire of Louis Bonaparte* (London: Lawrence and Wishart, 1984).

Marx, Karl, and F. Engels, *Basic Writings on Politics and Philosophy* (London: Collins, 1979).

——, 'Socialism Utopian Scientific' in *Basic Writings on Politics and Philosophy* (London: Collins, 1979).

——, *The German Ideology* (London: Lawrence and Wishart, 1985).

——, *The Communist Manifesto* (London: Penguin Classics, 2002).

Michel, Louise, *La Commune* (Paris: Editions Stock, 1978) (1898).

More, Thomas, *Utopia* (London: Penguin, 2006) (1516).

Moretti, Franco, *Atlas of the European Novel 1800–1900* (London: Verso, 2009).

Morris, William, *News from Nowhere* (London: Penguin Classics, 1986) (1890).

Morson, Gary S., *The Boundaries of Genre: Dostoevsky's Diary of a Writer and the Traditions of Literary Utopia* (Austin: University of Texas, 1981).

Nabakov, Vladimir, *Bend Sinister* (London: Penguin, 2007) (1941).

Orwell, George, *1984* (London: Everyman's Library, 1992) (1949).

——, *Homage to Catalonia* (Harmondsworth: Penguin, 2000) (1938).

Pacione, Michael, *Glasgow – A Socio-Spatial History* (Chichester: Wiley, 1995).

Pak, Y., *Organizatia truda i zarabotnaya plati v stroitelstve* (Moscow: Stroizdat, 1974).

——, *Ekonomika truda v stroitelstve* (Moscow: Stroizdat, 1978).

Pashukanis, Evgeny G., *Law and Marxism: A General Theory* (London: Pluto, 1989).

Platonov, Andrey, *The Foundation Pit* (London: Vintage, 2009).

Postgate, Raymond W., *The Builder's History* (London: The National Federation of Building Trade Operatives, 1923).

Price, Richard, *Masters, Unions and Men* (Cambridge: Cambridge University Press, 1980).

Pushkin, Alexander, 'The Queen of Spades' in *Collected Works* (New York: Everyman's Library, 1999).

Rabota soyuz stroiteli za 1924–1925 (Moscow:, 1926). Publisher uncertain.

Rashina (ed.), *Trud v SSSR, Statistiko, Economicheski obzop, 1922–1924* (Moscow, 1924). Publisher uncertain.

Remarque, Erich M., *All Quiet on the Western Front* (London: Vintage, 1996).

Rubin, Isaac Ilyich, *A History of Economic Thought* (London: Pluto, 1989).

Rudé, George, *The Crowd in History* (London: Serif, 1995).

Said, Edward, *Culture and Imperialism* (London: Vintage, 1994).

Saramago, José, *Blindness* (London: Vintage, 1995).

——, *The Cave* (London: Vintage, 2003) (2000).

Sbriglio, Jacques, *Guides D'Architecture: Marseille, 1945–1993* (Marseille: Edition Parenthèses, 1993).

Schulkind, Eugene, *The Paris Commune of 1871* (London: Historical Association Pamphlets, No. 78, 1971.

——, (ed.), *The Paris Commune of 1871: The View From the Left* (London: Jonathan Cape, 1972).

Schumpeter, Joseph A., *Capitalism, Socialism, and Democracy* (London: Routledge, 2010).

Sebald, Walter G., *Austerlitz* (London: Penguin Books, 2001).

——, *The Rings of Saturn* (London: Vintage, 2002).

——, *On The Natural History of Destruction* (London: Penguin, 2004).

Sennett, Richard, *Flesh and Stone: The Body and the City in Western Civilization* (London: Faber and Faber, 1994).

Sherwood, Marika and Kim, *Britain, the Slave Trade and Slavery From 1562 to the 1880s* (Liverpool: Savannah Press, 2007).

Shliapnikov, A., 'The Workers' Opposition', in *Selected Writings of Alexandra Kollontai* (Westport, CT: Lawrence Hill, 1977).

Shvidovsky, Oleg, *Building in The USSR* (London: Studio Vista, 1971).

Simmel, George, 'The Metropolis and Mental Life'(1903). Republished in Leach, N. (ed.), *Rethinking Architecture: A Reader in Cultural Theory* (London: Routledge, 1997).

Sindeyev, S., *Professionalniye Dvisheniye Rabochik stroiteli v 1917* (Moscow: Trud i Kniga,1927).

Skelley, Jeffrey (ed.), *The General Strike, 1926* (London: Lawrence and Wishart, 1976).

Smith, Steve A., *Red Petrograd: Revolution in the Factories 1917–18* (Cambridge: Cambridge University Press, 1986).

Speer, Albert, *Inside the Third Reich* (London: Phoenix, 1997).

Stiglitz, Joseph, *Globalization and its Discontents* (London: Penguin, 2002).

Stites, Richard, *Revolutionary Dreams: Utopian Vision and Experimental Life in the Russian Revolution*, (Oxford: Oxford University Press, 1989).

Strugatsky, Arakady and Boris, *Roadside Picnic* (London: Gollancz, 2007) (1977).

Suvin, Darko, *Metamorphoses of Science Fiction* (New Haven and London: Yale University Press, 1979).

Ten Years of Soviet Power in Figures. 1917–1927 (Moscow: Central Statistical Board of the USSR, 1927).

'The Production of the Built in Environment', *The Proceedings of the Bartlett International Summer School*, 1979–1995, Volumes 1–17.

Thompson, Edward P., *The Making of the English Working Class* (London: Pelican, 1980).

Trotsky, Leon, *The Revolution Betrayed* (New York: Pathfinder, 1989).

——— *Literature and Revolution*, (Ann Arbor: University of Michigan Press, 1971).

Virilio, Paul, *War and Cinema – The Logistics of Perception* (London: Verso, 1989).

———, *Bunker Archaeology* (New York: Princeton University Press, 1994).

———, *City of Panic* (Oxford: Berg, 2005).

Voline, *The Unknown Revolution* (New York: Free Life Editions, 1974).

Vonnegut, Kurt, *Slaughterhouse 5* (London: Vintage, 2000).

———, *Cat's Cradle* (London: Gollancz, 2010) (1963).

Wegner, Philip E., *Imaginary Communities – Utopia, the Nation, and the Spatial Histories of Modernity* (Berkeley, CA: University of California Press, 2002).

Wells, Herbert G., *The Time Machine* (London: Penguin, 2005) (1895).

———, *The Sleeper Awakes* (London: Penguin, 2005) (1889).

Zamyatin, Yevgeny, *The Dragon and Other Stories* (London: Penguin, 1983).

———, *Soviet Heretic* (London: Quartet Books, 1991).

———, *We* (London: Penguin, 1993) (1924).

Zola, Emile, *The Kill (La Curee)* (Oxford: Oxford University Press, 2008).

Zvorikin, *Razvitia stroitelnovo proizvodtsva*, (Moscow: Stroizdat, 1987).

JOURNALS AND PERIODICALS

Architects' Journal

Arkhitektura CCCP

Building Design

Housing and Construction Statistics Quarterly

Postroika

Stroitel

Stroitelstvo Moskvi

Stroitelnaya Promishlennost

The Financial Times

Guardian

The Times

Trud

Index